An Introduction to the UK Economy

Third edition

Colin Harbury
Professor of Economics
The City University
London

Richard G Lipsey
Professor of Economics
Simon Fraser University
British Columbia

PITMAN PUBLISHING
128 Long Acre, London WC2E 9AN

A Division of Longman Group UK Limited

© C D Harbury & R G Lipsey 1983, 1986, 1989

Third Edition first published in Great Britain 1989

British Library Cataloguing in Publication Data
Harbury, C. D.
   An Introduction to the UK Economy. – 3rd ed.
   1. Great Britain – Economic conditions – 19th century
   2. Great Britain – Economic conditions – 20th century
   I. Title   II. Lipsey, Richard G.
   330.941′082   HC255

   ISBN 0–273–03068–X

Text set in 9½/12 Bembo, by Tek Art Ltd.
Printed and bound in Great Britain at The Bath Press, Avon

Contents

commercial policy, exchange control, reserves · international co-operation: Bretton Woods · European Monetary System · world debt problem · concluding remarks: macroeconomic policy – a perspective. Questions and exercises · Appendix.

Preface

Economic theory is only useful if it is understood in the context of the real world. We originally wrote this book as a companion to the theory texts then available at the introductory level, including *An Introduction to Positive Economics*[1].

Now we have jointly written a new introductory text, *First Principles of Economics*[2], intended for complete beginners, especially A level economics students and candidates for the economics examinations set by the major professional bodies, such as the Institute of Chartered Accountants, Institute of Bankers, Institute of Actuaries, and Institute of Chartered Surveyors. This *Introduction to the UK Economy* is, we believe, a real companion to our theory book, though we hope that it will still go well with any other theory text. Our two books are amply cross-referenced to each other. The present book covers those aspects of the economy, both macro and micro, which we regard as important for understanding the relevance of economic theory.

We have gone out of our way not to clutter either our text with endless tables of indigestible statistics or our charts with numbers calculated to decimal-place accuracy. We believe that all a student can, or should, take away from a book such as this is an outline view of the economy's institutions and functions and its chief orders of magnitude, which date far less quickly than the detailed statistics.

Our illustrations have been designed to help our readers to retain visually most of the more important quantitative features of the UK economy. To this end we have deliberately employed a variety of diagrammatic styles and types, including straightforward graphs, pie charts, histograms and bar charts in two and three dimensions. We hope that they, together with the text, will assist readers to gain a general knowledge of the economic forest without having to try to absorb the detailed structure of every sectoral tree.

For the same reason statistical tables on which the various charts and diagrams are based have been relegated to an

1 The original book was Richard Lipsey's *Introduction to Positive Economics*, 6th edition (Weidenfeld and Nicolson, 1983). The new book is *First Principles of Economics* by Richard Lipsey and Colin Harbury (Weidenfeld and Nicolson, 1988). It is referred to throughout this book as Lipsey and Harbury, *First Principles*
2 Readers of Colin Harbury's *Descriptive Economics* (Pitman) may regard this third edition of *An Introduction to the UK Economy* as, more or less, an eighth edition of *Descriptive Economics*.

appendix in each chapter. We strongly recommend readers to add more recent data as it appears, and to refer also to the charts themselves. Although the data used for the book cannot remain current for long, we do not expect readers to find many diagrams which need alteration.

Among the many people whom we should like to thank, we would like to single out both our publishers who have supported the venture – especially Weidenfeld & Nicolson for their goodwill over a book in which they have no commercial interest.

The third edition   The passage of three years since the second edition and consequent need for updating of material throughout the book is a prime reason for this new third edition. In updating, we have not simply extended the timescale of charts, but thoroughly rewritten the text wherever necessary to take account of major changes such as the extensive privatisation measures of the 1980s. Such rewriting, in particular, now takes on a more international – especially European – coverage in the run up to 1992. In response to market pressure we also comment rather more than in previous editions on some of the policy issues discussed in the book. Finally, and also in response to the market, we have supplied a number of exercises at chapter ends.

The exercises have several aims: to foster the intelligent use of data; to encourage the collection of some original material of a simple kind; to put the student in direct touch with some of the more accessible economic statistics; to provide encouragement for updating of the book during the course of study; and to confront the student with facts and ideas which pose questions about the relationship between data on the UK economy and elementary economic theory.

Colin Harbury
Richard G Lipsey
January 1989

Data sources for questions and exercises

At the end of every chapter in this book are sets of questions and exercises. We would like to encourage you to attempt as many of them as you have time for. Doing so will give you valuable experience in collecting, presenting and interpreting simple statistical and other data from easily accessible sources. Many of the exercises are also designed to make you think about the relationships between facts about the UK economy and elementary economic theory. Incidentally, too, doing the exercises helps to keep the book up to date.

Some of the exercises call for the construction of graphs, usually of a kind to be found in the book itself. Nevertheless, a student who is uncertain how to draw and interpret graphs would be well advised to brush up with an appropriate text.[1]

More exercises are contained in Colin Harbury's *Workbook in Introductory Economics*, Pergamon Press, 4th edn 1987.

Sources are suggested for all exercises where they are needed, though some data is available in the appendices to chapters in the book. We give the source most likely to be easily accessible, using key initial letters as indicated below. However, there may often be other sources which are more up to date, more detailed, or more convenient, and many questions and exercises can be slightly modified if the recommended source is not available. (This last point may be helpful for students from countries other than the UK who want to relate the questions to their own national data.)

1 UK government sources

(a) General

Key	Publication	Frequency
AS	*Annual Abstract of Statistics*. Of inestimable value, with extensive coverage, containing statistics generally running over ten-year periods.	annual

---

1 There is an appendix on graphs in economics in Lipsey and Harbury, *First Principles*, pages 563–73.

Key	Publication	Frequency
KD	*Key Data*. A recent addition to government publications, with a fair coverage of material in *AS* over slightly shorter periods, but illustrated with charts and graphs.	annual
MDS	*Monthly Digest of Statistics*. Supplements *AS* and *KD* for recent trends.	monthly
ET	*Economic Trends*. Coverage overlaps with *MDS* to some extent, but many series illustrated with charts (and sometimes with commentary).	monthly *plus* annual supplement
EPR	*Economic Progress Report*. Very useful broadsheet brought out six times a year by HM Treasury, and covering current topics with relevant data. The April (Budget) issue is exceptionally useful. Can be obtained (free) from COI, Hercules Road, London SE1 7DU.	bi-monthly

(b) Specialised

Key	Publication	Frequency
BB	*United Kingdom National Accounts*. Known as the '*Blue Book*'. Contains series of national income statistics extending over 20 years. Exceptionally useful for the exercises in Chapter 7.	annual
FS	*Financial Statistics*. Supplements *MDS* for financial and monetary data, being more detailed on many matters.	monthly
RT	*Regional Trends*. A digest of most statistics that are available on a regional basis, including many economic ones.	annual

2 Other sources

Key	Publication	Frequency
NIER	*National Institute Economic Review*. Journal of the National Institute of Economic and Social Research, containing an Appendix with several key statistical series for major nations – USA, Japan, W. Germany, France, Italy, as well as UK.	quarterly
IFS	*International Financial Statistics*. Published by the International Monetary Fund with extensive, though compressed, financial statistical series for individual countries, together with world totals.	monthly
WA	*Whitaker's Almanack*. A handy source for several kinds of information not easily available elsewhere.	annual
T	*The Times*.	
FT	*The Financial Times*. Useful sources for current financial data.	daily
BEKS	*The British Economy, Key Statistics, 1900–1970*. A one-off publication by *The Times* newspaper, of exceptional value as a source of historical statistics for long-term trends. May be available in libraries.	–

A few other sources are mentioned in specific questions and exercises. Full details of UK official publications are listed in the annual publication of the Government Statistical Service, *Government Statistics*, obtainable on application from the Information Services Division, Cabinet Office, Great George St, London SW1P 3AL.

List of tables in appendices

1 The economy in outline

The UK economy is complex, and this book goes into a lot of detail. The purpose of this introductory chapter is to outline its most distinctive features within a reasonably long-term context.[1] Recent trends will receive greater attention when we discuss individual topics in later chapters.

The features we focus on now are:

- **Resources** – land, labour and capital
- **Production** – primary, secondary and tertiary
- **Foreign trade** – exports and imports of goods and services
- **Economic growth** and living standards
- **Unemployment**
- **The monetary system** – financial institutions and the price level
- **Government** – the economic role of the state

Resources

The resources of a society consist not only of the free gifts of nature, such as land, forests and minerals, but also of human capacity, both mental and physical, and of man-made aids to further production, such as tools, machinery and buildings. It is sometimes useful to divide these resources into three main groups – **land, labour** and **capital** – known as **factors of production**.

Land

Land in the UK is scarce relative to the population. Figure 1.1 shows the allocation of the 24 million hectares among

Fig. 1.1 Land use 1987 (relative importance of different uses)
Source: *Annual Abstract of Statistics*

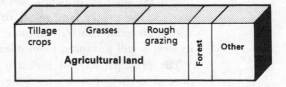

Tillage crops | Grasses | Rough grazing | Forest | Other
Agricultural land

---

1 For an introductory text concentrating on theory, see Richard G Lipsey and Colin Harbury, *First Principles of Economics,* (Weidenfeld and Nicolson, 1988). This source is hereafter referred to as Lipsey and Harbury, *First Principles.*

different purposes. The prime use is, of course, for agriculture, which accounts for nearly three-quarters of the total, or 18 million hectares. This is not all what could be called good agricultural land. Some 6 million hectares are at or below the margin of cultivation and classified as 'rough grazing', while over half of the arable land is under grass at any one time. The non-agricultural remainder includes forest (about 2¼ million hectares), inland water (⅓ million hectares) and around 25 thousand hectares which are in use for towns and villages in urban districts and rural areas.

A further breakdown of the 5 million hectares of land devoted to tillage crops is shown in Fig. 1.2. About three-quarters is devoted to cereal production, both for human and livestock consumption. Barley replaced oats as the foremost grain crop around 1960, though the area used for wheat has been slightly greater than that for barley since 1984.

Fig. 1.2 Land under tillage crops 1987 (relative importance of major crops) Source: *Monthly Digest of Statistics*

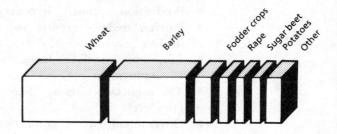

Something like 10 per cent of the available area is used for fodder crops, rape, sugar-beet and potatoes, the principal 'other' categories being vegetables, oats, fruit and flowers.

The shortage of good land suitable for arable cultivation makes the livestock population of the country a vitally important part of its agriculture for, by and large, livestock can thrive on poorer soils than growing crops like cereals and vegetables. In 1987 there were about 100 million chickens, 30 million sheep, half that number of head of cattle and about 8 million pigs on farms in the country.

The term land, as used by economists, conventionally includes those free gifts of nature commonly called natural resources, such as minerals and other raw materials lying above or below the land itself. Britain is not well endowed with high grade mineral deposits, though 2 or 3 per cent of its steel is still produced from domestic iron ore.

The principal natural resource in Britain at the present time is energy. For a very long time the main source of energy was coal. Discoveries of North Sea gas and oil in the 1970s led, as Fig.1.3 shows, to the displacement of coal from its dominant position as supplier of energy consumed in the UK. Britain has been self-sufficient in energy supplies since

1980. Estimates of the unexploited reserves of oil and natural gas are understandably imprecise and vary with new discoveries. Coal reserves are, however, substantial and the coal industry is capable of resuming a primary role when North Sea reserves run out.

Fig. 1.3 Inland energy consumption 1960 and 1987
Source: *Monthly Digest of Statistics*

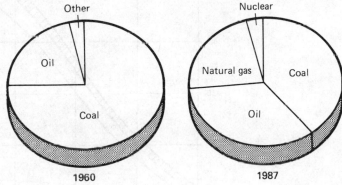

1960   1987

Labour

The supply of human resources is referred to by economists as labour – another factor of production. The amount that is available is called the **labour force** and depends, in the first instance, on the size of the population.

In 1801, when the first census was taken, the total population of Britain was roughly 12 million. Thereafter it grew at an astonishing rate As Fig. 1.4 shows, it doubled in 60 years, and by 1861 there were over 24 million people. It had more than doubled again by 1961, when the population was over 50 million. It had mounted to 56 million by 1971, slowing down to reach 57 million in 1988.

The population of Britain is by no means evenly spread over the whole country. It is clear from Fig. 1.4 that England, Wales, Scotland and Northern Ireland have very unequal shares of the total population. If the population of each of these countries is related to its size, however, the inequality is even greater, since England has over four-fifths of the people and only just over half the land, whilst Scotland has a third of the land but only about a tenth of the people. Wales has a tenth of the land but only a twentieth of the people and Northern Ireland has a twentieth of the land but a mere 3 per cent of the population. We can express these facts in another way by saying that in England there are about 900 people per square mile, in Wales about 350, in Northern Ireland less than 300 and in Scotland only about 175.

The reasons for these very unequal densities of population are to be found partly in differences in climatic conditions,

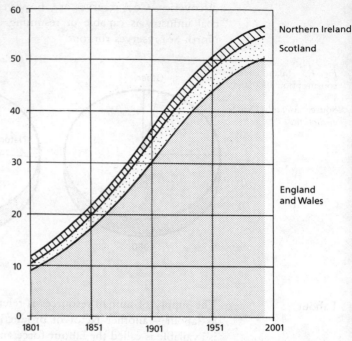

Fig. 1.4 Population since 1801
Source: *Annual Abstract of Statistics* and *Monthly Digest of Statistics*

Population (millions)

Northern Ireland
Scotland
England and Wales

but the overwhelming causes are economic. For all but a very select few of the population, where to live is decided for them by the whereabouts of the farms, factories, shops or offices at which they work to earn their living. When Britain was an agricultural country the population was fairly evenly spread over the good farming land. With the growth of industry the siting of factories became the predominant influence. We shall examine further aspects of the regional distribution of industry in Chapter 3.

The map (Fig. 1.5) reveals the main features of the geographical distribution of the population and shows the concentrations around the principal cities. At present something like four-fifths of the entire population live in urban areas and only one-fifth in the country. Even a good many of the latter work in towns. To emphasise the extent of urbanisation, notice that in 1988 there were 20 cities in the UK with more than a quarter of a million inhabitants, and seven conurbations – Greater London, West Midlands (around Birmingham), West Yorkshire, South East Lancashire (around Manchester), Merseyside, Tyneside (around Newcastle) and Central Clydeside (around Glasgow). These conurbations together occupied less than 3 per cent of all urban land, but housed nearly 30 per cent of the people.

The regional distribution of the population is continually changing. Rural depopulation and the growth of cities began

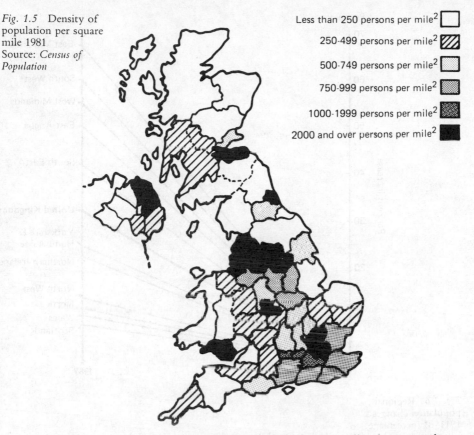

Fig. 1.5 Density of population per square mile 1981
Source: *Census of Population*

Less than 250 persons per mile^2
250-499 persons per mile^2
500-749 persons per mile^2
750-999 persons per mile^2
1000-1999 persons per mile^2
2000 and over persons per mile^2

with the industrial revolution, but not all urban areas have grown at the same rate. Figure 1.6 shows the changes in the geographical distribution of the population that took place since the Census of 1911. That period witnessed the greatest increases in population in the Midlands, South West, East Anglia and South East England, while Scotland, Wales, Northern and North West England experienced *relative* declines. These changes are the result of internal migration of workers and their families, attracted by employment opportunities in the areas involved, and natural increases of the populations themselves.

A fairly recent tendency, not observable from Fig. 1.6, is for people to choose to live in outlying suburbs rather than in the centres of large cities. In the interwar years this led to the sprawling conurbations mentioned previously. In order to prevent further erosion of the countryside, the government introduced a policy of designating 'green belts' of land, usually several kilometres wide, around larger cities, where urban building was virtually prohibited. With similar objectives in mind, over 30 'new towns', now with a combined population of over 2 million, were created under legislation passed in 1946.

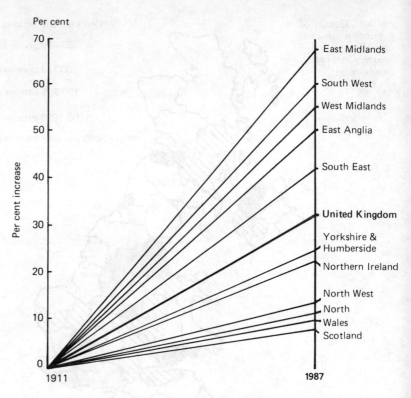

Per cent

70 — East Midlands

60 — South West

West Midlands

50 — East Anglia

South East

40 —

30 — **United Kingdom**

Yorkshire &
Humberside

20 — Northern Ireland

North West

10 — North

Wales

Scotland

0 —

1911   1987

Per cent increase

Fig. 1.6 Regional
population changes
1911–81 (percentage
increase in population)
Source: *Annual Abstract
of Statistics*

We started our discussion of labour as a factor of
production by looking at the size of the population.
However, only about half of the community can be regarded
as being available for work in the ordinary sense of the
word. The labour force, including both those in work and
those currently unemployed, numbers about 28 million.
What about the other 30 million? How do they spend the
time? Figure 1.7 provides the answer.

First, about half are growing up; the law prohibits the full-
time employment of some 12 million school pupils under the
age of 16, and they must therefore be excluded from the
labour force. At the other end of the scale there is a similar,
though smaller, group of women over 60 and men over 65
(the ages of entitlement to retirement pensions). The remainder includes housewives, students, the infirm, convicts,
people taking early retirement, and others. Most of these are
not counted as part of the working population, not because
they do not work, but because they are not paid a wage for
doing so. Some married women are given housekeeping
allowances by their spouses, for example, but by no stretch
of the imagination can any be thought of as being employed
by them!

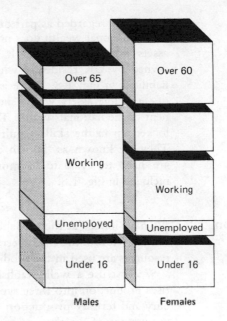

Fig. 1.7 The working
and non-working
population 1987
Source: *Annual Abstract
of Statistics*

Capital

The third and last factor of production consists of all those
man-made aids to further production, such as factory
buildings, machinery, plant and equipment, which are not
consumed for their own sake but are used to make other
goods and services, i.e. capital.

The size of the nation's capital stock is very large, valued
in the late 1980s at more than £1500 billion. It is difficult to
appreciate the significance of such a magnitude. One way of
putting it into perspective is to consider that it represents
something like the total output of the entire economy for
about four years.

Figure 1.8 shows the breakdown of the national capital
wealth of the community, with buildings as the largest item.
Notice also that dwellings account for over 40 per cent of the
total. These, it is true, are not capital goods of the kind we
described. However, they are long-lasting and, in the sense
that they help to provide for employment in the future, they

Fig. 1.8 Gross capital
stock 1987
Source: *UK National
Accounts*

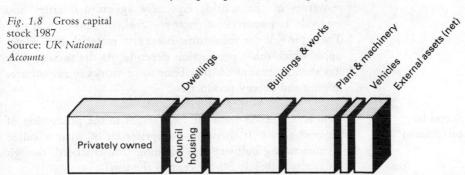

are usually regarded as part of the nation's capital resources.

The national wealth does not consist solely of the tangible assets mentioned above. It includes also external assets owned by UK residents, which are shown *net* of external liabilities in Fig. 1.8. There is, too, another important class of intangible assets which should be regarded as a component of the national wealth. This comprises assets which are locked up in the skills acquired by education and training. They are known as 'human capital'. Such intangible assets are hard to evaluate in money terms and they are not included in Fig. 1.8.

Production

We have looked at the available resources. We now continue our overview of the British economy by looking at how these resources are used in the production of goods and services.

We first use a well-established distinction which categorises production into three types, known as **primary, secondary** and **tertiary production**. Figure 1.9 shows the relative importance of the three types of production in present day Britain, according to the number of workers employed.

Fig. 1.9 Types of industrial activity 1987; percentage of total labour force engaged in primary, secondary and tertiary production Source: *Monthly Digest of Statistics*

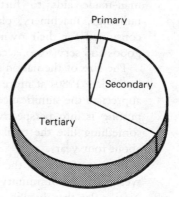

Primary

Secondary

Tertiary

Primary production This consists of all economic activity which is a first step in the productive process, i.e. the harvesting of the natural resources of the world, especially agricultural crops and minerals and sources of energy – coal, oil and natural gas. These provide the foodstuffs, basic raw materials and power upon which other production depends. At the present time less than 5 per cent of the labour force works in agriculture, mining and energy production.

Secondary production This is concerned with the later stages in the production of finished goods. It therefore comprises all of what is called manufacturing industry and building (construction), though today that is barely 30 per cent of the total.

Tertiary production   This involves the provision of **services** which either help other producers to do their jobs, e.g. transport, or satisfy consumer demands for such things as entertainment or hairdressing. As can be seen in Fig. 1.9, tertiary services employ about two-thirds of the working population. They include workers in transport, retailing, commerce, finance, government and the professions.

The fact that secondary and tertiary employment account for such a high proportion of the total is one indication of the advanced state of industrial development of Britain. This is clearly illustrated if we compare the situation today with that in the past. The proportion of the labour force engaged in primary production 100 years ago was about 25 per cent. Were reliable figures available for, say, 300 years ago, the contrast would be even more striking. At that time agriculture was almost the only important industry, and the proportion of the labour force engaged in primary production was correspondingly high. Manufacturing business was still rare and, in those days before railways and cars, transport was difficult and the numbers in government service and the professions were much fewer.

Employment in secondary production was the first to increase with the industrial revolution. Then, as technical advances raised productivity in industrial production, resources were released for the tertiary sector, while the output of manufactured goods was maintained and even raised. The relative importance of the services sector increased, gaining ground from secondary production.

Employment in manufacturing peaked at around 9 million in 1960, declining by a million by the end of that decade, and by another million ten or so years later. By 1988, manufacturing employment had dropped to just over 5 million. This process of **deindustrialisation** has come about as a result of complex changes, including the rapid advance of technology in the manufacturing sector. It has not been confined to the UK, though its implications for this country have been of considerable concern to some people, because of the traditional and important role that manufacturing has played in exports. The full impact of deindustrialisation on UK exports was sheltered by the development of North Sea oil. It remains to be seen whether the longer term pessimistic forecasts will, or will not, prove justified.

The pattern of   Figure 1.10 helps to show further details of the relative
production   importance of the main sectors of the economy. The service industries in the tertiary sector appear in the middle of the main block in the diagram. Finance and the professions employ over 5 million people, about a quarter of the total.

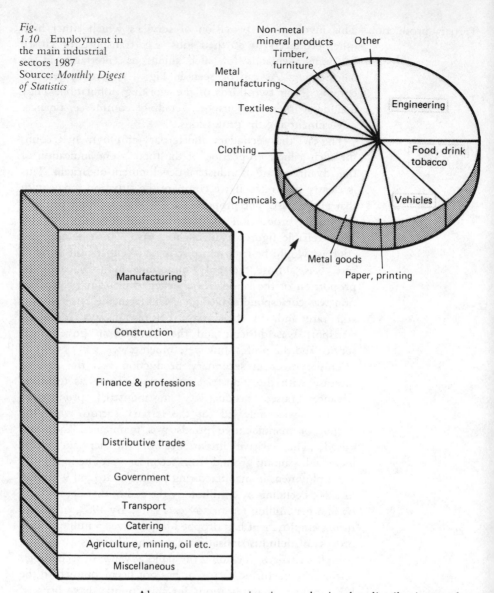

Fig.
1.10 Employment in
the main industrial
sectors 1987
Source: *Monthly Digest*
of Statistics

Non-metal
mineral products   Other
Timber,
furniture
Metal
manufacturing
Engineering
Textiles
Clothing
Food, drink
tobacco
Chemicals
Vehicles
Metal goods
Paper, printing

Manufacturing

Construction

Finance & professions

Distributive trades

Government

Transport

Catering

Agriculture, mining, oil etc.

Miscellaneous

About one person in six works in the distributive trades,
while fewer than one in ten is employed directly by the
central and local government. Many more work indirectly
for the state, e.g. in the capacity of teachers, nurses, doctors
and as other employees in the public sector provision of
education and health, and in other nationalised industries.
The last of these sectors has been declining considerably in
the 1980s as a result of the programme of privatisation (*see*
pages 47–8).

Note, however, that Fig. 1.10 relates to employees and,
therefore, excludes the self-employed, about whom there is
much less information, but who increased in number from 2
to 3 million during the 1980s.

Manufacturing industry, by itself, accounts for the employment of some 25 per cent of all those at work. The pie diagram in Fig. 1.10 has been included to show the relative importance of individual manufacturing industries. The dominant position of the engineering industry is at once apparent, since it employs 1 in every 4 factory workers. Food, drink and tobacco, vehicles (including shipbuilding), and paper and printing industries are the next largest groups. Together with engineering, these industries account for the employment of over half the manufacturing workforce. Among others, metal goods (a miscellaneous category including tools, cutlery, metal containers, etc.), chemicals, clothing, textiles, metal manufacture (mainly iron and steel), timber and furniture, and non-metallic mineral products (e.g. glass and ceramics) are sufficiently important to be separately distinguished.

Foreign trade

The United Kingdom is far from being an isolated self-sufficient country; instead it engages in a substantial amount of trade with the rest of the world.

In the last century Britain held a dominant position in world trade, especially in the export of manufactured products. A hundred years ago Britain supplied almost 40 per cent of such world exports, compared with less than 8 per cent today – Britain now takes fifth place after Japan, West Germany, the United States and France. Britain is also the fifth largest importer in the world. More relevant in some ways, however, is the role imports play in the UK economy. Over a quarter of all goods and services consumed in Britain are made up, directly or indirectly, of imports. This underlines the key place of foreign trade in the economic life of the country and may be contrasted with the situation in the USA or Japan, for example, where imported goods comprise notably lower proportions of the national income. (There are, of course, countries where the proportion of imports to national income is higher than in the UK, e.g. Belgium and the Netherlands – *see* page 113.)

Commodity composition

The traditional picture of Britain in the world economy in the past was characterised by great dependence upon foreign sources of supply for essential raw materials and foodstuffs, paid for by the export of manufactured products. This is no longer the case. The importance of primary products in the import bill has greatly diminished as a result of many factors, including the development of synthetics and the decline of some raw-material-using industries, such as textiles.

Figures 1.11 and 1.12 show the major changes that have

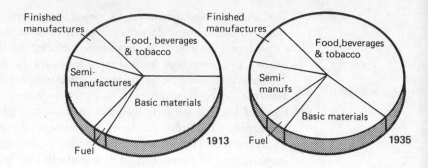

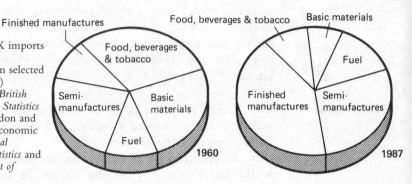

Fig. 1.11 UK imports (commodity composition in selected years 1913–87) Sources: *The British Economy, Key Statistics 1900–70*, London and Cambridge Economic Service, *Annual Abstract of Statistics* and *Monthly Digest of Statistics*

taken place in the composition of British foreign trade during the twentieth century. It can be seen that food, beverages and basic materials accounted for about three-quarters of total imports before the First World War, but for barely more than 15 per cent by 1987. The only material to have increased significantly has been fuel; though, thanks largely to North Sea oil, the UK had become a *net* fuel exporter by the 1980s. The corollary of the decline in imports of primary products, also seen in Fig. 1.11, is the great rise in the importance of manufactures and semi-manufactures, which nowadays account for over two-thirds of total imports. Since UK exports have remained mainly of manufactured goods (*see* Fig. 1.12), British overseas trade is best characterised as consisting predominantly of the exchange of manufactured goods with other countries. There have, however, been substantial changes in the relative importance of different kinds of manufactured goods which are exported. To a substantial extent these reflect shifts in the structure of industrial production.

Geographical distribution of trade

The geographical composition of UK trade is shown in Fig. 1.13. It has shifted very considerably from that of former times. Before the Second World War, the countries in the Commonwealth were the UK's major trading partners.

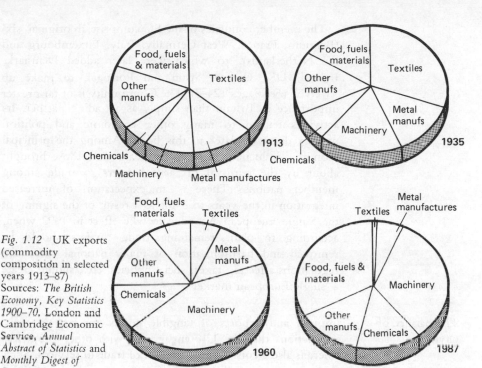

Fig. 1.12 UK exports (commodity composition in selected years 1913–87) Sources: *The British Economy, Key Statistics 1900–70*, London and Cambridge Economic Service, *Annual Abstract of Statistics* and *Monthly Digest of Statistics*

Fig. 1.13 Geographical distribution of UK foreign trade, 1987 Source: *Monthly Digest of Statistics*

Now the countries of Europe occupy the dominant position, accounting for about 60 per cent of UK imports and exports. By far the most important are the countries belonging to the European Community (EC). They alone were responsible for half of all UK overseas trade by 1987.

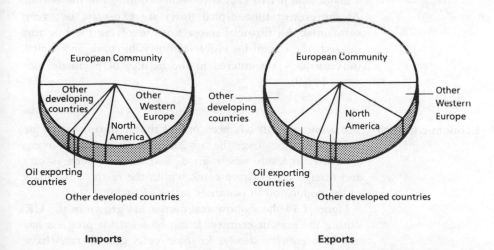

The member countries of the EC comprise an original 'six' (Belgium, France, West Germany, Italy, Luxembourg and the Netherlands), to which were later added Denmark, Ireland, UK, Greece, Spain and Portugal, to make up 'twelve'. (*See* pages 124–7). The Community is of far greater importance to Britain than simply as a trading partner. Its activities extend to many other economic and political matters discussed later in this book. Among the principal economic influences in the early years were those brought about by the removal of tariff barriers to trade among member nations. There is an expectation of increased integration in the years to come as a result of the signing of the Single European Act, due to take effect in 1992 when, according to plan, remaining trade barriers should be removed and harmonisation of many national rules and regulations affecting taxes, social policies, etc., should create a 'single European market'.

The balance of payments

Imports and exports of tangible goods are not the only transactions that the UK engages in with other countries. There is also a considerable amount of trade in services. Such trade is known as '**invisible**', in contrast with the '**visible**' **trade** in exports and imports of goods with which we have so far been concerned. Invisible earnings from the services of financial institutions, in the form of returns on overseas investments and from other sources, have played an important part in paying for the UK's excess in the value of imports over exports of goods.

Finally, we should mention international capital transactions – lending and borrowing on short-term and long-term account. As far back as the nineteenth century, Britain was a major supplier of capital for other countries in the world. At the present time capital flows are two-way, but very substantial. All financial transactions involving the UK and the rest of the world – visible and invisible trade and capital movements – are entered in the balance of payments (*see* pages 194–9).

Economic growth

Economic growth has been one of the dominant forces for industrial nations over the last 200 years. It has raised living standards to levels where goods and services, such as cars and foreign travel, have come within the reach of the mass of the population in countries such as Britain.

Figure 1.14 shows how real output has grown in the UK during the present century. It can be seen that progress has not been entirely steady. In some years growth rates have been high – up to 8 per cent. In others the rate has actually

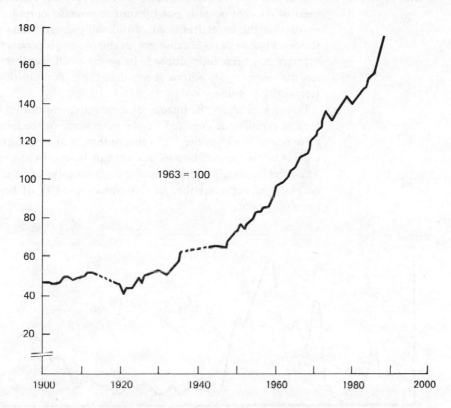

180 ─

160 ─

140 ─

120 ─

100 ─   1963 = 100

80 ─

60 ─

40 ─

20 ─

1900   1920   1940   1960   1980   2000

Fig. 1.14 Real output 1900–87
Sources: *The British Economy, Key Statistics 1900–70,* London and Cambridge Economic Service, *Annual Abstract of Statistics* and *Monthly Digest of Statistics.*

been negative, output falling by almost as much as it rose in the good years. However, the long-term trend has been unequivocally upwards. Since the end of the Second World War the rate of economic growth has averaged 2½ per cent per annum. This figure may seem low by comparison with some other countries, especially Japan, and, until recently, EC countries such as West Germany and France. However it is substantially higher than the average rate of growth in Britain earlier in the century, which was about 1 per cent before the First World War and is comparable to the 2 per cent achieved in the interwar period. Moreover, the cumulative workings of compound interest can lead to rather startling results: a growth rate of 2 per cent per year, if continued for a century, will lead to more than a sevenfold increase in real national income. Britain achieved a rate of 2½ per cent in the third quarter of this century. Such a rate causes output to double within a generation, as can be seen by inspection of the levels of output in 1957 and 1987 in Fig. 1.14. Material living standards rose by almost the same extent. Only *almost* because the population, among whom output needs to be divided, rose by about 10 per cent, so that income *per head* rose by rather less than gross output.

Unemployment

The account of economic growth in the previous section has been of *achieved* output, not maximum *potential* output. We know that the latter has been considerably greater than the former in some years because not all the country's productive capacity has been fully utilised. In so far as all workers are not fully employed, output is less than the maximum that is technically possible.

Figure 1.15 traces the history of unemployment during the present century, as depicted by the percentage of the labour force out of work. In the 19th century there was a reasonably regular trade cycle of booms and slumps lasting 8–10 years. The level of unemployment varied continuously; there were no *prolonged* periods either of full employment or of heavy unemployment.

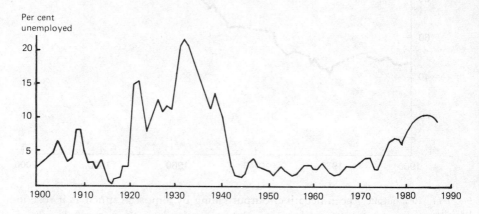

Per cent unemployed

Fig. 1.15 Percentage unemployment 1900–87 (figures for 1900–26 relate to the unionised labour force; for 1926–81 to the numbers registering as unemployed; and for 1981–87 to those claiming social security benefits)
Sources: *The British Economy, Key Statistics 1900–70*, London and Cambridge Economic Service, *Annual Abstract of Statistics* and *Monthly Digest of Statistics*.

The period between the two world wars presents a dismal picture of heavy unemployment. The unemployment of the 1920s was an isolated British phenomenon associated with the long-term decline in some of Britain's staple export industries. The high British unemployment rate was not matched elsewhere in the world in that decade; in the United States, for example, the mid-1920s was a period of boom. The 1930s, however, saw heavy unemployment throughout the world. At the worst point in the Great Depression one person in four was unemployed in the United Kingdom. A similar situation ruled in America and in most industrialised countries.

During the Second World War unemployment fell to an extremely low level indeed. After the war unemployment still fluctuated, but from 1945 until the early 1970s the fluctuations were over a much narrower range than in the 19th century.

In 1974 the world entered the worst recession since the Great Depression of the 1930s. Unemployment in the UK began a steady upward climb that took it from 2½ per cent in 1974 to 6 per cent in 1977, breaking the 10 per cent barrier in the early 1980s. Several changes in the definition of unemployment make it difficult to identify the exact peak reached in 1986. Even the official figure touched 12 per cent, though on bases comparable with earlier years the figure was certainly higher. Recent trends are reconsidered in Chapter 4 (*see* pages 235–9).

The monetary system

So far this chapter has discussed the *real* parts of the economy, that is to say the supply of the real resources of land, labour and capital and the production of real goods and services. However, the economy has another side to it, a *monetary* one, which reflects the fact that resources and goods are measured in terms of their prices or monetary values.

Money has traditionally been defined as anything that is generally accepted by virtually everyone in exchange for goods and services. It includes notes and coins, but the most important means of making payments today is through banks. Bank deposits, the sums standing to the credit of customers, are the prime constituent of what is regarded as money in the UK, though there are several alternative definitions of the money supply which will be discussed in Chapter 8 (pages 209–10).

The business of banking is mainly in the hands of the four large so-called **clearing banks** – Barclays, Lloyds, Midland and National Westminster. Against their deposit liabilities they hold a variety of financial assets, ranging from notes and coins in the vaults, through securities, to the loans and advances they make to customers, often by granting them overdraft facilities. It is the last of these which are of major importance in determining the quantity of money in existence.

The monetary sector of the economy, however, includes a great many other financial institutions, for example merchant banks, discount houses, building societies and insurance companies, which will be considered in Chapter 8. All deal in monetary assets of one form or another. Their activities may affect key economic variables, especially the general levels of prices, output and employment. Since the banks and other financial institutions can play important roles in these matters, the government often tries to influence them in pursuit of its policy objectives. The state has many ways of doing so. Several are carried out through the central bank – in the UK, the Bank of England – which is owned by the government and is its instrument of monetary policy.

The Bank of England can exert influence on the supply of

money by pressuring the banks to alter their lending policies. It has methods of influencing the size of their cash reserves, and in other ways affecting the banks' liquidity (the proportion of cash and other assets to total deposits). The Bank can also control the level of interest rates, i.e. the prices paid by borrowers or received by lenders of money, and in that way alter spending, and thereby also the price level, output and employment.

Inflation

Changes in the general level of prices affect real output. The strength and duration of this effect are controversial, but governments throughout the world have been worried by persistent inflation, which hardly needs describing to anyone alive today.

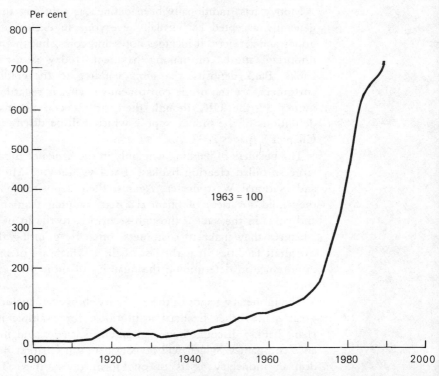

Fig. 1.16 Index of retail prices 1900–1988
Sources: *The British Economy, Key Statistics 1900–70*, London and Cambridge Economic Service, *Annual Abstract of Statistics* and *Monthly Digest of Statistics.*

Figure 1.16 shows the course of the *average* level of retail prices in the UK since 1900. It demonstrates that, apart from a very few years after the First World War and in the early 1930s, the general trend has been decidedly upwards. Indeed, by 1988 prices were approximately five times their level of 20 years before, or nearly 50 times those in 1900. Put another way, a 1988 pound had roughly the same purchasing power as 20 pence of a 1968 pound or as 2 pence at the beginning of the century.

The first 20 years after the Second World War were those of a fairly steady, if slow, rate of increase in the level of prices – 2 to 3 per cent per annum on average. Towards the end of the 1960s inflation started to accelerate and first reached double figures in the early 1970s. In 1974 the rate topped 20 per cent and the following year prices rose by more than 25 per cent in 12 months. The rate of inflation dropped again in the later 1970s but only fell below 10 per cent after 1982. In the following few years the rate stayed around 5 per cent. We discuss recent inflation in more detail in Chapter 9.

Government

The UK is a **mixed economy**. A great many decisions are taken by private individuals in markets where the forces of supply and demand work relatively free from government interference. However, there are important sectors where the state enters directly or indirectly into decision-making on the allocation of resources.

Figure 1.17 shows the long-term trends in the size of government activity as measured by the proportion of public expenditure to total national income since 1900 (government expenditure here excludes expenditure by the nationalised industries). This is only one of a number of indicators that can be used for the same purpose; indeed, the precise percentages obtained are sensitive to which indicator is chosen. However, there is no danger in drawing the general conclusion that the trend is of substantial growth in government expenditure. While not much more than 10 per cent of the national income passed through the government's hands at the beginning of the century, by 1970 the proportion had risen to over 40 per cent, which level has been

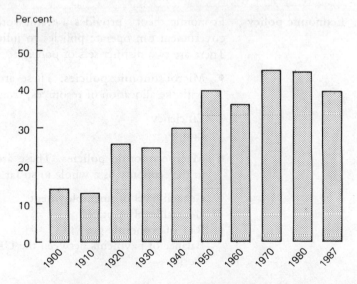

Fig. 1.17 Government expenditure as a percentage of GNP
Sources: *The Growth of Public Expenditure in the UK*, A T Peacock and J Wiseman (Allen & Unwin, 1967) and *UK National Accounts*

maintained until the late 1980s. Similar trends have been experienced by other countries.

There are many explanations for the growth of public expenditure which, of course, carried with it growing government income from taxation. They include major changes in the public's attitude to the role of the state in the provision of social services (the Welfare State) and decisions to take certain important industries into public ownership (nationalisation), especially in the early years after the Second World War.

There is also a technical reason why the public sector tends to grow relative to the rest of the economy. It is known as the **relative price effect**. Put simply, the reason is that productivity in government services rises more slowly than in manufacturing industry because of the small scope for mechanisation and, therefore, for economies of large-scale production. The prices of government services tend to rise in consequence *relative* to those of the rest of the economy (this is why it is called the *relative* price effect). Since the output of the public and private sectors is valued by reference to their prices (or costs), the size of the former has a natural tendency to increase relative to that of the latter. This is not, of course, an iron law. Governments can exercise control over the total expenditure from the public purse. Three Conservative administrations since 1979 were committed to reducing the size of the public sector. Various measures were set in train, including the transfer of several major activities into private hands, as part of the 'privatisation programme' (*see* pages 47–8). The percentage share, however, remained above 40 per cent, though planned public expenditure for 1988–89 was set to fall to 38 per cent.

| Economic policy | Economic theory provides a framework within which the government can operate policies to influence the economy. There are two distinct sets of policies: |

- **Microeconomic policies.** These are policies concerned with the allocation of resources, from the viewpoints of:

  Efficiency
  Equity

- **Macroeconomic policies.** These are policies applicable to the economy as a whole in so far as they concern:

  General level of unemployment
  General level of prices
  Rate of economic growth
  Balance of payments between the UK and the rest of the world

Economic policies in pursuit of these objectives are discussed at appropriate places throughout the book.[1] It may, however, be useful to indicate some of them in summary form here.

Measures related to efficiency

The measures in this category are especially varied. Many are directed to the private sector of the economy, where the state engages in interventionist actions to help certain industries and to regulate others. There are subsidies for industries thought to be in need of special assistance (e.g. agriculture); loans, grants and subsidised consultancy services for small businesses; measures designed to influence the regional location of industry; agencies for the investigation and control, where thought necessary, of monopolies, restrictive practices and mergers which might adversely affect the competitiveness of industrial sectors. Other agencies are more specialised, e.g. those regulating financial services; maintaining quality standards – especially in the case of products that are dangerous. These and many other measures are described later.

One other policy concerned with efficiency in the economy is that where the state itself engages in the provision of certain types of goods and services, because for one reason or another it is thought that private sector production is inappropriate.

Examples under this head include the provision of armies, navies and airforces for national defence, of the police and law courts for the administration of justice, and extensive parts of health and education services. These are, in the main, non-commercial activities financed by the state out of its general revenues and provided free to the community.

However, there is another group, known as the nationalised industries, which have been owned and operated by the state and which do levy charges for their services. These nationalised industries, which possess some of the characteristics of commercial enterprises, have been run by specialised agencies called **public corporations**. They enjoy a considerable degree of independence in the conduct of their day-to-day affairs, though subject to ultimate ministerial control.

The first appearance of nationalised industries can be traced to well before the Second World War, but the major period of extension of public ownership of industry in Britain occurred during the period 1945–51. Then the Labour Party first held a majority of seats in the House of Commons, and coal, electricity, gas, the railways and steel were taken over into public ownership.

1 See Lipsey and Harbury, *First Principles*, Chapters 23, 24, 31 and 37.

Nationalisation was, of course, a matter with strong political implications. Its value was, nevertheless, accepted by both Conservative and Labour governments from 1945 up to the 1970s. In their move towards much more reliance on free markets, however, the Conservative governments under Mrs Thatcher set about a major reversal of the policy, by returning a number of nationalised industries to private hands in the 1980s. Such denationalisation formed part of the policy better known as **privatisation** (*see* pages 47–8). The largest transfers are of telecommunications (British Telecom, 1984), gas (1986), airlines (British Airways, 1987), steel (1988), and electricity and water planned for 1989. Quantitatively, the effects of the policy can be seen in the fact that the total number of employees in the nationalised industries halved in the period 1980–87 – falling from a figure representing 8 per cent of the labour force to one of 4 per cent.

Measures related to equity

The government adopts some policies in order to make the allocation of resources among individuals fairer, i.e. more equitable. Two sets of policies are available. One is directed to redistributing income, leaving people free to decide how to spend it in their own best interests. The other provides certain goods and services free, or at less than cost, to all who want them, regardless of income. There are two instruments for redistribution which are of prime importance:

(a) the levying of taxes, especially on income earned and capital owned by individuals

(b) providing so-called transfer benefits in cash to individuals, e.g. retirement pensions, unemployment benefit.

The major fields in which the state provides goods and services free, or at a subsidised price, are education (from school to university), health and housing. Many such benefits have been effective in redistributing resources in the direction of greater equality. Some are 'means tested' in so far as they may be free to the poorest members of the population only, though possibly sold at subsidised prices to others.

Control of the economy as a whole

Since the Second World War, governments have usually taken on responsibility for trying to control the rate of inflation, the level of unemployment and the rate of economic growth of the national economy, and to exert an influence on the balance of trade between the UK and the rest of the world. Instruments available to these ends include (a) **fiscal policy**, which seeks to influence total spending through the government's own budget – changing its taxes and/or expenditure as required; and *(b)* **monetary policy** which tries to influence spending through interest rates and the supply of money. These policies are discussed in Chapter 9 of this book.

Questions and exercises

The questions which follow are designed to make you collect recent data, compare it with data in the book, and draw conclusions relevant to understanding the nature of the UK economy. (For key to symbols indicating suggested sources, *see* pages xi–xii).

1 Draw a chart on the lines of Fig. 1.6 showing the percentage changes in the population of each of the standard regions of the UK over the ten-year period leading up to the most recent year for which you can find statistics. Write a brief commentary comparing your figures with those for the longer period since 1900 in Fig. 1.6 (*AS*)

2 What is the population of your home town? What was it at the time of the 1951 Census, and 100 years ago? How does its changing size compare with that for the population of the country as a whole? Have you any idea why it may be the same, or different? (*WA may be helpful.*)

3 Calculate the proportion of the total agricultural area of the land in the UK used for cereal production in a recent year and the proportion of the value of output in the same year. Why are they not likely to be the same? (*AS*)

4 Obtain figures of total energy consumption by the main industry groups and place them in rank order. Do the same for those industries according to their growth (or decline) in output in a recent period. Are the heaviest consumers the fastest or slowest growers? What implications do your results have for energy scarcity in the future? (*AS*)

5 Prepare a table showing the gross capital stock, Gross National Product and net overseas assets of the UK for every other of the last ten years. Compare their sizes over the decade. Which have changed most? Which series gives the best indicator of how living standards may have changed? What do the other two series highlight? (*BB*)

6 Imagine you had £2500 to spend on consumer durables. Select some commodities from a local store or catalogue. Estimate the proportion of the total that would be on imported goods. Do you think the result of your calculation would be roughly the same as the proportion of total national expenditure which goes on imports? Check your conclusion with national statistics. (*AS, BB*)

7 Find the following figures for a recent year and for another year which is ten years previous to it:

(a) the number of unemployed workers;
(b) the rate of inflation for the year;
(c) the rate of growth of total output.

Which of the three have performed best? (AS)

8　Try to obtain the annual report of one of the large privatised public corporations which was sold to private investors in recent years. Extract its gross profit (income). Express this sum as a percentage of the total income of all public corporations.

9　Ask each member of your class to provide figures of the number of persons in their family above school leaving age, and of the number who are in the labour force. What would you expect the proportion in the labour force to be if the families of your classmates were, on average, typical of the nation as a whole? How typical are they?

Appendix

Table A1.1 Geographical distribution of population and land area in the UK (selected Census years)
Source: *Annual Abstract of Statistics*

Standard regions of England and Wales	Area (thousand) sq. km)	Population (thousands) 1911	1931	1961	1981
North	15.4	2 815	3 038	3 250	3 104
Yorkshire and Humberside	15.4	3 877	4 285	4 635	4 860
East Midlands	15.6	2 263	2 531	3 100	3 819
East Anglia	12.6	1 192	1 232	1 470	1 872
South East	27.2	1 744	13 539	16 271	16 796
South West	23.9	2 687	2 794	3 411	4 349
West Midlands	13.0	3 277	3 743	4 758	5 148
North West	7.3	5 796	6 197	6 567	6 414
Wales	20.8	2 421	2 593	2 644	2 792
Scotland	78.8	4 760	4 843	5 179	5 131
N. Ireland	11.0	1 251	1 280	1 425	1 562
United Kingdom	244.1	42 082	46 038	52 709	55 089

Table A1.2 Projected population of the UK to year 2015 (thousands)
Source: *Annual Abstract of Statistics*

Age group	1985	1995	2005	2015
0–9	7 008	7 976	7 662	7 134
10–19	8 428	7 030	7 981	7 669
20–29	8 850	8 408	7 004	7 851
30–39	7 914	8 712	8 243	6 850
40–49	6 595	7 788	8 568	8 103
50–59	6 120	6 307	7 458	8 229
60–69	5 686	5 386	5 624	6 670
70–79	4 226	4 191	4 062	4 322
80 and over	1 791	2 347	2 617	2 650

Table A1.3 Employees by industry, June 1988 (thousands)
Source: *Employment Gazette* (November 1988)

Agriculture, forestry and fishing	294	Other transport equipment	229	Hotels and catering	1 144
Energy and water supply	446	Metal goods n.e.s.	288	Transport and communication	1 353
Metal manufacturing	160	Food, drink and tobacco	538	Banking, finance, insurance	3 438
Chemicals and man-made fibres	349	Textiles, leather, footwear and clothing	495	Public administration and defence	159
Mechanical engineering	705	Timber and wooden furniture	209	Education	1 678
Electrical engineering	530	Paper products, printing and publishing	477	Medical and other health services; veterinary services	1 275
Office machinery and data processing equipment	102	Other manufacturing	234	Recreational services	526
Motor vehicles and parts	234	Construction	997	Sanitary services	419
		Wholesale distribution and repairs	933	Other services	1 012
		Retail distribution	2 085		

Table A1.4 Gross capital stock, UK, 1977 and 1987 (£ billion at 1985 prices)
Source: *UK National Accounts,* 1988 edn.

	1977	1987
Road vehicles	39.6	48.9
Railway rolling stock, ships and aircraft	29.5	15.9
Plant and machinery	345.1	455.1
Dwellings	415.8	524.7
Other buildings and works	442.5	546.8
Total gross capital stock	1 272.4	1 591.3

2 | Organisation of business activity

Economists theorise about business decisions and generally agree that such decisions are affected by the institutional arrangements within which they are taken. In this chapter and the next we deal with these matters and describe the structure of industry in the UK, most of which operates in the private sector of the economy, with which we begin. Later in the chapter we look at public sector business enterprises, including those which have changed hands as part of the privatisation programme of the 1980s.[1]

Private sector business organisation

We start with an explanation of the organisational features of modern firms. There are four main forms of private business organisation in Britain:

- Single proprietorships
- Partnerships
- Co-operatives
- Joint-stock companies (called corporations in North America)

The single proprietorship

The oldest and simplest form of business organisation is sole ownership. The distinguishing feature of this type of enterprise is not that all the work is necessarily done by one person, though this may be the case, but that the business is *owned* by one individual. Such businesses are easy to set up and the owner can easily maintain full control. However, the size of the firm is limited by the amount of capital that owners can raise for themselves and, moreover, owners are personally responsible in law for all the debts incurred by the firm. It is not surprising to find, therefore, that the single proprietorship is not now of much importance in the UK,

1 This chapter deals with material relevant to the theories discussed in Lipsey and Harbury, *First Principles*, Chapter 13.

although it still flourishes in a few sectors such as farming and shopkeeping.

Partnerships

More common than the single proprietorship is the partnership. Whenever a sole operator feels that the burden of the business is too great, the alternative of going into partnership with one or more other people may be attractive.

Partners may have complementary contributions to make. For example, an inventor may go into partnership with an accountant. However, a major reason for seeking a business partner is often that the capital needed for operations is more than a single owner can provide. In such circumstances a partnership with others who contribute shares of the capital and take out proportionate shares of any profits may be a suitable form of business organisation.

Partnerships, however, suffer in the same way as do single proprietorships in that each partner is legally liable for all the debts of the firm, even if they have been incurred by the activity of another partner. There is no limit to this liability, which extends to the whole of a firm's debts, regardless of the amount of capital which the individual partners have originally contributed. Thus, for example, in a two person partnership where one partner supplies £40 000 of the original capital and the other only £10 000, if the partnership incurs net debts to the extent of £25 000 and the first partner becomes bankrupt and unable to meet any of the debt, the partner who put down only £10 000 in the first place may have to meet the whole of the £25 000, even if it means selling his or her house and any other property in order to do so.

The risk of being in partnership with people who prove to be unreliable, unscrupulous or even merely inefficient is consequently great and partnerships persist only in relatively small numbers – often in family businesses, where mutual confidence is strong, and in certain professions where the form is traditional and in which their survival is aided by what are called **limited partnerships**. In these, certain partners enjoy liability only to the extent to which they have invested money in the firm, provided they take no part in the running of the business.

Co-operatives

The third form of organisation, co-operatives, applies to businesses which are controlled either by their workers, or by the consumers of their products. The former, _producer_ co-operatives, involve the sharing of profits among workers. These organisations were flourishing 100 or more years ago, but went into decline in the present century. In recent years they have enjoyed some revival, when workers have refused to accept management decisions to shut down businesses, and have taken them over and continued operations, e.g. in certain transport industries.

Consumer co-operatives operate mainly in the retail trade. The origins of consumer co-operation are found in the political movement associated with the name of Robert Owen. The first successful experiment was in Rochdale in 1844, co-operation in retailing expanding greatly after that. Today there are only about 200 retail societies, and their number has been falling steadily, partly as a result of amalgamations.

The distinctive feature of co-operative societies lies in their ownership. While other shops belong to individuals or are joint stock companies (*see* next section), co-operatives are, in a sense, 'owned' by those of their customers who pay a minimum deposit on a share in the business. The co-operatives sell to the general public but part, at least, of the capital comes from members, most of whom contribute only small sums, and there is an upper limit on the amount of share capital which may be held by any individual. Many districts have their own local 'co-op'; the members elect a committee of management from among themselves, which decides upon the general policy of the store and appoints a manager and full-time staff to do the work. The principle on which co-operative societies grew up was one whereby goods were sold at normal retail prices. At the end of each half year the profits, in the form of a 'dividend' of so many pence per pound of purchases, were distributed to members in proportion to their purchases during the period.

Consumer co-operatives have suffered from intense competition from other types of organisation and, like producer co-operatives, have been on the decline during the present century. Many retail outlets have closed and small societies merged. Modernisation has taken place, with the help of the Co-operative Wholesale Society (CWS), owned by the retail societies. The CWS is a large manufacturer and importer and also operates its own banking and insurance business. Outside the single sector of retail milk distribution, however, the retail co-operatives have so far failed to restore their former importance in retail trading. They were responsible for about an eighth of total retail turnover in 1950. By 1984 their share was only a twentieth.

Joint stock companies

The fourth and last type of business organisation, the joint stock company, is so important that we shall discuss it at much greater length.

Public prejudice against the joint stock form of organisation in the 18th and 19th centuries was strongly influenced by the abuses of company promoters at the time of the South Sea Bubble, and it was not until 1855 that the great privilege of **limited liability** was made generally available. Limited liability arises from the fact that companies are regarded in law as entities separate from the individuals who own them. A company can enter into contracts; it can sue and be sued; it can own property; it can contract debts; and its obligations are not those of its owners. Companies have a continuity of life unaffected, therefore, by changes in ownership, and they have become the most important form of business enterprise in Britain.

Such companies must include the word 'Limited' (or 'Ltd') in their name so that outsiders may know that the liability to meet the debts of the company is limited for every individual owner of the business (known as a **shareholder**) to the extent of the amount of capital that he or she has contributed or promised to contribute. The advantages of this privilege are substantial; two, in particular, are of outstanding importance.

Large amounts of capital become much easier to raise

This follows from the reduced risk to the individual investor, who knows from the outset the maximum amount of money he or she can lose, should the worst come to the worst. They will no longer be so afraid of venturing into business with other people whose names they may not even know. In fact, in many large companies there are hundreds of thousands, even millions, of shareholders, the vast majority of whom contribute only a minute proportion of the total capital of the business.

Transfer of ownership can take place with a minimum of formality

Limited liability removes the need for each shareholder to know every other shareholder personally. Consequently shareholders can sell their shares to anyone else. In other words, there is a distinct advantage, absent from a partnership, that the shares can always be sold quickly if one is in urgent need of cash. The great importance of this transferability of shares has given rise to the appearance of a specialised market place where shares are bought and sold. It is called the **Stock Exchange** (*see* pages 37–9).

The advantages which limited liability bestows on an individual company are matched, to some extent, by an increased risk to others, especially to companies and individuals who do business with it, and to minority shareholders whose interests may be lost sight of in very large companies. There is also a risk that unscrupulous company promoters may fraudulently try to raise funds for their own ends from the public. In an attempt to safeguard the community from such risks, a number of Companies Acts have been passed, mainly requiring publication of information about the state of the firm and its management.

There are two principal types of company, **public** and **private**. The latter must restrict its shareholders to 50 and is not permitted to offer its shares for sale to the general public. For these reasons private companies are not obliged to publish as much information about their affairs as are public companies, which, by EC law, must describe themselves as public limited companies (**plcs**). They are greatly outnumbered by private companies but tend to be much larger.

There are approximately half a million companies in existence, but only about 3 per cent are public companies. On the other hand, the great majority of large businesses in Britain are organised as public companies. Some indication of the importance of giant companies is given by the fact that the 100 largest groups of joint stock companies in manufacturing produce over 40 per cent of total output. (*See* pages 65–77 for a discussion of business concentration.)

Business accounts

The most important information that companies are required to publish is contained in their balance sheet and profit and loss account.

The **balance sheet** consists of a statement of the value of the business's assets together with its liabilities, or claims on them. There are two kinds of assets:

- **fixed assets** such as land, buildings, machinery and equipment;
- **current assets**, which are the result of business operations and include stocks of raw materials and finished products, debts due to the company from its customers and cash.

There is also a special kind of asset called **goodwill**, which is an estimate of the benefit deriving from a firm's reputation.

The **liabilities** of the company are financial claims on its assets. Since all assets must be owned by someone, they must be equal to the total liabilities. There are two classes of liabilities:

- liabilities to the owners of the business, i.e. the shareholders;
- liabilities to other creditors, including customers and those who have made loans to the company.

It should be realised that balance sheet valuations of assets are not necessarily as precise as they may appear. Assets are not all put up for sale continually, so that assessments of their value may be somewhat arbitrary. This can make comparisons of profit rates difficult, both among companies and, over time, within the same company. A simplified balance sheet of a typical company is shown below on this page.

A single balance sheet gives a picture of the financial state of a business at the time it is drawn up. To appreciate a company's prospects, however, it is necessary to compare balance sheets over a run of years, and to observe the progress that has occurred in the growth or depletion of the assets. A company's financial state may be best studied, however, with the help of the **profit and loss account**. Whereas a balance sheet relates to the financial position of a company at a particular *point of time*, the profit and loss account is a record of a company's operations over a stated *period of time*, such as a year. It is a statement of the residual profit or loss achieved by a company in the period, derived by taking the total revenue earned by a firm and subtracting all costs incurred in earning it.

Balance sheet as at 31 December 19–1

	£	£		£	£
Capital and liabilities			*Assets*		
Issued capital			Fixed assets		
Ordinary shares	x		Land, buildings	x	
Preference shares	x	x	Machinery, equipment	x	
Loan from XYZ Bank Ltd		x	Goodwill	x	x
Current liabilities			Current assets		
Sundry creditors		x	Stocks of raw materials	x	
			Stocks of finished products	x	
			Current debtors	x	
			Cash at bank	x	x
		£x			£x

Profit and loss account for the year 1 January to 31 December 19–1

	£	£		£
Expenditure			*Income*	
Fixed costs			Revenue from sales	x
Rent	x			
Research & development	x			
Managerial salaries	x			
Interest on bank loan	x			
Depreciation allowance	x	x		
Variable costs				
Wages	x			
Fuel used	x			
Raw materials used	x	x		
(Net profit for year		x)	(Net loss for year	x)
		£x		£x

A typical profit and loss account is shown above. Note the distinction, important in the theory of the firm, between **fixed** (or **overhead**) **costs** and **variable** (**prime**, or **direct**) **costs**.[1] Only the latter change as output changes, though the longer the period of time under consideration the more types of costs tend to be variable rather than fixed.

An important deduction from the *gross* profit of a business is that usually made to allow for the **depreciation** of its assets, which are subject to wear and tear and to obsolescence. Depreciation allowances are provided for in the accounts and must be subtracted from the revenue to arrive at the *net* profit. These depreciation provisions represent the value of capital equipment used up in the process of production. They must be deducted from the market value of current production in order to discover whether or not such production is profitable. It should be added that depreciation allowances are only estimates, which may be difficult to make in the face of uncertainty, especially about the future rate of inflation and hence about the future value of capital equipment.

The financing of the firm

Firms obtain finance for their operations in five ways:

- by selling (or issuing) **shares** in the business to buyers who then become owners
- by selling **bonds** to purchasers, who then become creditors of the business
- by **borrowing** from banks and other financial institutions
- by **reinvesting** the firm's profits
- by **taking over** or **merging** with other firms

[Handwritten margin notes: PREF. SHARES / DIVIDEND FROM SHARES – FIXED %; NO PROFITS – NO DIVIDENDS; ORD. SHARES (EQUITY); VOTING, PROFITS, CLAIM ON PROFITS; Preference & Ordinary Shares; PREF Shares PAID OUT before O.Share]

Share issues

There are two main groups of shares: preference shares and ordinary shares or equities

Preference shares, as their name implies, entitle their holders to shares in the firm's profits before other shareholders. The money they receive is known as a **dividend** and is usually fixed as a percentage of the capital invested. Courtaulds plc, for example, issued a 7½ per cent preference share which yields £7.50 for every £100 of shares held. So long as the company makes sufficient profit to meet the dividends of the preference shareholders, they all receive their dividends in full. Of course, if the company makes no profit at all, no dividends are paid (the dividend is then said to be 'passed'), but even if the company has a phenomenally

1 See Lipsey and Harbury, *First Principles*, Chapter 15.

profitable year, preference shareholders get no more than their fixed rate of dividend.

It is usually presumed, unless stated to the contrary, that preference shares are **cumulative**, i.e. when a dividend is passed, shareholders have the deficiency made good in a later year if profits recover. Often the right is evidenced by the word 'cumulative' being included in the name of the shares, e.g. those of Courtaulds plc. There may also be more than one class of preference share and, occasionally, participating preference shares are issued which allow the holders a share in profits over and above the stipulated figure. Preference shareholders may or may not be allowed a vote at company meetings, but they rarely have much power.

Holders of **ordinary shares** (or **equities**) usually do have voting rights and a residual claim on the company profits. Their dividend is not guaranteed, but is decided on a year-to-year basis when the profit position is known. The rate of dividend is declared as a percentage of the *nominal* value of the shares. It does not represent the profit rate for all shareholders − this depends upon the price paid for the shares. Tate and Lyle, for example, paid a dividend in 1988 of 39.3 pence on each of their £1 ordinary shares. Thus, a person who owns 100 shares receives £39.30. It is, however, unlikely that many shareholders paid exactly £100 for 100 shares. For them the rate of profit is not 39.3 per cent. In 1988, for instance, the price of one of these shares was around £800 so someone buying them would receive a dividend **yield** of about 5 per cent (£39·3 as a percentage of £800).

The income received by equityholders is liable to fluctuate from year to year, so that holdings of ordinary shares tend to be relatively risky investments. For an individual shareholder, however, a portfolio consisting of a range of shares in different companies reduces the risk. On the other hand, someone wanting to speculate in the hope of a high return can choose to invest in companies in risky lines of business, e.g. mine exploration (*see* pages 105–6 for some examples).

The risk attaching to shares depends, too, on the relative importance of equity to other issued capital carrying a fixed rate of interest (the 'gearing' ratio, *see* pages 36–7).

New issues

Companies wishing to raise new capital have a choice of four methods:

- They may opt for a public issue of shares to the general public. This is often done in co-operation with a specialist financial institution such as a merchant bank or an issuing house. Such issues are commonly guaranteed by 'underwriters' who, for a consideration, agree to buy any unsold shares at a price fixed in advance.

- A second method is an **offer for sale**, where the new shares are sold to an issuing house which then disposes of them to the public.
- Another alternative is a **placing**, whereby particularly small issues of shares are sold by arrangement, privately, to investors.
- Lastly, shares may be offered to the company's existing shareholders in what is called a **rights issue**. This method tends to keep the costs of the issue down, but the shares normally have to be offered on favourable terms.

Bond issues

Some part of a company's capital may be issued in the form of **debentures** (known also as **loan stock**, or **bonds**). Bondholders are sometimes confused with preference shareholders, with whom they have some common features, but a debenture is essentially different from a share of any kind. It may properly be regarded as a kind of IOU acknowledging a debt by a company to the purchasers of the bonds, who become creditors of the company, and who are also paid interest on the loan. The rate of interest on debentures is fixed in advance, such as the United Biscuit Company's 8 per cent debentures, holders of which have the prior right to receive this interest before any dividends are paid on preference or ordinary shares. The distinction between bonds and shares is thus clear.

However, hybrids exist, known as **convertibles**. These are bonds which carry an option to convert into shares at some time in the future, e.g. Storehouse plc's 9% loan stock which is convertible into equities at a fixed price of £100 loan stock for £6.60 (nominal value) of ordinary shares. Convertible loan stock has proved an attractive way of financing mergers and take-overs (*see* pages 73–5).

In the event of the company going into liquidation, i.e. being wound up, debenture holders, as creditors of the company, have a prior claim (together with any other trade creditors) to the return of their capital; their holding may even be secured by pledges attached to specific assets belonging to the company. The disadvantage of raising capital in the form of bonds is that the company must pay out interest even if there are no profits. Many a firm has been forced out of business because it could not meet its obligations in the form of fixed interest payments.

				HI plc			LO plc

Borrowing from banks

Businesses often borrow from banks to finance their operations. This form of finance is similar to that of issuing bonds, in that loans are at a rate of interest that must be paid regardless of whether the firm is, or is not, making a profit.

Gearing

The riskiness of any ordinary shares is liable to be affected by the ratio of equities to total capital. This is known as the **gearing ratio**, which is said to be high if the proportion of bonds and other fixed interest debt to equities is large (and vice versa).

The companies HI plc and LO plc in the example illustrate this point. Both have the same profits available for distribution in each of two years and the same total issued capital, but they have different gearing ratios. HI plc is highly geared, with 80 per cent of its capital in the form of 5 per cent debentures. When profits double in a good year from £5000 to £10 000 it would be possible to raise the dividend on ordinary shares sixfold from 5 to 30 per cent, after meeting the obligations to debenture holders. LO plc, on the other hand, is low geared, with only 20 per cent of its capital in 5 per cent debentures. The same doubling of profits would only permit a rise from 5 to 11¼ per cent for the ordinary shareholders.

		HI plc		LO plc	
	£		£		£
Capital	100 000	5 per cent Debentures	80 000	5 per cent Debentures	20 000
		Ordinary shares	20 000	Ordinary shares	80 000

Dividends

	Allocation of profits		Dividend rate per cent		Allocation of profits		Dividend rate per cent	
	Year 1	Year 2	Year 1	Year 2	Year 1	Year 2	Year 1	Year 2
	£	£	%	%	£	£	%	%
Capital								
Debentures	4 000	4 000	5	5	1 000	1 000	5	5
Ordinary shares	1 000	6 000	5	30	4 000	9 000	5	11¼
Total	5 000	10 000			5 000	10 000		

A real example of a very low geared company is Dowty (an engineering group), with less than 10 per cent of its capital needing to be serviced by fixed interest securities. It is difficult to find a very highly geared company, for the reason given above. Fodens, the commercial vehicle manu-facturer, was so highly geared, with over a third of its capital in fixed interest debt, that it underwent severe financial problems, ending in its being taken over in 1980.

Reinvested profits

We stated earlier that a major source of capital for new investment comes from **ploughing back profits** into the business. This is one of the easiest ways for the controllers of a firm to raise money. It implies holding back dividend payments in the short term, but it can lead to larger earnings for shareholders later. It is also by far the most important means, quantitatively speaking, of expanding businesses. Figure 2.1 shows that undistributed profits far exceed other uses of company profits. ('Other interest' is to banks and other lenders.)

Fig. 2.1 Allocation of company income 1987
Source: *UK National Accounts*

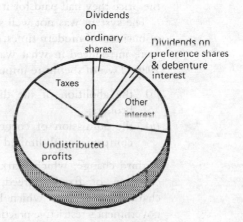

Dividends on ordinary shares

Dividends on preference shares & debenture interest

Taxes

Other interest

Undistributed profits

Take-overs of other firms

The final method of obtaining finance, which is especially important for businesses seeking expansion, is by the acquisition of one firm by another. Merger activity has been strong since the 1960s, though mergers tend to come in waves. Note, too, that the provision of finance is only one among several motives for amalgamations, which we discuss again on pages 73–5.

The Stock Exchange

One of the great advantages of the joint stock form of organisation mentioned earlier is that shares can be bought and sold with relative ease. The existence of the specialised market place, called a **stock exchange**, helps greatly in this respect.

The International Stock Exchange (formerly named the London Stock Exchange) is not concerned with raising new capital for companies, but with purchases and sales of *existing* shares. Such business has a long history and can be traced back to the informal meetings of traders in the eighteenth century at Jonathan's Coffee House in Exchange Alley. The modern stock exchange developed during the nineteenth century, stimulated by the Companies Acts and the institution of limited liability, mentioned earlier.

Prior to 1986, dealing in shares was conducted on the floor of the Stock Exchange by members of the Stock Exchange who, curiously enough, were not themselves permitted to enjoy limited liability but were, for the most part, organised as partnerships. Two distinct classes of member were recognised – **brokers** and **jobbers**. Brokers acted as agents for the general public for whom they bought or sold shares or bonds, charging a commission for the service. Jobbers were the 'middlemen' who were not allowed to deal with the public, but only with brokers (or each other). The jobbers' profit depended on the price they received for stock exceeding the price they had paid for it.

The system was not well suited to the nature and volume of business of modern times, and a number of major changes were introduced in what was called 'Big Bang' in October 1986. Two of the more important of these changes were:

(a) the abolition of the distinction between jobbers and brokers;
(b) the admission of corporate members (i.e. joint-stock companies with limited liability).

A third change, which sparked off Big Bang itself, was the cessation of fixed, agreed, minimum commission rates charged by dealers, which had been challenged under the government's restrictive practices legislation (*see* pages 161–2).

Although the consequences of Big Bang have not yet completely worked themselves out, they are considerable. Large financial corporations moved into the stock market. Several were internationally based, and over half of London's brokers became foreign-owned. Some of the strongest became **market makers**, performing the role previously done by jobbers. VDUs in city offices replaced the floor of the Stock Exchange building for business; the volume of transactions doubled, while commission rates on large deals halved. The entire set-up became much more competitive, quite soon forcing some less efficient and less well-capitalised entrants to withdraw – especially after the stock market crash on 'Black Monday' (16 October 1987) when share prices underwent a dramatic fall.

Securities traded on the Stock Exchange include shares and debentures of public companies and bonds issued by British and foreign governments. (UK government securities are known as **gilt-edged** because the likelihood of bankruptcy is virtually nil.) Not every public company's shares are dealt in on the Stock Exchange. To earn the right to a full Stock Exchange quotation, companies must comply with certain rules, including the offer of a minimum proportion of its shares to the general public. More than 5000 securities are quoted on the International Stock Exchange. However, to attract smaller, and mainly new, companies, an Unlisted Securities Market was established in 1980. 'Unlisted' is obviously a misnomer, but the 300–400 listed companies in that market have less exacting requirements to meet for disclosure and frequency of reporting.

Investors who wish to minimise risk can buy shares in investment trust companies, which carry a range of shares. Alternatively they can buy units in a **unit trust**. This is an organisation which holds a portfolio of securities, so that the purchaser of a unit participates in the benefits and risks attaching to all the shares in the portfolio. These units are especially attractive to small savers and can be bought and sold in small denominations and with a minimum of formality without necessarily going through the Stock Exchange.

Many investors intend to hold on for a relatively long time to the shares that they buy. Others are speculators, known as 'bulls', 'bears' and 'stags'. **Bulls** expect a price rise; they buy shares now, hoping for the price to increase later. **Bears** expect a price fall; they agree on a price now at which they are to sell shares in the future. They do not own the shares at this point, but hope to buy them at a lower price before the contract to deliver becomes due. **Stags** expect the market price of *new* shares to be higher than the price at which they are initially offered for sale. They contract to buy forthcoming issues of shares, hoping to sell them at a profit after trading begins.

| The control of joint stock companies | The standard theory of the firm is based on the assumption that businesses seek to maximise their profits.[1] The proposition has some intuitive appeal in the case of small firms, where the owners run their businesses, but a major criticism of the theory centres around the question of who actually controls the firm.

Companies are owned by their shareholders, with whom

1   See Lipsey and Harbury, *First Principles*, Chapter 16.

ultimate control therefore lies. However, this is something of an oversimplification. In order to discover where effective control really lies, it is necessary to consider three important issues:

- the power of personal and institutional investors
- the role of company managers
- the size distribution of share ownership

The power of personal and institutional investors

The capitalist system was built on the basis of the ownership of shares by private individuals. However, as the economy developed, joint stock companies began to appear in the financial as well as the industrial sectors. These were large-scale financial institutions, such as merchant banks, insurance companies, and pension funds operating to provide private sector pensions for employees on retirement. These institutions came to hold increasing quantities of ordinary shares in British industry, pushing personal investors into a position of much diminished importance. As Fig. 2.2 shows, in 1963 individual persons owned over half of the total value of ordinary shares; by 1986, their holdings had dropped to a quarter.

Fig. 2.2 The ownership of shares in companies 1963 and 1986
Sources: *The Ownership of Company Shares*, Central Statistical Office, and *Lloyds Bank Economic Bulletin*, 1988

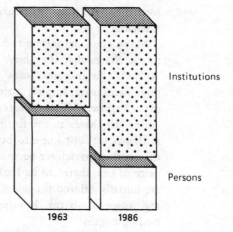

Institutions

Persons

1963   1986

The dominant position of financial institutions in the ownership of capital does not, of course, preclude private individuals from benefiting from the profitability of British companies. They merely benefit indirectly rather than directly.

It has, however, to be pointed out that the 1980s saw a substantial rise in the number of persons owning shares in British companies – from around 7 per cent of the adult population in 1979 to 20 per cent in 1988 (*see* Fig. 2.3). The new trend can be explained by several factors, including some growth in popularity of employee share ownership, and favoured tax treatment, but by far the most important influence was the government's privatisation programme (*see* pages 48 and 173–4). Sales of three large blocs of shares to the public – British Telecom, British Gas and Trustee Savings Bank – added almost 10 million shareholders.

It is important to realise that institutional shareholders are often large and, although individually they may not own very substantial proportions of the shares in a company, they may have a greater power than this would suggest because they may all act collectively. Indeed the greater the number, and the wider the spread among small shareholders, the greater the influence that a few large institutions may have.

The question of the control of companies as distinct from their ownership will be discussed shortly. First we need to see how joint stock companies make day-to-day management decisions.

Company management

Shareholders of large companies are generally remote from the company business. They rarely know enough about the affairs of the company to be involved in day-to-day decision-making, which is the concern of boards of directors. **Directors** are company employees, nominally appointed by shareholders at the **annual general meeting**, although they may often be (and for public companies are required by law to be) shareholders as well.

The power that shareholders are able to exercise over directors depends very much on the particular circumstances of a company. Often the power may be slight. This is especially the case where the distribution of shares is very wide and there are no really large shareholders. It is also the result of small attendances at company meetings. Absentee shareholders have the right to appoint 'proxies', or agents, to vote for them at the meeting, but as directors are in by far the best position to secure proxies, they themselves may be armed with an overwhelming number of votes and be able to control the decisions of the meeting.

The directors elect one of their number to be chairman and titular head of the company, and another (sometimes the same person) to be chief executive, or managing director, who is responsible, with the rest of the board, for running the company. Middle managers, such as the works manager, sales manager and other heads of department, are responsible to the board. Some part-time, non-executive directors may be appointed. They are often on the boards of several companies, and it is hoped that they are able to take a detached view of the efficiency of each.

Share ownership and control[1]   Effective control of a joint stock company lies in the ownership of the voting shares. Industrial democracy is based on the principle of one vote for every voting share held. Whoever can raise a majority of votes at company meetings can, therefore, control the meetings.

There is no general rule concerning the minimum percentage of total voting shares which qualify for a controlling interest. It is rare, except in small companies, that as much as 51 per cent is necessary. If ownership is widely diffused, and the majority of small shareholders are absent from a company meeting (as is often the case), the proportion of votes needed for effective control could be as little as 10 per cent. It would be an oversimplification to associate control of a company with a single individual. Groups of shareholders may act collectively, whether related by family or by common interests, as in the case of institutional shareholders.

It is thought, not unreasonably, that companies whose boards of directors collectively control a large number of voting shares may to some extent ignore the wishes of outside shareholders. They may, for example, be less concerned with trying to maximise profits for shareholders than with aiming for expansion of the firm to protect their jobs and raise their own remuneration. Some interest attaches, therefore, to identifying director-controlled and owner-controlled, i.e. shareholder-controlled, companies. Such a distinction is not, however, easily established, partly because full and up-to-date information on share ownership is not available. There are, indeed, some companies where directors appear to exercise control, but it is no easy matter to identify exactly which they are. Much depends on the distribution of non-directors' shareholdings. In this connection, the substantial increase in the number of personal shareholders since 1979 (*see* Fig. 2.3) should be seen as making their power more diffuse, especially in privatised corporations, where the size of the majority of holdings is very small. Of the million-and-a-half holders of British Telecom shares in 1986, for example, nearly 80 per cent owned fewer than 800 shares each.

Director power depends also on such matters as how many proxy votes the board acquires, the precise identity of the chairman and managing director (including their relationship to the founder of the firm and the founder's family), and other matters. Moreover, it must not be thought that, even where the directors are able to assemble enough votes to control meetings, they can necessarily ignore the views of other shareholders, particularly with regard to the level of

1   The importance for economic theory of the issues of ownership and control is discussed in Lipsey and Harbury, *First Principles*, Chapters 13 and 18.

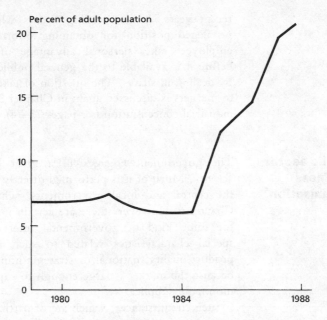

Fig. 2.3 Persons holding shares in Britain since 1979 Source: *Economic Progress Report*, 1988

Per cent of adult population

profits. This may be true for companies where a single firm or institution holds more than 50 per cent of the voting shares, but it is rare with large public companies.

Boardroom battles can take place, indicating that even the directors are not all of the same mind regarding policy. Ultimately, if the directors fail to operate a company effectively, they have to face the risk that outside interests (individuals, institutions or other companies) may try to acquire sufficient shares to give them a controlling interest and enable them to unseat the existing directors.

Take-over bids

The threat of hostile take-over bids (defined as those not agreed by the current board of directors) may be effective in keeping managers on their toes. However, sudden purchases of large quantities of shares can be extremely disruptive. They can cause great volatility in the prices of the shares of affected companies. This can, in turn, enable large profits to be made in the space of a few days by anyone with inside knowledge of what is going on. Rules have, therefore, been agreed to try to ensure that the 'game is played on a level playing field', to use the current jargon. This means, for example, that Stock Exchange dealings in shares may be suspended during a period of intense negotiations; and that a purchaser is required to offer to buy all the shares in a company as soon as their holding reaches 30 per cent. Rules to try to prevent insider trading have also been introduced, though few would contend that they could ever be 100 per cent effective, and the City has been embarrassed by some large, so-called insider trading that has come to light in recent years. Insider trading occurs when a person in a privileged position for obtaining information (e.g. as an employee) takes personal advantage of the information, before it is available to the general public, to make a profit by dealing in shares. The question of take-over bids leading to mergers is discussed again in Chapter 3, in the context of industrial concentration (*see* pages 73–74).

Public sector business organisation[1]

The government engages in a great deal of economic activity. Much of it is performed directly by departments of the central and local governments, which we discuss in Chapter 6. However, there are certain industries which call for some kind of governmental intervention because of special characteristics related to such matters as safety, product quality, national or strategic importance, or simply because the market is large enough to support only a single monopoly supplier.

Such circumstances, which are of particular importance in the areas of power supplies, transport, and communication, appear to make unfettered private enterprise an inappropriate form of organisation, though there is no general agreement on what is the best policy to adopt!

Broadly speaking, there are two alternatives available. One is to leave the industries in private hands, but to set up rules and regulations to control their activities. This option is discussed in Chapter 6. The second alternative is for the state itself to own and run the industries, which are said then to be nationalised.

Nationalised industries

(buses)

Nationalisation was a major policy of the Labour Government in 1945–50, when coal, gas, electricity, rail and some road transport industries were taken into the public sector. The public sector already included civil airlines, postal and telephonic communications, the BBC, and one or two others. Several major nationalised industries were sold back to private owners by the Conservative Governments of the 1980s, and others were scheduled for privatisation in the 1990s. However, the nationalised industries remained sufficiently important in 1988 (when they still accounted for the employment of about one in twenty of the labour force) for us to look briefly at the distinctive form of organisation within which they have been run. For, although the detailed structures of individual nationalised industries have varied, they have certain common features.

1 Issues of nationalised and publicly regulated industries are discussed in Lipsey and Harbury, *First Principles*, Chapter 19.

The public corporation	Nationalised industries in Britain are run by what are known as public corporations. The form and functions of these bodies differ somewhat from case to case, but in all of them there is a close resemblance to the boards of directors of joint

Parliament Control
Public A/c's Cttee.

stock companies. The chairmen and members of the corporations are appointed by the appropriate minister, e.g. Secretary of State for Energy, Secretary of State for Industry, but the corporations are otherwise free from day-to-day interference in the management of their affairs. Many members of the boards of nationalised industries come from private industry and, since 1978, have included civil servants and employee representatives. The major appointments are generally made for a fixed period of years, and matters of wages and conditions of service for the staff are generally determined independently from those in the Civil Service.

The control of nationalised industries	Since public corporations are to a certain extent independent bodies which do not have to face a shareholders' meeting every year, it is clearly important that they should have to submit to some control from outside. This happens in several ways.

In the first place, each nationalised industry is subject to a considerable measure of control from the appropriate minister, who appoints the members of the boards of the corporations and has general powers of direction over them. Ministerial powers are written into the individual Acts of nationalisation.

While ministers are not responsible to Parliament for the day to day administration of the nationalised industries, parliamentary control can be exercised through scrutiny by parliamentary committees such as the Public Accounts Committee. Since 1980, the Monopolies and Mergers Commission has also been called upon to investigate the efficiency of specific nationalised industries (see pages 160 ff). In addition, consumer councils have existed for some nationalised industries, e.g. electricity, gas, postal services and the railways. They are vehicles for the consuming public to voice their satisfaction, or dissatisfaction, with the way in which things are run.

Financial obligations of nationalised industries	Nationalised industries resemble commercial enterprises in several respects. Unlike many other government activities, they have not been intended to be financed mainly, if at all, from taxation, but to cover all or part of their costs by charging for their services. Some nationalised industries, however, have had recognised social obligations, e.g. to

provide postal services and rail transport to rural areas at less than full cost. Some, too, enjoy a monopoly position which can be exploited.

The financial obligations imposed on the nationalised industries have changed significantly over the years as a result of an increasing awareness of the commercial side of their operations and of a desire to compare their performance with that of companies in the private sector of the economy. Capital for development, over and above the capital generated internally, is borrowed from the central government, which, in turn, borrows from the market in order to obtain the best terms.

The terms of the original Acts of Parliament setting up the early corporations called for each industry to break even over an average of good and bad years. A substantial change in policy, however, followed the publication of two White Papers in 1961 and 1967. The second of these was particularly important in that, while recognising the existence of certain social obligations, it emphasised the commercial side of their operations and recommended that prices should be set to reflect long-run marginal costs, subject to the industry being able to cover its full costs of operation and to meeting its financial targets (*see* pages 171–2).

Pricing and investment in nationalised industries

The application of marginal cost pricing follows conclusions drawn from economic theory on optimal resource allocation.[1] This policy was adopted in many cases, including in the gas industry where it resulted in the (unpopular) earning of substantial short-run profits, justifiable in terms of the need to conserve an energy source, expected to be in long-term short supply. The pricing policy for the nationalised industries has not, however, always been strictly applied but has been allowed to lapse when it seriously interfered with other policy goals, especially for the control of inflation.

Marginal cost pricing was intended to establish a system whereby consumers of particular products pay for the cost of providing each product. This avoids any cross-subsidisation, so that profits made in one line of activity are not used to allow another to be carried on at a loss. However, this does still happen, for example, in the charge for posting a letter which is the same regardless of whether it is from Lands End to John O'Groats or from one house in Little Puddlecombe to another. There are two reasons for marginal cost pricing not being applied in such cases:

(a) the desire to subsidise certain classes of individual, e.g. those living in rural areas, or

(b) the need to keep down administrative costs

1 See Lipsey and Harbury, *First Principles*, Chapter 19, pages 214–5.

As far as investment policy is concerned, the earlier of the White Papers led to the setting of target rates of return on capital for each nationalised industry. The targets were arrived at after consideration of the social obligations of the different industries and their financial histories. They varied from 12½ per cent for electricity to a break-even formula for coal.

The second White Paper was more concerned with *new* investment than with the average rate of return on capital employed. Its main innovation was the introduction of a so-called test discount rate (TDR), intended as a measure of the real cost of using capital in the public sector of the economy. It could be changed from time to time, reflecting changes in the cost of raising capital. It was set at 8 per cent, but later raised to 10 per cent.

More recent developments in investment policy followed the publication of a third White Paper in 1978, which endorsed the general commercial approach of its predecessors. The recommendations of the 1978 White Paper were for the setting of financial targets for three to five years ahead and the adoption of a **required rate of return (RRR)** in real terms (i.e. allowing for inflation) of 5 per cent. The RRR should reflect the real cost of capital in the economy and form the basis for targets for individual industries. A further measure of control introduced was the **external financing limited (EFL)**, which can limit the amount a nationalised industry may raise from external sources in a particular year.

| Denationalisation and privatisation | As explained earlier, several major (as well as minor) nationalised industries were transferred to private ownership as part of the Conservative Governments' privatisation programme in the 1980s. Other parts of that programme are discussed in later chapters (*see* especially Chapter 6), but the denationalisation sales are relevant here. |

Figure 2.4 lists the principal assets that were sold off – the figures of proceeds of sale in the final column give an approximate idea of the size of the individual industries involved.

Note: The table excludes certain 'privatisation' sales such as the government's shares in British Petroleum, and shares in the Trustees Savings Bank, which were never nationalised industries in the sense that the term has been used in this book. However, it does include a number of industries which, though not run as independent public corporations, were nonetheless, state-run businesses. In these instances, the reasons for their having come into the public sector were unusual – for example, businesses such as British Rail Hotels which, unintentionally, were bought up as subsidiary components of major industries, or businesses such as Rolls Royce aero-engines, which were taken over as a temporary measure in order to help key industries in short-term financial difficulties.

Fig. 2.4 Major public sector asset sales 1981–88

Year	Company	Business	Sale Proceeds (£m)
1981	British Aerospace	aerospace	40
	Cable and Wireless	telecommunication	180
1982	National Freight	road haulage	5
	Britoil	oil	630
1983	Associated British Ports	seaports	50
	British Rail Hotels	hotels	50
1984	British Gas Onshore Oil	oil	80
	Enterprise Oil	oil	380
	Sealink Ferries	cross-channel ferries	65
	Jaguar cars	cars	300
	British Telecom	telecommunications	3900
	British Technology Group	miscellaneous	700
1986	British Gas	gas	4500
1987	British Airways	civil airline	900
	Rolls Royce	aero-engines	1400
	British Airport Authority	airports	1200
1988	British Steel	steel	2500
Proposed	British Electricity	electricity generation and distribution	
1989	British Water Authorities	water supply and sewerage	
onwards	National Coal Board	coal	
	British Rail	railways	
	Post Office	postal services	

At the foot of the table are listed the remaining nationalised industries. The first two, electricity and water, were announced as due for sale in late 1989, and some talk, albeit tentative, of privatising others had also begun. In so far as changes in ownership created privately-owned monopolies, in place of state-owned monopolies, new regulatory bodies were sometimes set up (e.g. OFTEL and OFGAS). These are discussed later (see pages 174–5).

Market structures[1] This chapter has dealt mainly with the legal and institutional framework within which private and public sector businesses make decisions. Economic theory tells us, however, that the behaviour of a firm is affected also by the kind of market in which it operates, and in particular by the number of firms in the industry and the type of product sold, both of which

1 The theoretical issues involved in market structure distinctions are discussed in Lipsey and Harbury, First Principles, Chapter 18.

influence the degree of **competition**.

We shall look at the size and concentration of firms in Chapter 3, but it must be admitted now that it is not easy to generalise about the degree of competition. The power that a firm can exercise over price, however, *can* be associated with market structure. Some structures allow the firm to set its own price while others make the firm a mere price taker, responding to prices set by the forces of market supply and demand. Figure 2.5 shows two contrasting products which typify the extreme cases. The graph shows the course of prices for a popular model of car and for a primary product, lead.

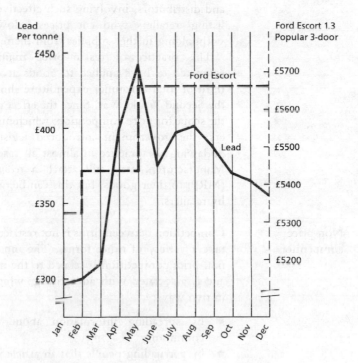

Fig. 2.5 Average monthly prices of Ford Escorts and lead Sources: *The Motor* and *The Times*. (The prices are those of 1987, but are typical of any year)

Within the car industry individual manufacturers enjoy some degree of monopoly power arising from the special features of their models, whether real or imagined by buyers. Within limits, therefore, the industry is able to set prices for itself. Such **administered pricing**, as it is called, can be contrasted with the behaviour of suppliers of many primary products, where the material is homogeneous and there are many producers. One such product is lead, the world price of which is free to fluctuate with changes in supply and demand. Figure 2.5 shows how much more volatile is the price of lead than that of the administratively set Ford Escort.

It should be added that the power of individual manufacturers may extend beyond fixing their *own* selling prices to setting minimum prices below which their customers may not *resell* their products. This applies in particular to the retail trade. Such price setting can be attractive to shopkeepers in so far as it protects them from cut-price competition from other shops. It is not surprising, therefore, that many manufacturers, acting partly in their own interests and partly in response to requests from retailers, long ago took steps to ensure that their products were sold everywhere at the same price. General conformity to such fixed prices frequently used to be maintained by collective agreement between the appropriate trade associations of manufacturers and distributors, involving such effective methods as 'black-listing' retailers who cut prices below those agreed and withholding further supplies from them.

This practice of **resale price maintenance (RPM)** is estimated to have applied to goods accounting for about a third of total consumer expenditure shortly after the end of the Second World War. Since the effect of RPM is to restrict the scope for price competition, which might benefit consumers, the government introduced legislation in the 1960s outlawing the practice in almost all cases (*see* pages 161–2). Manufacturers may still attach a *recommended* retail price (MRP) to their goods, but this can be, and often is, ignored by retailers.

Non-price competition	Competition between firms is not restricted to prices but may take a variety of other forms. The most important type of non-price competition is related to the nature of the product and is associated with **advertising**, which can increase sales in two ways:

- by spreading information about the existence of a commodity
- by persuading people that an article is worth buying

The way in which persuasion is achieved is not important from the point of view of the advertiser. Whether you are induced to buy a particular brand of detergent because you are told it contains a substance which has been 'proved' to wash whiter or whether it is because you have seen a picture of a television personality using it, the effect on sales of that detergent may be much the same. The tendency to emphasise persuasion is at the back of much of the criticism continually levelled at advertising. On the other hand, it is argued that the provision of information, especially about new products, is valuable and may help to build up sales to the point where costs begin to fall.

The scale of advertising expenditure in Britain, after a period of fairly steady growth, seems to have settled at a level representing fractionally less than 2 per cent of total consumer expenditure. Most advertising is done by manufacturers and is directed at final consumers, but some is organised by retailers. The press is the most important single medium for advertising. In fact, revenue from advertisements is a larger source of income for many newspapers than proceeds from sales. Television and radio advertising account for about a third of the total.

Questions and exercises

For key to symbols indicating suggested sources *see* pages xi–xii.

1   Call at the office of one of the major building societies in the district where you live and ask for a copy of their latest balance sheet and profit and loss account.

Calculate the proportion of total costs which are identifiable as fixed costs.

Suppose the accounts had to be prepared for a period of a month rather than for the year. Would the proportion of total costs which were fixed be any different?

2   From the list of London share prices select any 6 companies which have issued preference shares and list them in order of the fixed rate of interest which they pay.

Now make a note of the price of the shares (i.e. the price you would have to pay to buy now), and calculate the yield you would receive if you bought £100 worth of them. (*Hint* Divide £100 by the price of the shares. This gives you the number of shares which you will be able to buy. Now, using the fixed rate of dividend, work out how much you would earn each year on your investment. This is the yield of the share.)

List them again in the order of yield. Can you suggest any reasons why the order may not be the same? *(FT, T)*

3   Find out:

(a)   the gross trading profits of 'large' companies for the last five years
(b)   the total net assets of the companies for the same years

Express *(a)* as a percentage of *(b)* and set the results of your calculations alongside each other. Does there seem to be any relationship between them? *(AS)*

4   Obtain the average price each month for the last 12 months of:

(a)   a Vauxhall Cavalier, or similar model car
(b)   the London price of coffee.

Present the two series in the form of a graph, carefully

choosing scales which allow both prices to be on the same diagram. Which series shows the most variability? Can you explain why? ((a) *The Motor* or *Parker's Car Price Guide;* (b) *FT* or *T.*)

5   Find out the current prices of shares in the following privatised companies:

British Telecom; British Airways; Jaguar; and British Aerospace.

Compare their prices with those a year ago and, if possible, at the date they were sold to the public. Would you have made a good profit by buying at either of the earlier dates? (*FT* or *T*)

6   From the yellow pages of your local *Phone book*, find the proportion of the total number of businesses which appear to be joint stock companies in the following trades:

Funeral directors
Furniture manufacturers
Plumbers
Dress shops
Shoe repairers
Paint manufacturers

Would your results have been very different if you had been able to calculate the proportions on the basis of the value of total sales?

7   Draw a graph to show trends in the following over the past ten years:

(a)   the number of members of retail co-operative societies
(b)   the number of retail co-operative societies
(c)   the value of sales of all grocery retailers
(d)   the value of sales of groceries by retail co-operative societies

How far can the *difference* between the series (c) and (d) be explained by either series (a) or series (b), or both of them?

Note: For series (c) and (d) you will need to use index numbers of the value of sales. These simply represent the figures for each year as a percentage of those in one year – called the 'base'. (*AS*)

8   Draw a diagram on the lines of Fig. 2.1, showing the allocation of gross company income into the following categories for the last year for which statistics are available:

(a)   interest and dividends on preference shares
(b)   dividends on ordinary shares
(c)   UK taxes on income
(d)   undistributed income after taxation

Compare your diagram with Fig. 2.1 on page 37. (*AS*)

9   Calculate the proportion of the total value of company

securities quoted on the Stock Exchange that were of the following kinds:

(a) loan capital and preference capital
(b) ordinary (and deferred) capital

Try to find data for the same year as that used for exercise 8. Compare the proportions of (a) to (b) in the two exercises, and comment on the difference between the proportions, if any, that you found. (AS)

3 | Structure of British industry

This chapter deals with the structure of British industry as it has been shaped by the operation of market forces.[1] The subjects considered are as follows:

- the relative importance of different sectors
- productivity
- regional distribution of industry
- the size of firms
- industrial concentration

National output

Figure 3.1 shows the main groups of goods and services in the UK in 1987. It confirms the conclusion reached in Chapter 1 (*see* pages 8–9) that tertiary (service) industries are today substantially larger than primary production (mainly agriculture and energy supply) and secondary production (manufacturing and construction). All service sectors

Fig. 3.1 Value of national output 1987 Source: *UK National Accounts*

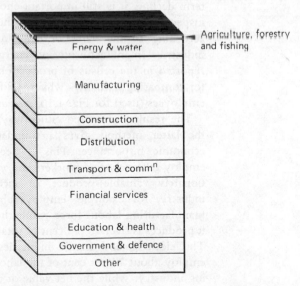

Agriculture, forestry and fishing

Energy & water

Manufacturing

Construction

Distribution

Transport & comm^n

Financial services

Education & health

Government & defence

Other

1 Theoretical analysis relating to the topics discussed in this chapter is to be found mainly in Lipsey and Harbury, *First Principles*, Chapters 16–18.

Fig. 3.2 Production
industries 1986 value of
net output
Source: *Census of
Production* 1986
Summary Tables,
Business Monitor PA
1002 (1988)

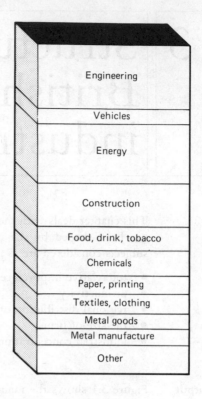

account for around 60 per cent of total national output – the
principal components shown in Fig. 3.1 are finance, distribution, education and health.

Although manufacturing industry has exhibited a long-
term decline, it is still important enough to warrant detailed
inspection. Figure 3.2 distinguishes the various sectors
according to the value of net output of the production
industries (manufacturing and energy) and construction as
reported in the census of production. This provides a basis
for comparing industries which is different from numbers of
employees (used for Fig. 1.10, *see* page 10).

The results, measured either way, are often similar, but
the latter method gives a sounder basis for comparing
economic importance. This is because an industry may
employ relatively few workers and yet produce a disproportionately valuable product, or vice versa. The chemical
industry, for example, employs about 6 per cent of the
manufacturing labour force, while the value of the chemicals
it produces is over 10 per cent of total manufacturing output.
The clothing and textile industries, on the other hand,
employ about 10 per cent of the labour force in manufacturing industry, while the net value of their output is nearer to
6 per cent of the total.

Fig. 3.3 Industrial production, 1987 (output as a percentage of 1980)
Source: *Monthly Digest of Statistics*

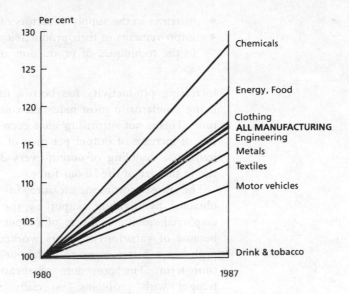

Per cent

- 130 — Chemicals
- 125 —
- 120 — Energy, Food
- 115 — Clothing **ALL MANUFACTURING** Engineering
- Metals
- 110 — Textiles
- Motor vehicles
- 105 —
- 100 — Drink & tobacco

1980   1987

Industrial change

It should be emphasised that Fig. 3.2 refers only to the pattern of output in one year, 1986. Figure 3.3 shows changes in the output of the various industrial sectors between 1980 and 1987 (after making allowance for changes in output prices).

The period was one during which output rose on average by approximately 17 to 18 per cent, so that one can pick out the relative performance of different sectors compared to this benchmark, as well as to each other.

Expanding and contracting industries

The most rapidly expanding manufacturing industry in the 1980s was chemicals – also, incidentally, the most consistent pace setter for the bulk of the period since the end of the Second World War. It was replaced for a relatively short number of years from the mid–1970s by energy, as output rocketed upwards following the discovery and exploitation of oil and natural gas under the North Sea. Energy production remained high in the 1980s, as did food. In contrast, output of the drink and tobacco sector barely held its own in absolute terms. Industries which contracted in *relative* terms were textiles and vehicles. Finally, among groupings which expanded at roughly the same rate as total output were clothing and engineering, although the latter is the average of a very broad category, covering both fast-growing sectors such as computers, and laggards such as mechanical engineering.

Productivity

Expansion in the volume of output can be traced to one of two causes:

- increases in the supply of factors of production
- improvements in their productivity arising from changes in the techniques of production and in factor performance

Increasing productivity has been a major source of rising living standards in most industrial countries for a very long time. This is not surprising since even an apparently modest rate of increase of output per man of 2 per cent per annum leads to a doubling of output every 35 years, without any rise in the size of the labour force.

The most common measure of productivity is that obtained by dividing output by the number of workers employed, giving a figure of output per head. However, because of variations in hours worked, output per hour is probably a better measure of labour's productivity in the short-term. The procedure of measuring productivity is fraught with problems, especially when attempting to measure output in the service trades. It is therefore wise to treat estimates of productivity with caution and to regard only broad orders of magnitude as significant.

Fig. 3.4 Labour productivity in manufacturing since 1950
Sources: *The British Economy, Key Statistics 1900–70*, London and Cambridge Economic Service, and *Monthly Digest of Statistics*

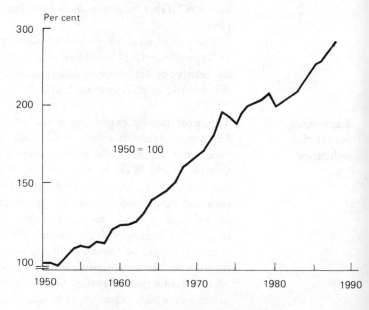

This warning is relevant when examining Fig. 3.4, which gives an index of labour productivity (1950 = 100). Since it is restricted to productivity in the manufacturing sector, it is probably fairly reliable as far as long-term trends are concerned. It can be seen that output per unit of labour has risen fairly steadily since 1950 at an average rate of approximately 2½ per cent per annum.

Productivity increases have varied widely from industry to industry, partly, of course, because of differences in the scope for the application of new technology. Computerisation, for example, is more easily applied to the chemical industry (which has had one of the fastest growth rates) than to the services of solicitors or hairdressers. In spite of certain exceptions, it is broadly true that productivity increases in manufacturing industry have tended to outstrip those in the tertiary (service) sector of the economy.

It is instructive to compare output per employee between sectors of the UK and between the UK and other countries. Figure 3.5 supplies information on these matters for the year 1985. Productivity is here measured in value terms, expressed in pounds sterling, and leads to the conclusion that within the UK productivity is highest in financial services and energy and lowest in distribution and in textiles and clothing. The diagram also gives comparable figures for three major competitor nations in the EC – West Germany, Italy and France. It may be seen that the UK is the leader in financial services, construction and chemicals, but lags behind the others in several sectors, especially in textiles and clothing, metal products and distribution.

Fig. 3.5 Comparative productivity: UK, West Germany, Italy and France, selected sectors, 1985. Source: *Eurostat*

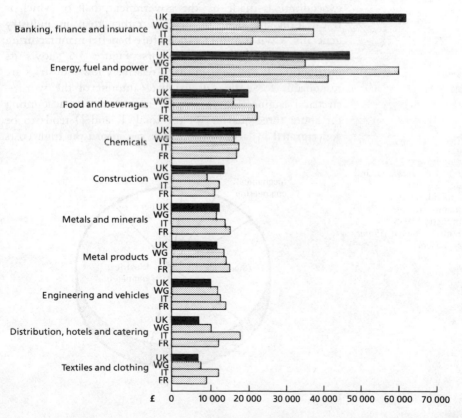

It must be appreciated that comparative productivity measures of the kind on which Fig. 3.5 is based are the result of many complex factors. Observed differences among nations may be due to variations in the amount of capital per employee, in the scale of output, in industrial relations, and in what is called R and D (standing for research and development), etc. There is an obvious link between each of these and output per employee.

As it happens, differences in capital expenditure per unit of output are not currently too great. Most member countries in the EC have proportions standing between 17 and 19 per cent of the total. The UK's figure lies towards the lower end of the range. However, in previous years the UK figure has tended to be significantly below that of several of its major competitors. The relevance of this should not be overlooked, given that most capital expenditure takes time, sometimes several years, before it becomes fully effective.

As far as expenditure on R and D is concerned, differences among nations are probably a little greater than differences in capital expenditure, though it is difficult to secure precisely comparable statistics. The UK expenditure approximates that of France, and lies between a high for West Germany and a low for Italy. However, more than 40 per cent of UK expenditure is made by the government, half of which is research in the field of defence rather than in industry generally. Civil R and D expenditure benefits manufacturing industry more than other sectors. Figure 3.6 shows its distribution. It can be seen that a relatively few industries are responsible for a disproportionate amount of the work – electrical engineering, aerospace and chemicals accounting for about three-quarters of the total. R and D tends to be concentrated in large firms which can afford the high costs

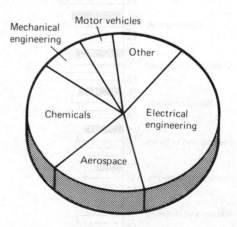

Fig. 3.6 Research and development expenditure, manufacturing industry, 1986
Source: *Annual Abstract of Statistics*

involved in modern technological research, not to mention the willingness to accept the risks of failure. However, small firms have been responsible for some major innovations.

A final comment on the reasons for international differences in labour productivity puts the question in a wider context. Output per employee is higher in Japan than in most EC countries, and has been so for many years. So too is capital expenditure related to total output, and expenditure on R and D.

Productivity in the short-term

So far we have discussed long-term trends, but productivity also fluctuates in the short-term. Output per person tends to fall at the beginning of downturns in economic activity as firms hold on to their labour, dismissing the workforce only when the decline in sales is perceived to be lasting. In contrast, productivity typically rises at the start of upturns in output for the opposite reason, as employment rises only some time after increases in output. This pattern is not always strongly exhibited, but it was quite marked in the recession which lasted from 1973 to 1977 and the recovery after 1981 (see Fig. 3.4).

The location of industry

Economic theory tells us that profit-maximising firms tend to locate their businesses where costs are lowest relative to revenues. This basic underlying principle is relevant to the geographical distribution of industry in the UK, although it needs to be applied in the context of government intervention to influence location decisions (see Chapter 6, pages 164-6).

We already know something of the regional distribution of the population (see Fig. 1.5, pages 4-6). This gives a first approximation to the location of industry too, since the need to be near both labour supplies and markets for the sale of products are two important determinants of location.

Figure 3.7a shows the geographical spread of different industries. It should be examined in conjunction with Fig. 3.7b which shows the standard regions used in official statistics. In Fig. 3.7a each area has a column to itself, with spaces for the main industries. Where a ● appears, the regional percentage of the total area labour force in that industry is more than that for the country as a whole. Thus, wherever there is a ●, the region is to some extent specialising in that particular industry. Wherever there is a blank the region is not specialising in that industry, although, of course, it may well be producing some of the goods in question.

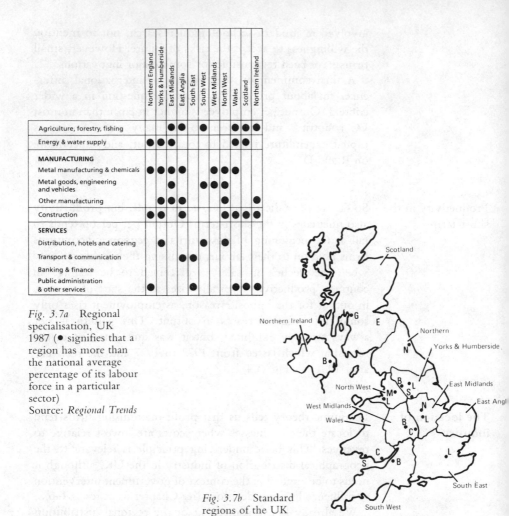

	Northern England	Yorks & Humberside	East Midlands	East Anglia	South East	South West	West Midlands	North West	Wales	Scotland	Northern Ireland
Agriculture, forestry, fishing		●	●		●				●	●	●
Energy & water supply	●	●	●					●	●		
MANUFACTURING											
Metal manufacturing & chemicals	●	●	●	●			●	●	●		
Metal goods, engineering and vehicles				●			●	●	●		
Other manufacturing		●	●	●			●				●
Construction	●	●		●			●	●	●	●	
SERVICES											
Distribution, hotels and catering	●				●	●					
Transport & communication			●	●							
Banking & finance											
Public administration & other services	●				●			●	●	●	

Fig. 3.7a Regional specialisation, UK 1987 (● signifies that a region has more than the national average percentage of its labour force in a particular sector)
Source: *Regional Trends*

Fig. 3.7b Standard regions of the UK

Northern England	Centred around Tyneside, the Northern region of England used to be particularly dependent on the heavy industries of coal, iron and steel, shipbuilding and chemicals. Well over a third of the labour force is still employed in energy and manufacturing, which is now more diversified.
Yorkshire and Humberside	This is another diversified manufacturing region. Its specialisations include engineering, metal manufacture, and clothing and textiles.
Midlands	The Midlands is divided into West and East regions, the former being substantially the larger. Both concentrate more on manufacturing than any other region. Both also specialise in metal manufacture. The West Midlands is the more important in the field of engineering, including (road) vehicles, much of the heavy sections of which are in the 'Black Country' around Birmingham and Wolverhampton.

The East Midlands industry tends to be lighter and includes more clothing and textiles, and food, drink and tobacco. The East Midlands also has a sizeable agricultural sector, as well as taking in the coalfields of Derbyshire and Nottinghamshire.

East Anglia

East Anglia is the smallest employment region in Britain, but the proportion of its labour force in agriculture (over 4 per cent) is the highest. It also has a fair share of manufacturing industry of various kinds, especially food processing, and is an important tourist area.

South East

The South East region employs over a third of the entire UK labour force. It includes London, which concentrates predominantly on non-manufacturing – hence the specialisation in banking and finance, as so many offices of banks, insurance companies and other financial institutions are in the City. London is the pivot of road and rail networks, and the site of many government departments.

The South East is also an important producer in agriculture, engineering and vehicles and employs more than the national average of its workforce in distribution and public administration and other services, which include education and health.

South West

The South West employs more workers in agriculture than any other region, and is second only to East Anglia in being relatively heavily specialised in that sector. Like East Anglia, its industry includes food processing. The industrial centre is Bristol, where engineering and aerospace equipment flourish, while the region's coastal resorts account for the high employment in hotels, catering and distribution.

The North West

The North West region, encompassing Manchester and Liverpool, is the second largest in Britain. It is also strongly industrial, specialising in all the major industrial groups. The region's traditional strength, textiles, has long been overshadowed by other industries, including engineering, much of it heavy.

Wales

Wales is sparsely populated and largely mountainous. However it does have more than the national average percentage of workers in agriculture. It has traditionally been a coal mining area, although only a very small percentage of its labour force remains in that industry now. Wales specialises in metal manufacture and chemicals, but iron and steel has been on the decline for several years. The range of manufacturing industry has, however, been widening to include engineering, plastics and clothing. Decentralisation of government departments explains some of the specialisation in public administration and defence.

Scotland

Scotland is a good deal larger than Wales, but it is also sparsely populated and mountainous. Its agricultural labour force is substantial, but the proportion of the total working in that industry is only marginally above the national average. The centre of industry is in the central lowlands around Glasgow, and exploitation of North Sea oil and gas accounts for the specialisation in energy.

Northern Ireland

Northern Ireland has the smallest labour force of any of the regions of the UK – about half a million, but only East Anglia is more highly specialised in agriculture. Industry is diversified, and includes food processing, clothing and textiles. The region has, of course, suffered for many years from political unrest, which has not helped the economy, and the unemployment rate is the highest in the UK.

Changes in
location

We have discussed regional specialisation as it exists in the UK today. For the greater part of this century, however, there has been considerable redeployment of industry over different parts of the country. The decades between the two world wars were outstanding, and witnessed a striking growth in the relative importance of Southern England and the Midlands at the expense of Northern England, Merseyside, South Wales and Scotland.

Two factors account for these changes. In the first place there was a tendency for industrialists to move southwards when erecting new factories because they were attracted by the growing market of Greater London. Moreover, the development of electricity as a source of power released them from the need to be near coalfields. The second explanation is the one that carries more weight. As we saw earlier, not all industries were expanding at the same rate and, in fact, some were declining. Most of the new and expanding industries, such as engineering, vehicles and electrical goods, were those in which the South and the Midlands were specialising, while the staple industries of the 19th century, especially textiles, coal and shipbuilding, largely concentrated in the North of England, Scotland and South Wales, were declining in importance.

The period since the end of the Second World War has seen a continuation of the same broad trends, to which have been added more recent trends as some of the newer industries began to decline and be replaced by others. The influence of the government's regional policy can also be observed in the changing scene post–1945, especially with regard to stemming the growth in the South East. (*See* Chapter 6, page 164). Figure 3.8 shows which regions have gained and lost population in the years between the 1971 Census and 1987. It may be compared with the longer term trends, since 1911, in Fig. 1.6 on page 6.

Fig. 3.8 Regional population changes 1971–87
Source: *Annual Abstract of Statistics*

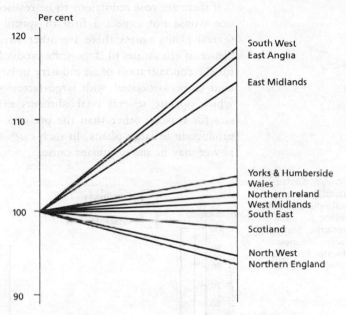

	South West
	East Anglia
	East Midlands
	Yorks & Humberside
	Wales
	Northern Ireland
	West Midlands
	South East
	Scotland
	North West
	Northern England

Industrial concentration[1]

One of the many outstanding features of industrial development in the past 100 years has been the growth in the size of firms and an increasing concentration of industry in a relatively few large concerns. The days when the majority of goods were produced by a great many small businesses have disappeared. The typical unit in many industries today is the giant corporation. Two of the many reasons for this development are of special importance. First, in many industries costs per unit of output fall as production expands, giving rise to what are known as **economies of large-scale production**. This obviously gives a cost advantage to large firms. The second is the appearance of **market power** for a firm which dominates an industry. Such a firm does not have to accept the market price as given but may be able to fix prices, restrict output and/or stifle innovations which threaten the demand for its product.

1 The theoretical issues dealt with in the rest of this chapter are examined in Lipsey and Harbury, *First Principles*, Chapters 17 & 18.

The size of
establishments

Any one business enterprise may consist of a number of individual factories and plants, officially known as **establishments**. We start by considering their size distribution. This may, in turn, reflect the relative importance of economies of large-scale production as distinct from a desire for market power.

If there are cost reductions to be realised within a factory, one would not expect a firm to spread its output among several plants unless there are other advantages to be had. Hence, if economies of large-scale production are responsible for the concentration of an industry in large firms, they will tend to be associated with large factories too. Large firms which operate several establishments may have grown in size for reasons other than the presence of falling costs of production in large plants. In such cases a desire for market power may be the dominant cause.

Fig. 3.9 Size of manufacturing establishments 1986 Source: *Census of Production,* Summary Tables, Business Monitor PA 1002 (1988)

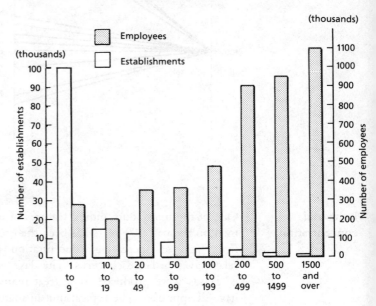

Although the information on which Fig. 3.9 is based is probably incomplete in its recording of very small establishments, it reveals that they are by far the most numerous. Of the total of 150 000 manufacturing establishments, nearly three-quarters employ fewer than 10 workers, while about 90 per cent employ under 100.

Nonetheless, large-scale production is dominant in manufacturing. The 1500 establishments employing more than 500 workers each, which represent less than 2 per cent of the total, are so large that altogether they employ over 40 per cent of the entire manufacturing labour force. Furthermore, the 315 largest establishments of all, each of which has more than 1500 workers on its payroll, account for nearly a quarter of total employment in manufacturing.

Large-scale production is, of course, much more common in some industries than in others. An idea of this is given in Fig. 3.10 which shows the percentage of total employment in establishments with 1000 or more employees. We find that the prime large-scale industry is motor vehicle manufacture, where large establishments are responsible for the employment of over half of the labour force. In metal manufacture large establishments account for nearly 40 per cent of total employment, and in electrical engineering and chemicals for about 30 per cent. The Figure shows, however, that there are industries, especially in timber and furniture, clothing and textiles, where large plants are uncommon.

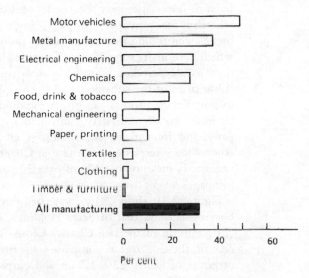

Fig. 3.10 Employment in large establishments 1986 (percentage of total employment in establishments with 1000 or more workers) Source: *Census of Production*, Summary Tables, Business Monitor PA 1002 (1988)

The size of business enterprises

The concentration of industry in large establishments is, as we have seen, considerable. However, businesses (which are usually companies in manufacturing) may own several establishments. For example, the 100 largest businesses in manufacturing industry in the UK operated nearly 4000 establishments between them in 1986.

The private sector of industry in Britain is not organised in such a way that all establishments are autonomous bodies. In some cases an independent company may own a single establishment, but this is not necessarily the case and we need to look deeper into the links that exist between industrial units in order to identify where control lies and business decisions are taken. We therefore have to distinguish between the following:

- **establishments** (or **plants**)
- **companies** which may own one or more establishments
- **enterprises** comprising *groups* of companies under the overall control of a single company

Note, however, that the term **firm** is used to cover the business organisation where decisions are taken. Firms may, therefore, either be independent or part of a group.

The growth of firms   Firms may grow by internal expansion or by merging with other firms.

When **internal expansion** is the method of growth, a company itself expands. When **mergers** take place, a business enterprise can be created by the acquisition of existing companies or the creation of new ones, leading to a network of firms ultimately under the control of one of them. In such cases use may be made of **holding companies**, whereby the principal company, known as the 'parent', owns a controlling interest in one or more other companies, which become its subsidiaries. The subsidiaries may, in their turn, own controlling interests in other companies, which are subsidiaries of the subsidiaries. In principle there is no limit to how far the process can go. A pyramid of companies can be built up, all ultimately controlled by the holding company. (So long as its shareholdings are sufficient to give controlling interests – as we saw in Chapter 2, this does not necessarily mean ownership of over 50 per cent of the shares (*see* pages 42–3.)

Figure 3.11 shows, by way of illustration, one such business empire, that of Sears Holdings, built up under the chairmanship of the late Charles Clore. The Sears group is one of the 50 largest companies in Britain, with a sales turnover of nearly £2½ billion and employing over 60 000 workers. There are about 400 companies in the group and control is exercised through several pyramidal tiers. There are even larger groups in the country. A few more familiar names in the top dozen (in rank order by size in 1988) are BP, Shell, ICI, British Telecom, GEC, Ford, Sainsbury, Marks and Spencer, Tesco and British Aerospace.

Remembering the definition given above of a business enterprise, we can examine the extent to which concentration exists among enterprises of different size in British industry. Figure 3.12 throws light on this subject. It shows the proportions of total manufacturing output accounted for by *enterprises* of different size; it must not be confused with Fig. 3.9 which relates to *establishments*.

Concentration in large enterprises is very considerable. Nearly 150 000 enterprises were identified in the 1986 census

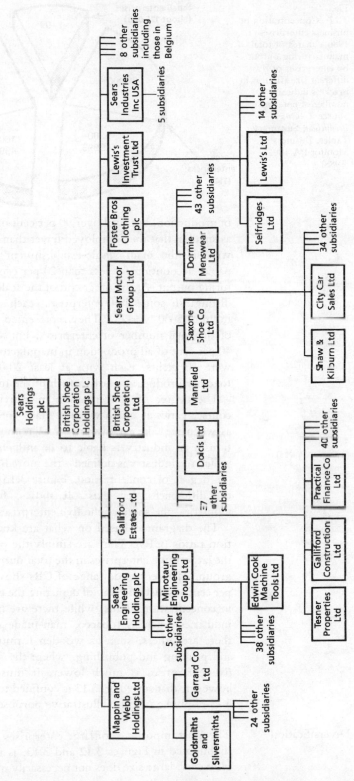

Fig. 3.11 Company structure: the Sears group 1988
Source: *Who Owns Whom*

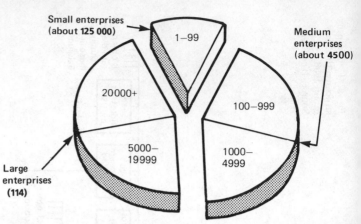

Fig.
3.12 Concentration in business enterprises 1986 – shares of total manufacturing output by enterprises of different size (figures in brackets indicate number of enterprises)
Source: *Census of Production*, Summary Tables, Business Monitor PA 1002 (1988)

of production, but well over 90 per cent of them were classed as small in that they employed fewer than 100 workers. They were in the main single-establishment independent companies accounting for less than 20 per cent of total manufacturing output. At the other end of the scale, however, we can distinguish some 114 enterprises, each employing a minimum of 5000 workers. They represented less than 1 per cent of the total number of enterprises, but accounted for some 40 per cent of all production in manufacturing. Among them were 20 giants, each with at least 20 000 employees and together producing nearly a fifth of the total output.

The degree of concentration in individual industries, of course, varies as much when we take enterprises as our unit as when we take establishments. The measure of concentration in an industry is liable to be influenced by the way in which the industry is defined – the more narrowly, the higher the degree of concentration. Figure 3.13 illustrates some of the differences that exist. It shows, for certain selected industries, the share of the five enterprises in total sales.

The diagram is based on what are known as **concentration ratios (CRs)**. They are simply the percentage shares of the largest five enterprises in the total output of each industry group. The very wide range of CRs shown – from 10 to 99 per cent – is just one way of depicting the extent of differences in concentration. Thus, while there are highly concentrated industries, such as tobacco, man-made fibres and cement, there are others, such as wooden furniture, machine tools and printing and publishing, where the share of the largest five enterprises is much lower. It must be remembered, however, that since Fig. 3.13 is confined to selected industries it can only be used for illustrative purposes.

Diversification

The great importance of large enterprises in British industry, highlighted in Figures 3.12 and 3.13, is not open to doubt. However, large size does not necessarily imply the possession

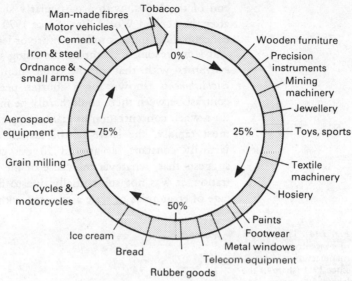

Fig. 3.13 Concentration ratios, selected industries, UK 1986 – percentage of total net output by the five largest enterprises (the percentage for each industry is measured separately, clockwise from the 12 o'clock origin)

Source: *Census of Production*, Summary Tables, Business Monitor PA 1002 (1988)

of great market power. Market power depends on controlling a large part of one market, e.g. selling a high percentage of the industry's sales. Large size often arises when a single firm diversifies into a number of markets – indeed, many of the UK's industrial giants are multi-product businesses. The Sears group of companies depicted in Fig. 3.11 on page 69, for example, has widely diversified interests including engineering, motor distribution, the gold and silver trade and the ownership of department stores, backing its chains of shoe shops. Another example is Grand Metropolitan, whose chief interest in hotels is supplemented by others in breweries (Watney, Mann and Truman), milk supply (Express Dairies), bookmakers and entertainment (Mecca).

The extent of diversification among large corporations is not easily quantified. As when measuring concentration itself, the results obtained by using various measures are liable to be sensitive to the way in which industry groups are defined. The narrower the definitions, the greater the observed diversification. However, a study made of changes in diversification in British industry up to the 1970s showed that, although there were a few sectors where diversification had declined, in most cases it had increased.

Changes in concentration

Attention has so far been directed to the extent of concentration in British industry in the 1980s. We should also look at past trends in the degree of concentration both in the economy as a whole and by sector. Figure 3.14 shows the share of the largest 100 enterprises in total manufacturing output. The share of these giants rose from about 15 per cent in the first decade of the century to over 40 per cent at the end of the 1960s, with a particularly sharp rate of increase after the Second World War. Since 1970 the level of overall concentration appears to have more or less stabilised.

It is interesting to compare the rising share of the top 100 *enterprises* with that of the same number of the largest *establishments* (shown for a shorter period of time). The contrast between them could hardly be more marked. At the time when concentration in giant companies was proceeding most rapidly, the share of the largest establishments was virtually constant, at around 10 per cent. This strongly suggests that, whatever the cause of the increase in concentration, it was not substantially due to firms taking advantage of economies of scale associated with large plants.

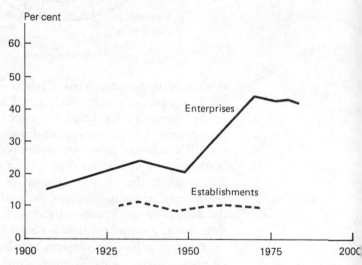

Fig. 3.14 The growth of concentration in manufacturing industry since 1911 (share of the largest 100 enterprises and largest 100 establishments in total output)
Sources: *The Evolution of Giant Firms in Britain,* S J Prais (Cambridge University Press, 1981) and *Recent Trends in Concentration in British Industry*, P E Hart (NIESR, 1984)

Within the trend of increasing overall concentration of industry in relatively few businesses, it is necessary to look at what has been happening in different sectors. This is difficult to measure because of the changes that occur, particularly over long periods of time, in the nature of products offered for sale. However, studies based on the most comparable industry groups reach conclusions on trends in sectoral concentration that match those in overall concentration, as far as the time pattern is concerned (the size of the increases in concentration being rather less sharp). The post-war decade of most rapid concentration growth' was the 1960s. One study estimated the average CR3 (i.e. the percentage of total output by the largest 3 enterprises) in a sample of 42 industries to have been 29 per cent in 1951, 32 per cent in 1958, but 41 per cent in 1968. Since that date

1 Hart, P E and Clarke *Concentration in British Industry, 1935–75* (1980) and Hart, P E *Recent Trends in Concentration in British Industry* (1984) (National Institute of Economic and Social Research).

very little change was observed in sectoral concentration.[1] It must be added that our summary runs only in terms of *average* concentration, and that all industries do not move in line together. Some sectors grew at above average rates and, even in the period of rapid growth of concentration, some industries experienced falling concentration (e.g. fruit and vegetable products and agricultural and electrical machinery).

Mergers

It was mentioned earlier that businesses can expand by internal growth or by the acquisition of other companies. While the former method has undoubtedly been an important one, especially in earlier times, growth by merger has been on the increase and is estimated to have been the cause of at least half of the increase in concentration since 1970. Mergers tend to come in waves. They were running at a rate of about 750 per annum from the early 1960s, peaking in 1968 and in 1972. Thereafter merger activity waned somewhat, until the next wave in the mid-1980s, which was characterised less by the number of mergers (which had actually dropped to around 400 p.a.) than by being between giant firms, so called mega mergers, and increasingly involved corporations based overseas. Thus take-overs of Britoil, Distillers, Imperial, Rover and Rowntree have all been of companies in the top 100 in the UK. International consortia of companies have been formed to bid for some of the very largest giants, e.g. in early 1989 for GEC, the thirteenth largest corporation in Britain, with a capital value of about £6 billion and employing over 150 000 workers.

Some mergers take place between companies of roughly equal size. In other cases a small firm may be taken over in such a way as to lose its identity virtually completely. From the point of view of concentration of the *control* of industry, however, the most important aspect of amalgamations between companies concerns the nature of the businesses. It is useful to distinguish three types of merger.

1 **Horizontal mergers** are those between firms producing similar products, e.g. the Dolcis and Manfield shoe chains in the Sears group (*see* Fig. 3.11) or more recently, between British Airways and British Caledonian.
2 **Vertical mergers** involve the absorption of suppliers or outlets, e.g. the acquisition by Dunlop of rubber plantations or the purchase by a brewery of public houses which sell its beer direct to the public.
3 **Conglomerate mergers** lead to a diversification of interests – the Sears group is a good example, since there is little in common between the product lines of some of its companies, e.g. shoe shops, engineering and property development.

It is not always easy to place a particular merger in the correct category. Some amalgamations may not appear, on the surface, to have elements of either the vertical or horizontal merger about them. They may, however, conceal less obvious matters, such as disposal of by-products or utilisation of expertise in a related field which might explain such otherwise unlikely combinations as detergents, plastics and ice cream manufacture in the Unilever group.

Horizontal mergers have been the predominant type in post-Second World War Britain, with vertical integration being insignificant. Conglomerate mergers gradually increased in importance in the 1960s and 1970s, accounting for about a third of the total by the late 1970s, though falling back temporarily until the 1980s mergers wave.

Horizontal mergers and, to an extent, vertical ones tend to increase the power of a company over its market. Conglomerate mergers, in contrast, often have the aim of diversification in order to reduce risks by spreading them. They may also increase bargaining power in the financial markets in which a firm raises capital.

Increasing concentration may well be associated with increasing market power. But, in a curious way, greater concentration may even heighten competition if it leads diversified giant companies to enter each others' markets. There is little doubt, however, that merger activity, especially in the last twenty years, has been an important determinant of increasing concentration. Whether the mergers have paid off is a different matter. Studies of the effects of amalgamations on company profits suggest that it was not uncommon for the financial situation to be no better after the merger.

Co-operation among firms

The emphasis so far in this section on industrial concentration has been on the power of business enterprises based on common ownership. However, there are avenues of co-operation open to separate firms which fall short of the full pooling of sovereignty involved in amalgamation. Some of the most common arrangements among firms take place through a **trade association**. This is a very wide term and includes any body of employers who have agreements with each other. The Confederation of British Industry (CBI) is such an association though not a typical one. It acts as industry's spokesman on economic and labour matters where a national voice is desired.

In individual industries, trade associations usually have a more specific role. Their functions vary from industry to industry and include the carrying out of research and publicity. They may also cover activities such as regulating the output or fixing the price of products in the industry and organising the machinery for carrying through policies. Some trade associations have made arrangements for allocating shares of the market to constituent firms on a predetermined basis, involving the setting up of a central sales organisation, often referred to as a **cartel**. Agreements of this kind can have much the same effect as more complete mergers between firms in so far as the restriction of competition is concerned, although they may be less stable. Legislation was passed in the 1950s limiting the operation of such practices by firms acting together, and an illustration of a complex set of organised links among many separate companies in the electric lamp industry is shown in Fig. 3.15. (It predates the Restrictive Practices Act of 1956.)

There are other devices for inter-firm co-operation, such as that of the **interlocking directorate**. A link between firms is contrived by one or more persons becoming directors of several companies. This practice is common in the area of banking and finance, but is rather less so in manufacturing industry.

Firms also get together for the exchange of information or joint action of one kind or another. They may have unwritten understandings, often called 'gentlemen's agreements', or more formal undertakings. An example of this is the old understanding between Imperial Chemical Industries and Unilever, whereby the former agreed to refrain from competing with the latter in the production of soap. Another example is where a group of local builders decides not to compete for building contracts, but to allocate new orders received by any of them in rotation. A third involves the exchange of 'know how' between companies, extending in some cases to a pooling of patents. Such arrangements are frequently not well publicised and it is consequently difficult to find out what is going on. Governments have to assess the seriousness of these matters, as well as others related to business concentration, and take a view on what, if anything, to do about them in their competition policy (which we consider in Chapter 6, pages 160–64).

| **Multinational corporations** | The second half of this chapter has been written from a narrow nationalistic point of view – as if industrial concentration was simply a question of such matters as market shares by British-owned companies selling in the UK market. Such is not the case. |

Many firms operating in the UK are owned, wholly or partly, by persons or companies located elsewhere – e.g. BP has subsidiaries in well over 50 foreign countries. These

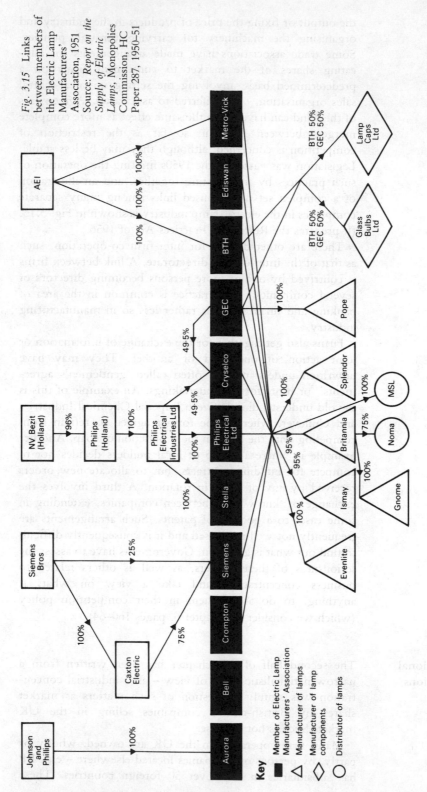

Fig. 3.15 Links
between members of
the Electric Lamp
Manufacturers'
Association, 1951
Source: Report on the
Supply of Electric
Lamps, Monopolies
Commission, HC
Paper 287, 1950–51

Key

■ Member of Electric Lamp
  Manufacturers' Association
◁ Manufacturer of lamps
◇ Manufacturer of lamp
  components
○ Distributor of lamps

international mega-giants are known as **multinational** or **transnational corporations**. They dwarf the typical large national enterprise described earlier. The value (in £s) of turnover in the world's largest company (C Itoh of Japan) was nearly thirty times that of the Sears group, which we cited as a typical UK giant. By the same measuring rod, even the smallest of the top 25 multinationals (Matsu-Shita) was eight times that of Sears. Again, of the top 25, 21 had their HQ in either Japan or the USA. Only one was UK-based (BP), one West German (Mercedes-Benz), one Italian (IRI) and one Anglo-Dutch (Shell). To put these corporations in another perspective, according to the 1986 Census of Production, some 20 per cent of UK output was produced by 'foreign' firms.

For a variety of reasons, recent trends in international investment flows have greatly increased the importance of multinational corporations. Not least among the factors behind the trend is the desire by companies to exploit world markets without worrying about tariff and other barriers to international trade. (*See* Chapter 5, page 122). Thus, the acquisition in 1988 of the chocolate manufacturer Rowntree of York by the Swiss giant, Nestlé, was at least partly explicable in terms of a desire by a non-EC member country (Switzerland) to avoid the discrimination it could expect after the 'single market' comes in 1992 (*see* pages 122–5) by acquiring a UK-based subsidiary.

A second advantage enjoyed by multinationals is their ability to distribute the fruits of technological advance amongst their subsidiaries, and to locate production of components where costs are lowest. A potentially disturbing aspect of this power is that the multinationals are, by the same token, able to manipulate their global tax bills. This they do by what is known as 'transfer pricing' – that is, selling components among subsidiaries in different countries at prices which result in accounting profits being highest where tax rates are lowest. From the viewpoint of economic policy, multinationals may cause major problems, which are to an extent intractable; though country groupings such as the EC may be better placed to take some appropriate action.

Questions and exercises

For key to symbols indicating suggested sources *see* pages xi–xii.

1   Using both the oldest and the latest figures you have available, calculate the proportion of total wage earners in industrial groups according to whether you consider the product of that industry to be primary, secondary or tertiary in nature. Compare your results. (*AS*)

2   Prepare a graph to show two series relating to mergers in the UK over the past ten years:

(a)   the number of companies acquired
(b)   the total expenditure on acquisitions
(c)   Now add a third series, comprising *(b)* deflated by the retail price index to give the expenditure on acquisitions in 'real terms'.

Inspect the graph and try to answer the question of whether *(a)* we are experiencing a merger 'wave', and *(b)* whether the current trend in mergers is biased towards large or small amalgamations. *(AS)*

3   From the latest edition of *Who Owns Whom* in your local library prepare a chart on the lines of Fig. 3.11 of one of the following PLCs:

Grand Metropolitan
Thorn-EMI
Lonrho
Hanson Trust
Pearson

Does the company you selected appear to be more or less diversified than Sears in Fig. 3.11?

4   From the library obtain a copy of the latest issue of *The Times 1000*, a publication containing details of the finances of the largest 1000 companies in Britain. Add up the profits earned last year in the largest 20 profit earners.

   Next refer to the *Annual Abstract of Statistics* and extract the figure for the gross trading profits of all companies for the same year. (Use the table headed Corporate Sector Appropriation Account in the section 'National Income'.) Calculate the proportion of total company profits earned by the top 20 companies.

   Repeat the calculations for an earlier year. Does the degree of concentration in large companies appear to have changed at all between the two dates? *(AS, BB)*

5   Construct a table showing the ten industries, listed in rank order of output (or employment), which expanded most, and the ten which contracted most in the last ten years. Repeat the exercise for the last five years. What new trends, if any, are observable? *(AS)*

6   Find out how many people are employed in the firms in which three of your relatives or friends work. Assemble the information derived from the whole of your class and prepare a table showing the size of firms for everyone concerned, grouping firms by size into the following classifications:

less than 100 employees   1000–20 000 employees
100–999 employees   over 20 000 employees

Calculate the percentage of the total in each group. Compare the results with those in Fig. 3.12. (AS)

7 Prepare a table listing, for each of the major industrial groups in manufacturing, for each of the past five years, the year-to-year changes in

(a) employment of male and female workers;
(b) output per head;
(c) capital expenditure (net).

In which sectors has productivity increased most and least? Does the information you have gathered throw any light on what may have caused any changes in productivity? (AS)

8 Select three of the standard regions of the UK and make a note of their manufacturing specialisations. Using the set of local telephone directories in the public library, attempt to identify a number of companies in each region involved in its specialised product groups. Do your findings support the •'s in Fig. 3.7? (AS)

9 Arrange a visit to one or two local factories. Try to find out in each case:

(a) how long it has been situated in its present site, and why it was put there in the first place
(b) whether it is an independent company or a subsidiary
(c) whether capital investment grew last year compared to the previous year
(d) how many employees it has on its books
(e) how fast its output has been growing
(f) whether output per employee rose or fell last year compared to the previous year

Where possible compare any answers you get with the average for the industry and for all industries together. (AS)

Appendix

Table A3.1   Industrial output* in the UK, 1977 and 1987
Source: *Annual Abstract of Statistics*

	£ million	
	1977	1987
Agriculture, forestry and fishing	3 307	5 901
Energy and water supply	8 625	24 184
Manufacturing	37 972	85 552
Construction	7 840	21 524
Distribution, hotels and catering; repairs	17 057	48 963
Transport	6 955	16 227
Communication	3 259	9 688
Banking, finance, insurance, etc.	15 034	63 903
Ownership of dwellings	7 516	20 180
Public administration, defence and social security	8 964	24 895
Education and health	11 198	31 681
Other services	6 867	22 366
Total	134 594	375 064
Adjustment (for statistical discrepancy/financial services)	–5 656	–22 827
Gross Domestic Product	128 938	352 237

*GDP by industry (*see* page 187 for definition of GDP).

Table A3.2   Industrial output, UK, 1978–88 (1985 = 100)
Source: *National Institute Economic Review* (November 1988)

	Energy	Manu- facturing	Metals	Building materials	Chemicals	Engineer- ing and allied	Food, drink, tobacco	Textiles, clothing	Other manufacturing	Construction
1978	70.8	105.7	112.1	118.3	91.1	105.9	98.2	117.1	110.6	105.3
1979	83.7	105.5	116.8	117.3	93.4	103.6	99.7	115.7	113.0	106.0
1980	83.3	96.3	88.7	105.7	84.0	96.2	99.0	98.1	101.0	100.2
1981	86.4	90.6	94.1	94.2	83.5	88.3	97.3	91.0	94.1	90.1
1982	91.6	90.8	91.5	96.1	83.7	89.3	98.8	89.6	91.7	91.8
1983	96.8	93.8	93.9	96.6	91.5	92.4	100.0	92.6	93.5	95.5
1984	88.8	97.7	93.6	100.3	96.9	96.9	100.8	96.0	98.5	98.9
1985	100.0	100.0	100.0	100.0	100.0	100.0	100.0	100.0	100.0	100.0
1986	105.4	100.9	99.6	101.3	102.0	99.3	100.8	100.8	104.6	103.3
1987	105.0	106.8	108.2	106.6	109.0	104.1	103.4	103.2	115.4	111.4
1988*	103.6	112.8	120.6	114.9	113.1	110.3	106.3	102.0	124.9	121.0

* First half of year

Table A3.3 Labour productivity, UK, 1978–88 (1985 = 100)
Source: *National Institute Economic Review* (November 1988)

| | Output per person employed in | | Output per person-hour |
	whole economy	manufacturing	in manufacturing
1978	87.8	79.3	78.9
1979	89.5	79.7	79.2
1980	87.6	76.6	78.1
1981	89.2	79.2	81.8
1982	92.6	84.5	86.2
1983	97.0	92.0	93.4
1984	98.0	97.3	97.8
1985	100.0	100.0	100.0
1986	102.3	103.0	103.3
1907	105.3	110.5	110.2
1988*	108.5	116.9	116.1

* First half of year

Table A3.4 Size of establishments and enterprises in manufacturing, UK, 1986
Source: *Census of Production (Business Monitor PA1002,* 1988)

	Analysis by number of employees (thousands)								
	1–9	10–19	20–49	50–99	100–199	200–499	500–999	1 000–1 499	1 500 and over
Establishments									
Number of establishments	101 981	17 328	12 602	5 939	3 767	2 850	945	262	315
Total employment	323	241	400	417	532	875	643	315	1 132
Enterprises									
Number of enterprises		125 503			2 239	1 449	508	188	356
Total employment		1 146			310	447	353	228	2 291

4 | Distribution

Economics is concerned not only with the production of the goods and services which constitute the national 'cake', but also with how the cake is divided up among individuals. In dealing with this latter subject economists refer to the distribution of national income.[1]

Distribution of income

The forces of supply and demand operate in the markets for factors of production and in so doing affect the distribution of income, though this is influenced also by government intervention. There are two distributions to be considered:

- distribution according to the size of individuals' incomes
- distribution among factors of production.

Size distribution

We look first at the current degree of inequality in income distribution in the UK. Figure 4.1 presents this information in a convenient, if unusual, way, making use of what is known as a **Lorenz curve**. This shows how much of total income is accounted for by given proportions of persons. The percentages measured on both axes are *cumulative* so, as we move along the horizontal axis, we look at the shares of the bottom 1 per cent, 2 per cent, etc., of the population and then read off their shares on the vertical axis. For example, the bottom 20 per cent of persons received about 6 per cent of total income, the bottom 50 per cent about 22 per cent of income and so on. We can compare the Lorenz curve at any time with the *line of absolute equality*. This is drawn in the diagram as the diagonal going through the origin. It indicates absolute equality because all points along it show that a given percentage of the population receives exactly the same percentage of total income, i.e. the bottom 1 per cent receive 1 per cent of total income, the bottom 5 per cent receive 5 per cent, etc. Hence the further the Lorenz curve bends away from the diagonal, the greater the degree of inequality.

The simple single line of the Lorenz curve gives a full description of the distribution of income among persons (strictly speaking the data refers not to persons but to 'tax units', whereby the incomes of most husbands and wives are

---

1 The theory of distribution is covered by Lipsey and Harbury, *First Principles*, Chapters 20–21.

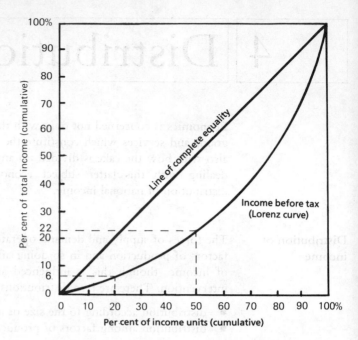

Fig. 4.1 Distribution of income before tax, UK 1984–85
Source: *Economic Trends*, November 1987

Per cent of total income (cumulative)

Line of complete equality

Income before tax
(Lorenz curve)

Per cent of income units (cumulative)

counted as one). We have already seen that the diagram shows the bottom 20 per cent receive only about 6 per cent of total income. We can see also that the bottom 80 per cent receive 54 per cent of total income, which means that the top 20 per cent receive 46 per cent. Why should this be so?

The answer to this question is complex. The distribution of income shown by the Lorenz curve is partly the result of economic forces, partly caused by the socioeconomic system of the country, and partly because of various kinds of action by the government. We shall consider the last of these in Chapter 6. Here we shall discuss the influence of market forces. They are relevant because a part, at least, of the income of most individuals comes as a reward for their services as factors of production.

Factor shares

Chapter 1 of this book began by explaining that economists usually classify resources, or factors of production, into three main categories – land, labour and capital. Each of these factors receives an income – known respectively as rent, wages and salaries, and interest. There is also a fourth kind of income, called profit, earned by a factor, which is sometimes given the name **enterprise**. Of course, a single individual may receive income from more than one source, e.g. wages from employment, interest on capital lent to industry and rent from land.

The factor (or **functional**) distribution of income is shown in Fig. 4.2. It must, however, be understood that the divisions shown in the diagram (derived from published statistics) do not correspond precisely to the concepts used in economic theory, though they come closest in the case of income from employment. Gross trading profits include interest on capital as well as pure profit; self-employment income contains an element of labour income as well as interest and profit; while rent is the return on land and buildings rather than pure economic rent. (**Economic rent** is a payment to any factor of production in excess of its transfer earnings[1] – some data relating to this concept is given in Fig. 4.15 page 105)

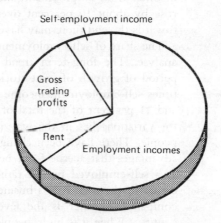

Fig. 4.2 Factor distribution of income, UK, 1987
Source: *UK National Accounts*

The largest share, about two-thirds of the total in 1987, accrued to labour in the form of wages and salaries. Rent took about a tenth as much as this. The gross trading profits of the private and public sectors are the pool from which dividends and interest are paid. In the diagram, profits are shown before any depreciation allowances are made (see page 33). *All* proportions are shown gross before the deduction of any taxes on income. Self-employment income cannot be regarded as the reward to a single factor of production, as with the first two main categories; it is rather a mixture. Part represents income for work done and part a return on capital invested, either in a business or in education and training to acquire the qualifications without which such professional earnings would not accrue. Self-employment income is about 10 per cent of the total.

Trends in the shares of factor incomes

Figure 4.2 showed the shares of the chief factors of production as they existed in one particular year, 1987. These shares are not always the same. The share of capital tends to be high in years of prosperity, when profits are high.

1   See Lipsey and Harbury, *First Principles*, pages 233–6, for the theory of economic rent.

Labour's share falls accordingly in such boom periods and rises, for the opposite reason, when trade is less flourishing. That is not to say that *wages* tend to be high in depressions, only that the *share of employment income* is large. In absolute terms, wages may be high or low.

Apart from short-term fluctuations, some longer-term trends are observable in factor shares. If we look back to the 1870s we can see a fairly stable share of wages alone, which persisted until about the middle of the present century. It should be added, however, that the proportion of wage earners was falling at the same time. Taking account of all incomes from employment, the share of wages and salaries rose by about 10 per cent over this long period, although towards the end there may have been a slight fall.

The share of self-employment income is more complex to analyse. The long-term trend was downward during the period of growth of joint stock companies. In more recent times self-employment income has accounted for between 8 and 11 per cent of the total of factor incomes. One reason for variations lies in the way in which taxes are levied on people. There have been changes from time to time in the advantages that accrue from being treated for tax purposes as a self-employed person rather than as a wage or salary earner or the owner of a business organised as a joint stock company. Another is the level of unemployment in the country. When it is high, people may seek to set themselves up in small businesses, often assisted by payments made in compensation for being declared redundant. There certainly was a substantial increase in the number of self-employed persons during the 1980s (from 2 to 3 million), but this was reflected in only a very modest increase in the share of self-employment income in the total of all domestic incomes (8·7 per cent 1979–80 average compared with 9·3 per cent 1986–87).

The income of any factor of production (and hence the share in total income that it is able to command) depends on the price that is paid for it, and on the amount that is used. Economic theory tells us that the forces of supply and demand determine the prices of factors of production just as they do of those of goods and services, although, as usual, government intervention affects the actual incomes of individuals. The remainder of this chapter will examine the background within which these forces work, with particular attention being paid to the labour market.

The supply of labour

The number of persons in the community able and wishing to work depends in the first instance on the size of the total population and its age (and to some extent its sex) distribution.

Population size

We saw in Chapter 1 that the population of the UK grew rapidly during the 19th and early 20th centuries, and appears now to have stabilised at around 57 million.

The size of the population depends on:

- birth rates
- death rates
- the balance of migration movements

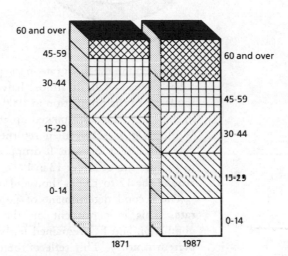

Fig. 4.3 Age
distribution of the
female population 1871
and 1987
Source: *Annual Abstract
of Statistics*

The **birth rate** (defined as the number of babies born per 1000 of the population) is determined by the age distribution of the female population and by family size. The number of women of child-bearing age in the population in 1987 is shown in Fig. 4.3; for purposes of comparison the figures for 1871 are also given. Not only was the proportion greater during the Victorian period of rapid population growth, but the numbers in the 0–14 age group, coming up later to fertility, were also very much higher.

The next diagram, Fig. 4.4, shows that by the interwar years family size had also changed dramatically from that of the 19th century. The contrast between the two periods is startling. Whereas every fourth Victorian family had at least 9 children, only 1 in 40 in the later period had as many. The reasons for this tremendous fall in the size of families are interesting even if they are not all understood. They are clearly associated with increasing knowledge and use of contraceptive techniques, which in turn reflect other changes – the growth of the middle classes (who tend to have fewer children), the emancipation of women, and changing attitudes towards family life and parental responsibility.

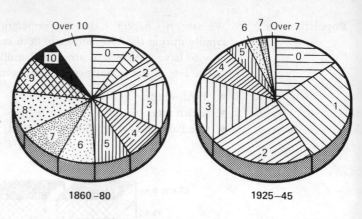

Fig. 4.4 Size of families 1960–80 (England and Wales) and 1925–45 (Great Britain) – number of children per family Source: *Report of the Royal Commission on population*, Cmnd 7695, 1949

1860–80   1925–45

The trend in the birth rate in the present century has shown a fairly steady fall. It almost halved from a rate of 29 per thousand of the population in 1900 to one of 16 per thousand in the 1930s. The rate picked up after the end of the Second World War as servicemen returned home to raise families deferred during the war. It dropped once more in the 1960s, to a minimum of under 12 in 1977, since when it has hovered around the 12 to 13 per thousand mark.

The second determinant of population size is the **death rate**. This is dependent on the age distribution of the population and has remained fairly constant throughout the present century. This reflects the opposing influences of an aging population and of a decline in mortality rates for most age groups, resulting from medical advances and rising living standards. The current situation may be summarised as that the average baby can expect to live to be 71½ if a boy, or 77½ if a girl. By comparison, average life expectancies at the beginning of the century were 49 and 52 respectively.

Finally, **migration** affects the size of the population. Throughout the 19th century, migration was an important factor restraining the growth of Britain's population; the range of opportunities, particularly in America, ensured that emigrants greatly outnumbered immigrants. Towards the end of the century immigration into Britain had also assumed sizeable proportions, but in the 60 years after 1871 there was a *net* loss from migration of the order of 4 million. In the 1920s most foreign countries put up barriers to immigrants and the balance of movements between the censuses of 1931 and 1961 was reversed, to become one of a net gain of some half a million people. This figure, however, conceals the fact that after the Second World War Britain reassumed her traditional role as a country of emigration, chiefly to the Commonwealth (especially Australia and Canada), and that this movement was offset in the late 1950s by increasing numbers of immigrants, again mainly from the Commonwealth (especially the West Indies, India and Pakistan). Net immigration around 1960 approached 150 000 per annum. This prompted the government to pass the Commonwealth Immigration Acts, the first in 1962, which gave it power to restrict immigration from the Commonwealth. A sharp fall in the number of immigrants followed, and for the next twenty years there was a net loss of more than three quarters of a million people through migration. Since 1982 the position reversed itself into a small net inflow of around 40 000 per annum, due rather more to a fall in outward migrants than to a rise in numbers of immigrants.

Activity rates

The **working population**, sometimes called the labour force, is not the same as the total population. It comes largely from those in the age group 16–65 and, as we observed in Chapter 1, involves only about half the total population – about 27 million.

The size of the labour force in a given population depends on many factors, including conventional views as to the proper age of retirement, the level of pensions, attitudes towards family life and responsibilities, the legal minimum school-leaving age and the tendency for young people to continue education after that.

The ratio of the working to the total population, expressed as a percentage, is known as the **activity rate**, or the **participation rate**. The rate varies naturally with age, especially for females, as many women leave work for at least a few years while they are bringing up young children. However, changing social attitudes have brought about a major upward shift in the participation rate for married women, which more than doubled (from 20 to 50 per cent) in a generation. In the middle age range (25–54) the female rate for the UK is significantly higher than that for Italy and West Germany, though about the same as that for France.

Occupations

Men and women are not evenly represented in the various occupational groups. For one thing, manual work accounts for about half of men's jobs but only a third of women's (see Fig. 4.5). Men are well represented in most occupational groups, while women tend to be concentrated in a relatively few, especially in clerical (including secretarial), professional (including teaching and nursing), and personal service (including catering, cleaning and hairdressing). Note, too, that the occupational structure in Britain has been changing considerably in recent years. Technological advance has led to the replacement of an increasing number of manual jobs

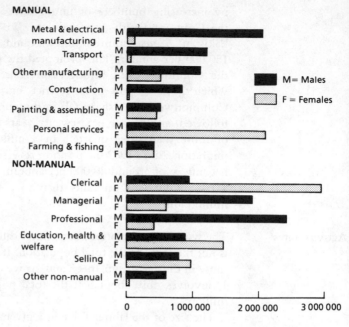

Fig. 4.5 Occupations of male and female workers, 1985
Source: Department of Employment

MANUAL

Metal & electrical manufacturing
Transport
Other manufacturing
Construction
Painting & assembling
Personal services
Farming & fishing

NON-MANUAL

Clerical
Managerial
Professional
Education, health & welfare
Selling
Other non-manual

M = Males
F = Females

0 1 000 000 2 000 000 3 000 000

by machines; and growth of the service sector in the economy and professionalisation of more and more skills has taken place.

Unemployment

The reader could be excused for assuming that when we used the term 'working population' we were considering all the people actually at work. That is not the case. The term includes members of the labour force who happen to be currently unemployed for one reason or another.

Several types of unemployment are distinguished in economic theory.[1] Two are of relevance here:

- **frictional unemployment**, which is associated with the normal turnover of labour as people move from one job to another;
- **structural unemployment**, which occurs when the structure of the economy is changing, with some industries declining while others expand; and where mismatches occur between workers made redundant in declining industries and not employable in expanding industries, at least not without retraining and/or relocating.

The precise level of general unemployment, measured as a percentage of the total labour force, is very sensitive to definitions of (a) who to count as unemployed, and (b) who

1 See Lipsey and Harbury, *First Principles*, pages 483–6.

to count in the total labour force. We discuss these matters in Chapter 9 (*see* pages 236–7). In the present chapter our concern is with certain aspects of the distribution of unemployment, which varies with a variety of circumstances. We consider here variations in unemployment that are associated with different regions of the country, different ethnic groups, different occupational groups, the age and qualifications of employees, and according to the length of time without work.

Regional unemployment

As we saw in Chapter 3 (*see* pages 62–5), regions tend to specialise in different industries. Hence it is not surprising to find that, when the structure of industry is changing, frictional and structural unemployment tends to vary among regions because of mismatches between the location of job vacancies and of unemployed seeking work. Figure 4.6 shows unemployment rates for each of the standard regions of the UK. Those with the lowest levels were the South East, East Anglia and the South West. Those with the highest were Northern Ireland, Scotland, Northern and North West England, and Wales. It must, of course, be appreciated that these are regional averages. Looking at smaller localities one can find much greater variation. For example, in 1988 the unemployment rate was as high as 30 per cent in Strabane, 20 per cent in Girvan (Scotland), Carmarthen (Wales) and South Tyneside, while it was less than 3 per cent in Winchester and Tunbridge Wells.

It is no coincidence that the regions of the country with relatively high unemployment rates happen to be relatively concentrated in the older declining industries, such as shipbuilding, steel and textiles. The unemployment rate in the West Midlands, which is a major producer of cars, illustrates the same point. During the first 20 years after the end of the Second World War the vehicle industry flourished and unemployment rates in the West Midlands were relatively low. In 1988 the car industry was no longer so prosperous, so the region's rate of unemployment was above the national average.

Unemployment and race

Unemployment rates vary among workers of different ethnic origin. The government survey on which Fig. 4.7 is based showed that rates for ethnic minorities were, on average, roughly double those for whites. Pakistani/Bangladeshi workers suffered particularly severely, with Indian/Guyanese being the least badly affected. Although some part of the differentials in the diagram may be explained by differences in age, qualification and region, a significant difference remains when these factors are taken into account.

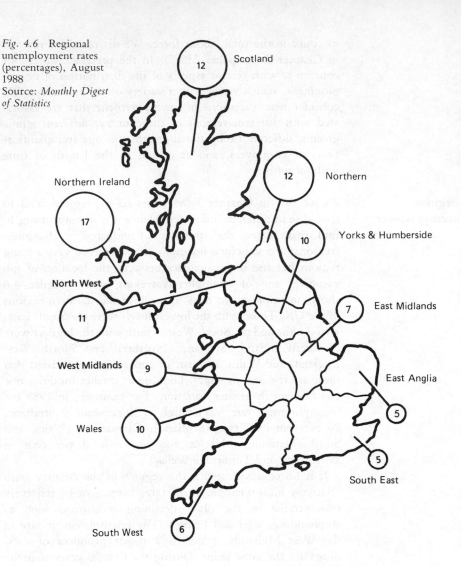

Fig. 4.6 Regional unemployment rates (percentages), August 1988
Source: *Monthly Digest of Statistics*

Scotland 12

Northern 12

Northern Ireland 17

Yorks & Humberside 10

North West 11

East Midlands 7

West Midlands 9

East Anglia 5

Wales 10

South East 5

South West 6

Other characteristics of the unemployed

The government conducts an annual Labour Force Survey (LFS) which allows the identification of characteristics of the unemployed from time to time.

The latest (1987) LFS showed variations in unemployment according to type of job and age of employee. Unemployment was found to be lower in non-manual than in manual occupations. The range was great – from rates of 3 per cent among professional/managerial occupations to 21 per cent among general labourers. Observed variations in unemployment associated with age showed the highest rates in the 16–24 year-old age bracket, while the 45 to retirement category had the lowest rates.

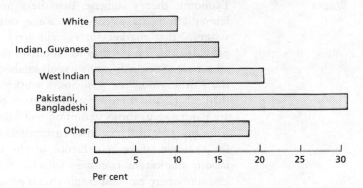

Fig. 4.7
Unemployment rates
by ethnic origin, 1986
Source: *Employment
Gazette* 1988

**The duration of
unemployment**

Another aspect of the distribution of unemployment which
deserves attention is the length of time that those affected
remain out of work. This is important because a major
feature of the high unemployment in recent years was that
the jobless stayed unemployed for longer.

There are several ways to measure unemployment duration. Two of the most important involve asking *(a)* the
currently unemployed, and *(b)* those finding new jobs, how
long they have been out of work. The former measures
uncompleted, and the latter *completed*, spells of unemployment.
The former is used in Fig. 4.8 which shows, therefore, the
distribution of uncompleted spells of unemployment in 1988.
The extent of the problem of chronic unemployment is
starkly clear in the diagram. No less than 45 per cent of
unemployed men and 30 per cent of unemployed women
were out of work for over a year. This pattern has persisted
throughout most of the 1980s. In the previous decade, when
the general level of unemployment was much lower, the
incidence of long-term joblessness was very much less as well.

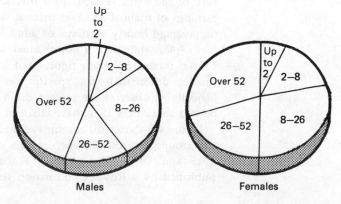

Fig. 4.8 Duration of
unemployment 1988
(number of weeks out
of work)
Sources: *Monthly Digest
of Statistics* and
Employment Gazette

Wages

Economic theory suggests that the supply and demand for labour affects its price – the **wage rate**. The theory also suggests that market forces will tend to equalise wages, provided that no barriers to labour mobility exist, and that all people are equally skilled at all kinds of work. Of course, the world is not like this. Some workers are more efficient than others, and there are many barriers to movement. Some are natural, e.g. those stemming from difficulties in moving from one part of the country to another. Others are artificial; for example, there is evidence of the existence of a **dual labour market** in countries such as the UK – a primary market, where pay and employment prospects are good, and a secondary market with high unemployment and low pay – and little movement between them, with many low-paid workers trapped in the secondary market.

We cannot examine all conceivable kinds of wage difference in this book, but concentrate on the following:

- differences among occupations
- differences among industries
- differences by age and sex
- differences among regions

Occupational wage differences

To a large extent occupational wage variations may be attributable to the skills needed to perform particular jobs. For example, the head chef at the Savoy Hotel is paid more than the unskilled cleaners and dishwashers there. It is hardly surprising that people with innate talents, and others who take the time and trouble to acquire skills, should earn higher incomes. How much higher? That is not an easy question to which a general answer can be given, because there is no unambiguous way of measuring the relative skills needed for different occupations. A first attempt to throw light on the subject might make use of the distinction, used by official collectors of statistics, between what are called skilled manual and unskilled manual workers. A first crude measure of the extra rewards paid for skills is to compare the earnings of manual and non-manual workers. In April 1988 the average hourly earnings of adult male manual workers was £4.46, while that of non-manual workers was £7.49. Of course, these are average figures and conceal both larger and smaller differentials for specific skills. It is difficult to generalise further about present differentials, but more can be said about how these have changed over time.

Figure 4.9 shows the earnings of men in certain occupational groups, expressed as percentages of average earnings in 1913 and 1978. The diagram is based on sample data published by a Royal Commission set up to report on the

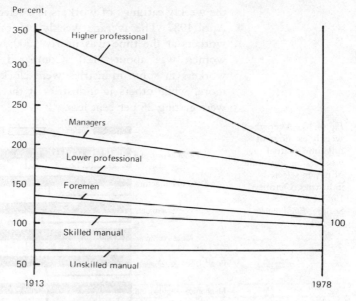

Fig. 4.9 Occupational wage differences (males) 1913 and 1978 (earnings for each occupation are shown as a percentage of average earnings) Source: *Report No 8 of the Royal Commission on the Distribution of Income and Wealth*, Cmnd 7679, 1979

distribution of income and wealth. Too much should not be read into evidence of this kind that extends over so long a period when so many conditions were changing. It serves one very useful purpose, however, in emphasising that a long-term narrowing of differentials was taking place over the half century to 1978. The trend was doubtless the result of changing forces on both the supply and demand sides. On the supply side has been increasing labour mobility, as more and more people have been acquiring qualifications of one sort or another. On the demand side, the forces have been less obvious. One possibility is that advances in technology have resulted in the automation, or computerisation, of some highly-skilled tasks.

In the shorter and more recent period since 1977, the evidence is that the spread of earnings has been widening rather than narrowing. To illustrate, consider two representative employees, one close to the top and the other near the bottom of the earnings distribution. In 1977, the former was paid almost exactly double that of the latter. By 1986, the better paid employee's earnings were nearly 2½ times those of the lower paid. The reasons for the widening of the spread of earnings in recent times are not yet fully understood. They may include such characteristics of the 1980s as a higher general level of unemployment than had existed for 40 or more years, and increased scarcity of certain kinds of skilled labour.

Industry wage differences

A second source of differences in wages is related to the industry in which people work. Figure 4.10 shows details of the weekly earnings of workers in a selection of industries in April 1987. The average weekly pay of adult male manual workers at the time was nearly £200, while the figure for women was about £120. Compared to these averages, workers in some industries were clocking up 25 per cent more, while others in industries at the bottom of the table were getting 25 per cent less.

Fig. 4.10 Average weekly earnings of full-time manual workers on adult rates of pay in selected industries, October 1987
Source: *Employment Gazette*

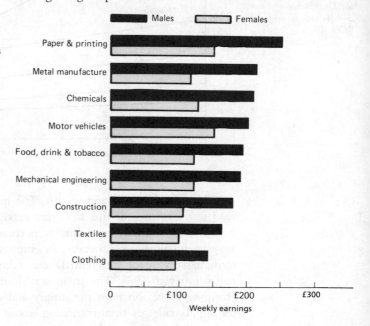

There are two reasons for the order of industries in the diagram. The first relates to the different conditions prevailing in particular industries at any time, e.g. differences in the proportion of skilled to unskilled workers and of men to women, in hours worked, in firm and plant size, and in the relative strength of trade unions. The second reason concerns industry differentials over time. It must be remembered that businesses expand and contract, and that changing wages may reflect alterations in the underlying conditions of supply and/or demand.

Age and sex wage differences

It is commonly believed that people tend to be paid more as they get older. This is certainly true up to a point. The average earnings of male manual workers aged 18–20 are less than two-thirds of the average for all workers.

What happens later on in life depends very much on the job – and it is dangerous to generalise. However, there is usually a plateau when earnings stop rising, or even fall. This is reached at younger age groups for manual workers than for non-manual, and earlier for women than for men.

As Fig. 4.10 shows, a man is much more likely to earn

more than a woman, regardless of the industry in which he works. Average earnings of women in all industries in October 1987 were between a half and two-thirds those of men and, although they differed from industry to industry, the figure is fairly representative. The reasons for this are many and complex and may well reflect an element of discrimination against women, despite the passing of the Equal Pay Act of 1976 (*see* Chapter 6 pages 152–3). However, the explanation probably lies also in the fact that women are concentrated relatively heavily in low-paid occupations and industries, as well as that they receive lower wages or salaries for identical work. Additionally, some women may be less job-committed than men, because of stronger feelings of family responsibility. They are under-represented in higher education and they tend to spend less (or to have less spent on them by employers) on vocational training, and they are less likely to join a trade union. Women, on average, also work shorter hours than their male counterparts, which keeps down their earnings, especially where they decide to forego hours paid at high overtime rates. Sex differences in *hourly* earnings are substantially less than in *weekly* earnings.

Regional wage differences

The final source of differences in wages is the region in which one works. Wages tend to be highest, on average, in Greater London. Figure 4.11 shows the average hourly earnings for manual workers in each region as a percentage of those in the capital. It can be seen that variations are considerable, with most regions having figures less than 80 per cent of those in London. Regional wage differences are, in the main, no more than a reflection of the basic forces with which we have already dealt. Behind the statistics lies the fact that regions differ in the proportions of their labour forces in different industries. We have observed something of the extent of variations in earnings by industry, and these obviously affect the regional statistics. Earnings differentials reflect also the state of local labour markets. It is no accident, for example, that earnings are highest in Greater London and lowest in Northern Ireland.

Non-pecuniary advantages and disadvantages

The discussion of wage differences has centred entirely on variations in *money* earnings. However, this is not the whole story. An economist once coined the term 'non-pecuniary advantages and disadvantages' of different occupations, in order to emphasise that some people would be happy with relatively low-paid jobs if there were compensating (i.e. non-pecuniary) advantages to go with them. An outdoor job

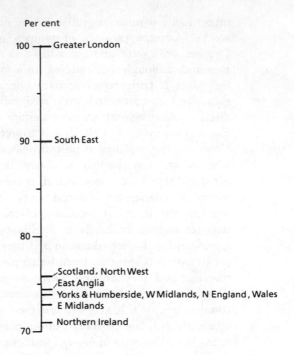

Fig. 4.11 Regional wage differentials (average weekly earnings of full-time adult male manual workers for each region shown as a percentage of those in Greater London)
Source: *Regional Trends*

appeals to many people more than one in an office or factory; an interesting one (e.g. teaching!) more than a dull routine one; a job with long holidays more than one with short; and so on.

These and similar characteristics are difficult, if not impossible, to quantify, but there are other kinds of non-monetary rewards that *are* quantifiable. They are commonly referred to as **fringe benefits** and include such 'extras' as the use of company cars, subsidised lunches, housing, etc. The Royal Commission on the Distribution of Income and Wealth (*see* below page 154) made a special study of this subject in 1978 and found benefits over and above monetary remuneration to run from around a fifth to a third of total pay, on average. It should be added that such fringe benefits may have been particularly high in that year for reasons associated with a government policy of pay restraint, but they should not be overlooked at any time when discussing wage differentials.

Trade unions[1]

Our discussion of the supply of labour and wages has already made passing reference to the trade unions. It is now time to consider them in more detail.

1 See Lipsey and Harbury, *First Principles*, pages 242–6, for economic analysis of trade unions.

Historical development	Trade unionism had its origins in the pitifully low standard of living of the average 19th century worker and his family. The explanation of the standard of living throughout the world lay in the small size of the total national output relative to the population. In 1800, even in the wealthiest of countries, an equal division of national income among all families would have left everyone in poverty by present standards.

Poverty had existed for centuries. It was accentuated, however, by the twin processes of urbanisation and industrialisation. The man who was moderately content working his land usually became restive and discontented when he moved into a grimy, smoky, 19th century city, took employment in a sweatshop or a factory, and settled with his family in a crowded, insanitary slum. (Of course, many moved because they had no choice, having been driven off their land by the enclosure movements. Thus we cannot assume that they made a free choice in the belief that the urban life was preferable to their rural one. Their rural life had been destroyed; the urban life was simply preferable to starvation.) Stories of suffering during the Industrial Revolution could fill many volumes. One example will at least illustrate some of the conditions that lay behind the drive for change and reform.

'In the cotton-spinning work, these creatures (the workers) are kept, fourteen hours in each day, locked up, summer and winter, in a heat of from *eighty to eighty-four degrees*. The rules which they are subject to are such as no negroes (i.e. slaves) were ever subjected to. . . . The door of the place wherein they work, is *locked, except half an hour, at tea-time*, the work-people are not allowed to send for water to drink, in the hot factory: even *the rain water is locked up*, by the master's order. . . . If any spinner be found with his *window open* he is to pay a fine of a shilling! . . . for a large part of the time, there is the abominable and pernicious stink of the *gas* to assist in the murderous effects of the heat. . . . the notorious fact is, that well constitutioned men are rendered old and past labour at forty years of age, and that children are rendered decrepit and deformed, and thousands upon thousands of them slaughtered by consumption (tuberculosis), before they arrive at the age of sixteen. . .'[1]

Out of these conditions came the full range of radical political movements from revolutionary socialism, which

1 *Political Register*, Vol LII, William Cobbett, 20 November 1824, as quoted by E Royston Pike in *Human Documents of the Industrial Revolution in Britain*, Allen & Unwin, 1966, pages 60–1 (parenthetical inserts added).

today we call Marxism or communism, to Fabian socialism, which tried to effect change gradually through existing political systems. Out of them also came the union, which was to some extent a club providing protection for unemployed, disabled or retired workers, and to some extent a negotiating agent. For a long time unions were resisted by the full power of both employers and government.

The union organisers perceived that 10 or 100 men acting together had more influence than one man acting alone. The union was the organisation that would provide a basis for confronting the power of employers with the collective power of workers. However it was easier to see the solution than to achieve it. Employers did not accept organisations of workers passively. Agitators who tried to organise other workers were often dismissed and blacklisted; in some cases they were physically assaulted or even killed. In order to realise the ambition of creating some effective power over the labour market, it was necessary to gain control of the supply of labour and to have the financial resources necessary to outlast employers. There was no 'right to organise', and the union usually had to force a hostile employer to negotiate with it. Since early unions did not have large resources, the employer had to be attacked where he was weakest.

All of these considerations explain why it was the unions of the highly skilled and the specialist types of labour that first met with success – it was easier to control the supply of skilled than unskilled workers. Secondly, a union of a small number of highly skilled specialists could attack the employer's weakest spots. Even then unions had their ups and downs. When employment was full and business booming, the cost of being fired for joining a union was not so great. During times of depression and unemployment, however, the risks were greater and we can observe cyclical swings in membership with gains in booms and setbacks in slumps – a pattern that persisted into the present century, as can be seen from Fig. 4.12 which charts trade union membership since 1920.

There was a substantial drop in the number of unionised workers during the depressed interwar years. More recently, membership fell again substantially in the 1980s, when unemployment was high, from a peak of 13¼ million in 1979 to 10½ million in 1986. Part of this decline can also be explained by changes in the structure of the economy, and the reduced employment in particular industries, e.g. in mining and manufacturing, where unionism has traditionally been strong.

Fig. 4.12 Numbers of trade unions and of members since 1920 Source: *Annual Abstract of Statistics*

Trade union membership

Total union membership is under half of the total number of employees in the UK. However, there are sectors which are strongly unionised and others which are weak. It is difficult to illustrate the variations from industry to industry and from occupation to occupation with published statistics. There are two main reasons for this. One is the classification system, which covers very broad groups within which there are both strong and weak sectors. The second reason is that several unions, including some of the largest, have members extending over a range of different industries. In 1986 nearly 4 million people belonged to general unions.

Let it, first, be said that unionism is, not surprisingly, stronger among full-time as against part-time employees, and among manual compared with non-manual workers (though more and more white collar and professional workers have joined trade unions in recent years). In order to make comparisons among industries, Fig. 4.13 is based on full-time workers only. It shows industries where unionism is especially strong – postal and communication services, energy (which includes coal mining), transport (which includes the railways) and government service. It also shows others where unionism is especially weak – retail distribution, building and construction, and the hotel and catering trades.

High union membership is a source of power for unions when negotiating with employers. This is reinforced where **closed shops** operate. These are arrangements, agreed with employers, where only members of the union may be employed. About a quarter of the workforce were in closed shops in the early 1980s, but the number is falling as legislation discouraging them is introduced (*see* Chapter 9, page 252).

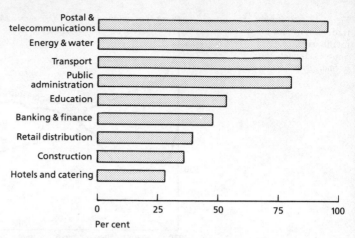

Fig. 4.13 Trade union membership 1986 (trade union members as a percentage of numbers employed in selected industries: full-time workers only) Source: *Employment Gazette*

Trade union structure

The 10½ million trade unionists in 1986 belonged to 335 unions, most of which were very small. Over half had fewer than 1000 members each, while the 24 largest accounted for about 80 per cent of total membership.

In the main, the very large unions have grown over the years as a result of amalgamations – e.g. the new Federated Union of Managerial and Professional Officers was formed in 1986 by the merging of 18 separate unions. Some unions are organised on an industry basis, such as the National Union of Mineworkers. Others, especially the older ones, are organised on a craft basis, like the National Graphical Association. However, the largest unions of all are either general unions covering a wide range of industries and/or occupations, such as the Transport and General Workers' Union with nearly 1½ million members, or multi-craft unions like the Amalgamated Engineering Union.

The central body of the trade union movement is known as the Trades Union Congress (TUC), to which most unions, especially the large ones, are affiliated. The TUC is often regarded as the representative voice of trade unions, and it negotiates with the government and national employers' associations. However, its formal powers are limited in that individual unions are not obliged to observe decisions taken at its annual conference. The standing of the TUC suffered a major blow in 1988 when one large union, the electricians' EETPU, was expelled for taking part in negotiations with employers of a kind which met with the disapproval of the majority of other unions.

Collective bargaining

Trade unions are concerned with all aspects of the employment of their members. Their major functions are related to wages, hours of work and unemployment, but extend to general working conditions such as safety, holidays and promotion procedures. In some cases unions also aim to play an influential role in management itself, including seeking representation on boards of directors.

Unions provide some benefits directly for their members, financed out of their subscription income. However, their main role is to engage in collective bargaining with employers. In the inflationary times in which we live, negotiations usually take place at least annually and lead to a series of 'wage rounds' of pay increases. Comparability with workers in similar industries or occupations, and the profitability of the business, are generally the major issues discussed.

In the majority of cases negotiations are successful, in that the bargaining sessions produce an agreed package, sometimes associated with productivity commitments on the part of unions. Negotiations take place at many levels and can cover a variety of subjects. Wages are usually the central issue, but hours and conditions of work, redundancy, allegations of victimisation of individual workers by management, etc., may also be involved. Government intervention in wage bargaining is discussed in Chapter 9 pages 251–2.

Trade disputes

If the parties fail to agree, an industrial dispute follows. At such a time the union may call on its members either to come out on strike or to take other action, such as refusing to work overtime. Employers, on the other side, may decide to close down the business, dismiss staff, or implement their offer even when it has not been agreed.

Disputes, of course, involve loss of production and Fig. 4.14 shows the numbers of days lost as a result of stoppages of work since 1920. The first point to make is that the average number of days lost has been substantially lower in the postwar period than in the 1920s. Secondly, notice the tendency for disputes to involve substantially more disruption in some years since 1970 than in earlier postwar years. A high proportion of the total number of days lost is also often attributable to a very few disputes. Of the 27 million days lost in 1984, for example, 22 million can be put down to the strike in the coal industry.

It may be worth while adding a general comment on where Britain fits into the international scene. Britain's strike record is often regarded as something of a national disgrace. However the picture is not quite as dreadful as some people may have thought. Although the UK does not have the best record in the international league table, when compared with such countries as Japan, the Netherlands and West Germany, neither is the UK at the bottom. Canada and Italy, in particular, have a worse record on average than the UK.

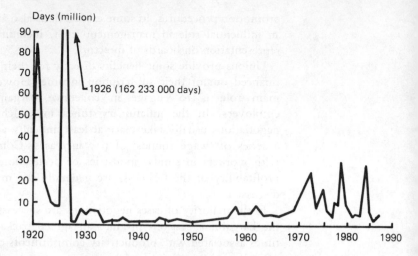

Days (million)

1926 (162 233 000 days)

Fig. 4.14 Industrial
disputes since 1920 –
number of working
days lost as a result of
industrial disputes
Source: *Annual Abstract
of Statistics*

However, strikes tend to come in waves and, when they do come, their effects can be widespread and serious, particularly if they involve wholesale disruption of power and communication services, thereby threatening indirectly both industry and the home.

Other factors of production

The bulk of this chapter has been devoted to a discussion of one factor of production, labour. This is not unreasonable, partly because incomes from employment take by far the largest proportion of the total, but mainly because of the great importance of labour in the economy as a whole. In a sense, too, some of the material in the preceding sections can be taken as illustrative of productive factors generally.

Although there are special features related to the incomes of other factors of production, especially to rent and profits, it is a little difficult to find much descriptive material that is useful for economic analysis on such matters. Nonetheless, we end this chapter by highlighting some features concerning rent and profits.

Rent[1]

To an economist rent is not just the return received by the factor of production, land; it is a surplus that can accrue to any factor of production which possesses some specific characteristic that others do not. A common example is the so-called **rent of ability** earned by film stars, which greatly exceeds their potential earnings in other occupations. Figure 4.15 has been prepared to try to illustrate the differential nature of the earnings received by individuals with different abilities. The figures must in no way be taken to be precise

1 Economic rent is discussed in Lipsey and Harbury, *First Principles*, Chapter 20.

measurements of the economic rents accruing to different skills. It could be argued, with justification, that at least some of the differentials are part of the returns for the education and training that some people decide to undergo. However, in so far as entry into certain trades and professions included in the diagram may be due to a shortage of talents, or may even be artificially restricted, some part of the earnings differentials are of the nature of economic rent.

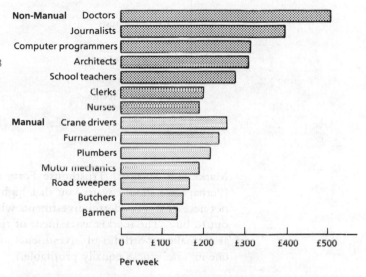

Fig. 4.15 Average gross weekly earnings of adult men, selected occupations, April 1988 Source: *New Earnings Survey* (Department of Employment)

Profit

What the man in the street calls **profit** economists call the **return on capital**. As well as an amount that would be earned on a riskless investment, the return includes, in most cases of equity investment, a substantial risk premium. The riskier the investment in some classes of enterprise, the higher must be the return on those ventures that succeed. The high return on the successful ventures averages out with the losses on the unsuccessful ones, to provide an incentive for people to risk their capital *before* they know whether their particular venture will succeed or not.

Figure 4.16 gives information on the relative riskiness of investing money in a number of different companies as measured by the yields on their ordinary shares (*see* Chapter 2 pages 33–4 for a definition of dividend yield). The companies in the diagram were chosen to represent a range of different degrees of riskiness in their business and have, correspondingly, a range of yields. Riskiest of all are some mining companies where output in future years is something of a gamble. Other relatively risky investments are certain finance companies, and even Tottenham Hotspur is not as safe a bet as are large industrial companies such as GEC,

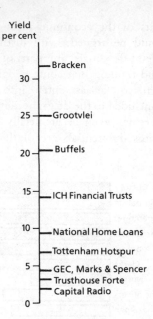

Fig. 4.16 Dividend
yields on selected
equities
Source: *The Financial
Times*, 22 December
1988

Marks and Spencer, Trusthouse Forte and Capital Radio.
(Perhaps we should warn you that high yielding shares are
not necessarily wonderful investments which one should rush
out to buy. The market assessment of risk ought to be such
as to make a portfolio of investments in mining shares and
one in 'safe' stocks equally profitable.)

Questions and exercises

For key to symbols indicating suggested sources *see* pages
xi–xii.

1　The Inland Revenue publishes figures of the numbers of
incomes in different size brackets and the total income
accruing to each bracket. For the most recent year that you
can find statistics, prepare a table showing the *percentages*
(a) of the total number of incomes, and *(b)* of the total
income in each bracket.

　Now add the percentages cumulatively – so that each row
in the table shows the percentage for *(a)* and for *(b)* – for all
brackets smaller in size. (For example, the first row might
show the percentage of incomes as being 10 per cent. If the
next row shows the percentage as being, say, 4 per cent, the
cumulative percentage would be 14 per cent.)

　Plot the data in your columns of cumulative percentages to
yield a Lorenz curve, as drawn in Fig. 4.1. How much
inequality of incomes exists in the year you have chosen?
Would you judge that to be greater or less than the degree of
inequality in 1984–5 (*see* Fig. 4.1)? (*AS*)

2   Prepare a graph showing, for the past ten years, the percentages of total factor income arising from the following three sources:

1 employment income;
2 self-employment income;
3 all other factor income.

Work out for which of these ten years series 1, 2 or 3 was *(a)* highest, and *(b)* lowest. Can you offer any explanations for the years which you identified? (*AS*)

3   Construct a table showing the age distribution of the total UK population last year, using the following age groups: Under 5, 5–24, 25–65 and over 65 (or some other similar age groupings).

Now try to find an old copy of the *Annual Abstract of Statistics* (preferably at least ten years old) and extract similar data, but from the table 'Projected Resident Population of the UK', choosing the figures for last year (i.e. the same year as your first table).

What differences are there between the projections and the actual? To what might any such differences be due? (*AS*)

4   Find out the numbers of *(a)* males *(b)* females in employment, and the total numbers of males and females in the population, between the ages of 18 and 65 for men and 18 and 60 for women.

Calculate the activity rates for the two groups.

Now repeat the exercise, but this time add the numbers of *unemployed* males and females to the totals.

What differences do you find? What meanings could you attach to these differences? (*AS*)

5   Trace an outline map of the UK from an atlas and divide it into regions as in Fig. 3.7b. Shade areas where unemployment rates are equal to the average for the whole country, and hatch those where they are below the average. Compare the result with Fig. 4.6. (*RT, ET, KD*)

6   Prepare a chart on the lines of Fig. 4.9 showing the percentage change in earnings of workers in each of the following industries over the last *five* years. Which have changed most and what differences in rank order are there?

Food, drink and tobacco	Banking and finance
Electrical engineering	Textiles
Agriculture	Chemicals (*AS*)

7   *Whitaker's Almanack* lists the names and membership of the main trade unions registered in Britain. Find out the names and total membership of the largest ten unions. Then obtain the total number and membership of all trade unions in the UK from the *Annual Abstract of Statistics*. Calculate the proportion of the total accounted for by the top ten. (*WA, AS*)

8 Collect figures showing the number of industrial stoppages of work in the main industrial groups in Britain for the past two calendar years. Work out the proportion of total stoppages accounted for by each group and compare your results. Are there any great changes, and do you know why? (AS)

9 Prepare a comparative table for male and female manual workers for a recent year showing:

(a) average weekly earnings;
(b) average hours worked;
(c) calculate average hourly earnings for the two groups. (NB Base your data on the numbers of workers on adult rates of pay.)

Then calculate the ratio of male to female earnings and hours as in (a), (b) and (c), and write a short commentary on your calculations. (AS)

Appendix

Table A4.1 Regional unemployment rates (per cent), UK, August
1988
Source: *Monthly Digest of Statistics*

North	11.9	West Midlands	8.8
Yorkshire and Humberside	9.6	North West	10.8
East Midlands	7.3	Wales	10.4
East Anglia	4.7	Scotland	11.5
South East	5.2	Northern Ireland	16.9
South West	6.1	UK	8.1

Table A4.2 Average weekly earnings of manual workers (full-time workers on adult rates of
pay), UK, October 1987 (£s per week)
Source: *Employment Gazette* (April 1988)

	All manu- facturing industries	Food, drink and tobacco	Mineral extraction	Chemicals and allied industries	Metal manu- facture	Mechanical engineering	Metal goods	Electrical engineering	Motor vehicles
Males	198	199	216	220	193	185	179	211
Females	131	121	138	124	132	124	127	155

	Textiles	Clothing and footwear	Timber furniture, etc.	Paper, printing and publishing	Energy and water	Construction	Other transport equipment
Males	163	143	175	254	222	181	198
Females	102	97	128	152	164	105	139

Table A4.3 Trade unions – numbers and membership, UK, 1980–88
Source: *Employment Gazette* (May 1988)

Year	Number	Membership (million)
1980	438	12.9
1981	414	12.1
1982	408	11.6
1983	394	11.2
1984	375	11.0
1985	370	10.8
1986	335	10.5

Table A4.4 Industrial stoppages (working days lost) 1987
Source: *Employment Gazette*

	(thousands)
Working days lost through stoppages which began in year	
Analysis by workers involved:	
Under 100 workers	85
100 and under 250 workers	155
250 and under 500 workers	164
500 and under 1000 workers	212
1000 and under 2500 workers	185
2500 and under 5000 workers	219
5000 workers and over	2525
Working days lost, all stoppages	
Analysis by industry:	
Mining and quarrying	217
Metal manufacture	36
Engineering	197
Shipbuilding	158
Vehicles	67
Textiles, clothing	50
Other manufacturing	88
Construction	22
Transport, communication	1 705
Other non-manufacturing	1 007

5 | International trade and development

Very few nations in the modern world are isolated from each other. They engage in trade in goods and services and in financial transactions of many kinds. The total record of international payments and receipts is to be found in the balance of payments of a country, which will be discussed in Chapter 7. For the present, we shall ignore purely financial transactions and concentrate on questions of the international allocation of resources and on patterns of trade.[1]

The basis for trade International specialisation is no different in principle from interregional specialisation, which was examined in Chapter 3. We saw how different parts of the UK tend to concentrate on certain lines of economic activity. The reasons for this relate to their natural and acquired endowments of factors of production – the size and quality of their labour forces and their particular skills, the quantity and fertility of the land, the mineral resources below it and the amount of capital equipment that has been accumulated in the past.

In one important respect international variations in factor endowments are of greater significance than are interregional variations – factors of production are much more freely mobile *within* countries than *between* them. The reasons are largely linguistic and political, stemming from the existence of national frontiers which impede factor movement. However, there are also social and psychological barriers reflected in different national life styles, which discourage labour, in particular, from moving in search of the highest paid employment, regardless of where it may be. Moreover, the very existence of national governments and national currencies often leads to state intervention to protect industries from foreign competition.

Most international trade is based upon relative scarcities or abundances of different factors of production, which in

1 The theory related to the issues discussed in this chapter is covered in Lipsey and Harbury, *First Principles*, Chapter 22.

turn give rise to relative cost advantages and disadvantages for individual countries when producing particular goods and services. In certain cases the disadvantage may be of an extreme kind, in the sense that a country may be incapable of producing something at all. In the main, however, these differences are due either to the uneven dispersion of minerals over the world or to the existence of regional variations in climate. Canada, for example, is rich in nickel deposits, Spain and Italy in mercury and South Africa in gold, while Britain has virtually none of these metals. Moreover, with a temperate climate Britain cannot grow such tropical and subtropical products as coffee, tea, cotton, rubber or cocoa. The only way in which Britain can obtain these and similar products is by importing them from abroad in exchange for goods and services which Britain produces for export.

Most trade, however, is between countries who have what is known as a comparative advantage in the production of some goods, which they export, and a comparative disadvantage in the production of others, which they import. This means that, although a country could produce the goods that it imports, the relative costs are such as to encourage specialisation in some and importation of others.

The major trading nations

Before looking at the detailed structure of the trade of the UK, we should put the country in perspective by taking note of the major world trading nations. Figure 5.1 shows the values of total imports and exports of the ten leading trading nations, which together are responsible for about 60 per cent of all international trade. It is immediately apparent that there are great differences among these leaders. The scene is dominated by the United States, West Germany and Japan, which together account for about a third of world exports and imports.

The UK occupies fourth or fifth position these days. This is a great change from the early part of this century, and earlier, especially on the export side where this country traditionally dominated the field. Around 1900, the UK was responsible for approximately a third of total world exports of manufactured goods. By 1950 that share had fallen to less than a quarter. By 1980 the proportion was below 8 per cent. Since then the position has become more stable. This is illustrated in Fig. 5.2, which shows how the exports of the five leading trading nations have performed *relative to the world total*. Thus, between 1980 and 1987 the UK regained some of its position as regards France and the USA, though continued to lag behind Japan and, to a much smaller extent, West Germany.

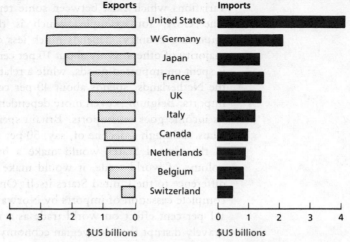

Fig. 5.1 Major
trading nations; values
of exports and imports
in US dollars, 1987
Source: *International
Financial Statistics*

The size of a country's exports or imports can be very
misleading as a guide to the significance of foreign trade to
that nation. A very large country can have an extensive
foreign trade which is nevertheless *proportionately* small in
comparison with that of a much less important nation. A
useful measure of the importance of foreign trade to a
country is the relationship between the value of its imports
and its total national income. Figure 5.3 shows the very wide

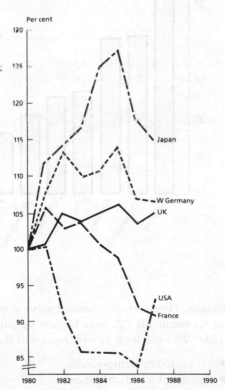

Fig. 5.2 Export
performance of leading
trading nations since
1980 (the series for
each country shows the
volume of exports
relative to the world
total)
Source: *National
Institute Economic
Review*

variations which exist between some representative nations. The USA, for example, which is the world's leading importing country, depends much less on imports than the majority of others. Only about 10 per cent of its total income is spent on imported goods, while a relatively small country, the Netherlands, spends about 40 per cent of its income on imports. Belgium is even more dependent on trade: over half its income goes on imports. Britain spends about a quarter. Thus, although a decline of, say, 50 per cent in foreign trade in the United States would make a big hole in the total volume of world trade, it would make comparatively little difference to the United States itself. On the other hand, the complete cessation of imports by Norway would have barely a 1 per cent effect on world trade as a whole, but it would gravely disrupt the Norwegian economy.

The trade of the UK

The aggregate importance of trade to the UK has been summarised in Fig. 5.3, i.e. imports as a percentage of total

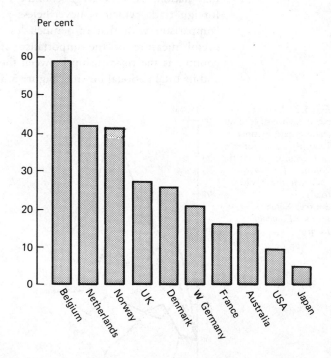

Fig. 5.3 Imports as a percentage of national income (GDP) for selected countries 1987 Source: *International Financial Statistics*

income. However, the detailed ways in which trade impinges on economic life can only be seen by studying the pattern of trade. We now look at two aspects of the trade of the UK:

• commodity composition
• geographical distribution

Commodity trade   The commodity composition of UK trade in 1987 is shown in Fig. 5.4. It is important to stress that this composition is *not* typical of earlier periods. Chapter 1 described the major shifts that have taken place in British overseas trade during the present century – the reader is urged to review that section, and in particular Figures 1.11 and 1.12 (pages 12 and 13).

The pattern of imports today is one where manufactures and semi-manufactures account for about three-quarters of the total, whereas prior to the First World War their share was less than a quarter. The traditional 19th century picture of the UK, exporting manufactured goods in exchange for imports of primary products, has been eroded over the century, at first gradually and then at an accelerating pace

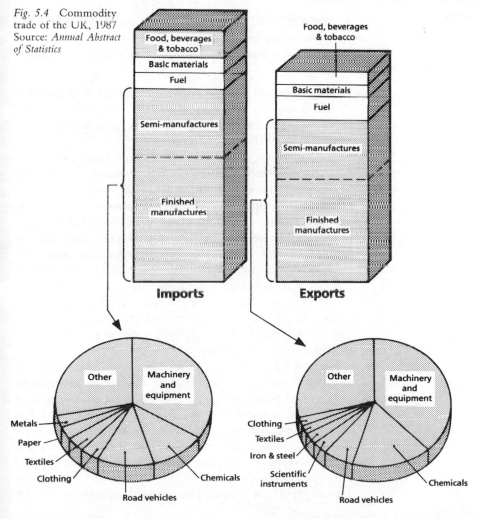

Fig. 5.4 Commodity trade of the UK, 1987
Source: *Annual Abstract of Statistics*

since the 1960s. British foreign trade now consists predominantly of the exchange of manufactured goods with other countries. The only raw material whose import increased significantly in recent years was fuel, although, as can be seen from Fig. 5.4, Britain became a fuel exporter as a result of the oil discoveries in the North Sea.

Although manufactures remain the solid backbone of Britain's exports, there have been substantial shifts in their composition. These reflect, in part, changes in the structure of British industry itself noted in Chapter 3. Textiles and iron and steel, for example, made up approximately half of total exports in 1913. By 1987 their share had dropped to less than 5 per cent and their place had been taken by machinery, chemicals and vehicles, as Fig. 5.4 shows.

Import penetration and export sales ratios

Two different aspects of commodity trade worthy of attention are:

- the extent to which foreign imports compete with domestically produced goods
- the relative importance of exports to total home production

Figure 5.5 throws light on both these matters for a selection of industries. The top lines show the percentages of UK export sales; the lower lines show the percentages of the foreign share of the UK markets.

The large share of some British markets taken by foreign suppliers is not necessarily a cause for concern. One should look also at the export performance of British industries, shown in the diagram by the ratio of exports to total sales. We find, in fact, that many of the industries where there is heavy import penetration are also ones where exports account for high proportions of output by UK firms. For example, the manufacturers of office machinery (which includes data processing equipment) sell over 90 per cent of their output overseas – almost the same proportion as foreign firms take of the UK market; and the export/sales ratio exceeds the imports/home demand ratio in both chemicals and mechanical engineering.

Figure 5.5 presents only a snapshot picture of the situation in a single recent year. It should be added that the trends in both import penetration and export/sales ratios have been of steady and appreciable increases in both figures. For manufacturing industry as a whole, import penetration rose from 17 to 35 per cent between 1971 and 1987, while exports as a percentage of sales rose from 19 to 30 per cent over the same period. In the previous section we described British foreign trade as being characterised nowadays by an

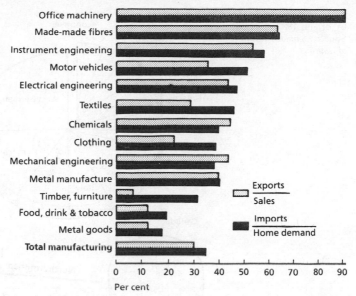

Fig. 5.5 UK import penetration and export sales ratios for selected industries, 1987
Source: *Annual Abstract of Statistics*

interchange of manufactures. We see now that this applies as much *within* industry groups as to exports of manufactures as a whole.

Geographical distribution of UK trade

The geographical composition of UK trade is illustrated by three diagrams; Fig. 5.6 traces the major shifts in percentage distribution by destination of British exports, and Figures 5.7 and 5.8 show details of Britain's main markets and suppliers in 1987.

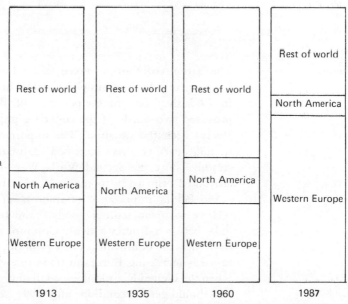

Fig. 5.6 UK exports (percentage distribution by destination in selected years 1913–1987)
Sources: *Abstract of British Historical Statistics*, B R Mitchell and P Deane (Cambridge University Press, 1962), and *Annual Abstract of Statistics*

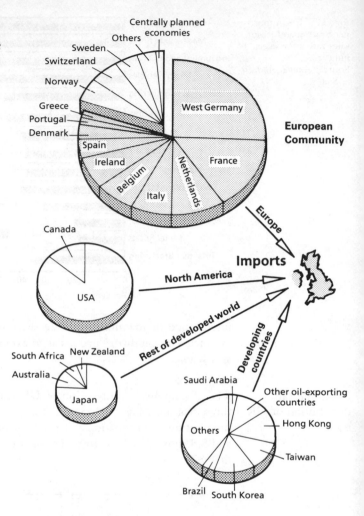

Fig. 5.7 UK imports by origin, 1987
Source: *Annual Abstract of Statistics*

Europe

The nations of Europe, taken as a whole, are at once the largest group both as suppliers and as markets for the UK. In 1987 they bought 60 per cent of British exports and provided two-thirds of the country's imports. This has not always been the situation. The importance of Europe as a trading partner has increased substantially, and fairly steadily, since the Second World War. The growth can be attributed principally to the changed structure of UK trade – the fall in importance of imports of primary products relative to manufactured goods – and to declining trading links between Britain and the Commonwealth, which used to occupy the dominant trading position. The postwar trend towards increasing European trade received a boost in 1973 when the United Kingdom joined the European Community, and should get a second one after 1992 (*see* page 125).

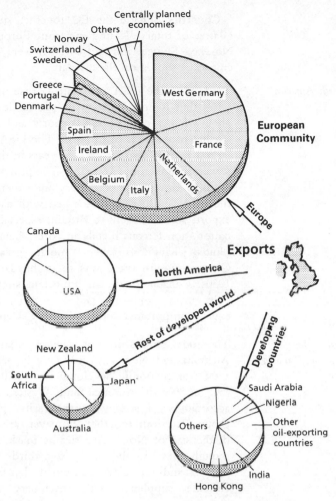

Fig. 5.8 UK exports by destination, 1987 Source: *Annual Abstract of Statistics*

Figures 5.7 and 5.8 divide Europe into two parts – members of the EC, and the rest. The former can be seen to be much the more important of the two; in 1987 the EC accounted for 50 per cent of UK exports and a slightly higher proportion of imports from all sources. The situation may be compared with that of the 1960s when those proportions were less than a third.

Within the EC, West Germany is Britain's major market and supplier of imports (mainly machinery and manufactured goods including cars and chemicals). Next in importance are France (which sends Britain manufactures and food) and the Netherlands (dairy produce and other foodstuffs), followed by Italy, Belgium and Ireland. The shares of the other EC member countries can be seen in Figures 5.7 and 5.8.

Countries outside the EC together supplied less than a quarter of total UK imports from Europe. Of them, only Norway, Switzerland and Sweden were sufficiently important to be shown on the diagram.

North America Trade with the USA and Canada rose in the early postwar years, but is now back to its prewar level, accounting for about 15 per cent of UK exports and supplying a rather smaller proportion of imports. The USA has been Britain's largest market apart from two years in the late 1970s, when it was overtaken by Germany. The principal goods the USA sends to Britain are machinery and other manufactures, but the USA is also richly endowed with natural resources and exports some of them to Britain, especially cereals, tobacco, cotton, non-ferrous metals and ores. Canada's links with the United Kingdom were much greater when intra-Commonwealth trade was in its heyday, especially in the 1930s. Canada is still an important supplier of wood and pulp, metals and ores and foodstuffs, and ranks roughly equal in importance today with, say, Denmark.

Rest of the 'developed' world The four nations in this category, Japan, South Africa, Australia and New Zealand, may be said to have reached a state of economic development broadly comparable with that of North America and Western Europe; they are accordingly, if somewhat arbitrarily, placed in the same group. The four together, however, are only about a third of the size of North America as markets for UK exports, though they supply nearly two-thirds of the imports of Canada and the USA combined. Japan heads the list of Britain's suppliers, with machinery and manufactures, including motor vehicles. Australia, New Zealand and South Africa were of far greater importance in the days of Imperial and Commonwealth preference (*see* page 123), as was Canada, and remained so for the first postwar decade. Exports to the UK from Australia consist principally of foodstuffs and minerals; from South Africa they are a little more varied and include manufactured goods as well as cereals, metals, fruit and vegetables; from New Zealand they are substantially foodstuffs.

Developing countries The final group of countries are the 'developing', or less developed countries. They include the so-called oil-exporters, which first sprang into prominence following the quadrupling of the price of crude oil in 1973–74. They then became of considerable importance, both as oil suppliers and as growing markets for UK exports, until exploitation of North Sea oil when output expanded. By 1987 this group of countries (of which Saudi Arabia is the largest) supplied only about 2 per cent of UK imports, but still took double that proportion of exports.

A host of other developing countries are included in the 'others' section in Figures 5.7 and 5.8. Few are of sufficient importance to warrant specific mention, but it is worth noting Hong Kong, as a supplier of miscellaneous manufactures, but from whom we import less than we do from Denmark. India is marginally more important as a market for UK goods than Hong Kong.

The terms of trade

The trading patterns outlined in the previous sections are the result of many forces. Prime among them are the prices of goods in different countries. Prices are affected by the rate of exchange between currencies, which will be discussed in Chapter 9. We can, however, make a start on this subject by looking at what are known as the **terms of trade**. These are defined as export prices as a percentage of import prices, calculated by dividing the price level of exports by that of imports.

The movements of the UK terms of trade since 1970 are plotted in Fig. 5.9. The diagram shows the sharp deterioration which followed the oil price shock of 1973–74 (*see* page 195), when the prices of many other primary products which the UK imports (cocoa, zinc, etc.) also rose substantially. The general trend in the 1980s was for a gradual improvement in the UK's terms of trade, although there were some short-term deviations.

Export competitiveness

The terms of trade give an impression of the average prices of British imports and exports relative to each other. To ascertain the competitiveness of British goods requires a comparison of UK export prices relative to those of our

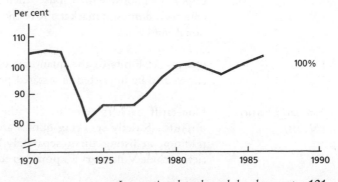

Fig. 5.9 Terms of trade, UK since 1970 (quantity of imports obtainable for a fixed quantity of exports) – an upward movement corresponds to an improvement in the UK's terms of trade
Source: *Annual Abstract of Statistics*

competitors. This is a complex matter, reflecting comparative rates of inflation and of exchange rates between sterling and other currencies. In the 1970s the net outcome of these factors worked generally unfavourably to the UK compared with, especially, Japan, West Germany, other EC countries and the USA. However, in the 1980s UK export prices operated in the opposite way, rising on the whole less than those of many other such countries (*see* Fig. 5.10). (The reader is warned that the figures on which the diagram are based are particularly sensitive to the choice of base year for the comparisons. You are advised to attempt question 5 at the end of this chapter.)

Fig. 5.10 Export competitiveness: export prices relative to the world average, selected countries, 1980–87 (a figure greater than 100 means that the countries' export prices became less competitive) Source: *National Institute Economic Review*

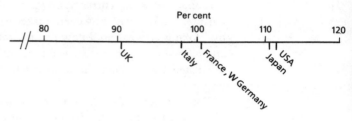

Trade restrictions

International trade does not all take place in completely free markets. Most governments take some actions designed to discourage certain imports and to encourage certain exports. Since one country's imports are another country's exports, it follows that the net effect of all measures is to lower the volume of world trade and reduce the scope for gains from trade based on comparative advantage. Three methods of restricting imports may be distinguished:

- tariffs
- quotas
- non–tariff barriers

Tariffs

The traditional means of restricting imports is through **tariffs** (also called **import duties**). These are taxes placed on imported goods which raise their prices in the levying country's domestic market above the prices ruling in international markets.

Quotas

Quotas set limits to the quantities of certain goods that are allowed to be imported in a stated period.

Non-tariff barriers (NTBs)

Non-tariff barriers refer to all other measures that reduce imports. (Strictly speaking quotas are NTBs, but we follow tradition in listing them separately.) Major non-tariff barriers include **Voluntary Export Agreements (VERs)** in which one country agrees to restrict its exports to a second country (usually to avoid more severe import restrictions which the second country is threatening to impose.) A different set of NTBs involves harrassment of goods at the border by unnecessarily complex and costly entry procedures, or the application of stricter standards for safety, quality, etc., than are applied to similar goods produced domestically.

Measures to encourage exports

The two most common practices designed to encourage exports are **dumping** and **export subsidies**. Dumping is variously defined. It can refer to sales in a foreign market at prices below those in the domestic market, or below cost of production. Export subsidies may be given to exporting firms, allowing goods to be sold abroad at reduced prices.

Importing countries attempt to offset 'unfair' export practices by levying anti-dumping, or countervailing, duties. Properly used, such 'trade remedy laws' do not distort trade. Misused, they can become potent non-tariff barriers, restricting trade. Partly because tariffs were drastically reduced during the decades that followed the end of the Second World War (see pages 127–8), countries have made increasing use of anti-dumping and countervailing duties in the past ten years in situations when the exporting country was not engaging in obviously unfair practices. Other non-tariff barriers have also been increasingly used over this period.

UK commercial policy

UK commercial policy has to be seen in two contexts – one with regard to the world as a whole, and another with regard to particular groups of countries.

The starting point should be that of the stand in support of free trade that Britain took from the middle of the nineteenth century, and which, with relatively minor exceptions, lasted until the early 1930s. The period of world economic depression in the 1930s also caused a collapse in the volume of international trade, and in 1932 the UK introduced protective tariffs on all imports, barring some foodstuffs and raw materials. Later the same year the idea of giving favoured tariff treatment to countries of the Commonwealth was born – Imperial (later Commonwealth) Preference.

The Imperial Preference system was responsible for a great increase in intra-Commonwealth trade. During the Second World War, however, new markets were developed and after the war the UK turned to establish links with the countries of Western Europe.

The European Community (EC)

The prime regional group with which the UK is linked is, of course, the European Community, the origins of which are to be found in the disruption caused in Europe by the Second World War, in subsequent US (Marshall) aid to the stricken countries, and in the establishment of the Organisation for Economic Co-operation and Development (OECD).

The first move in the direction of a common market came about with an economic union between Belgium, Luxembourg and the Netherlands (Benelux) shortly after the end of the war. They then joined France, Germany and Italy in 1952 to form the European Coal and Steel Community, aimed at creating a unified market in these products. Five years later the 'Six', as they then were, signed the Treaty of Rome, establishing the EEC and outlining a programme for the elimination of tariffs between themselves, and a unified schedule of import duties for outsiders.

The UK was at first reluctant to join the EEC (European *Economic* Community), as it then was, partly on political grounds and partly because of British links with the Commonwealth. Instead, Britain made an agreement with Austria, Denmark, Norway, Portugal, Sweden and Switzerland (and subsequently Finland) to set up the European Free Trade Association (EFTA) in 1960. The aims of EFTA were more modest than those of the EC. In one particular way they were attractive for Britain. Although tariffs were to be abolished within the Association, a common *external* tariff was not included. This allowed the UK to continue Commonwealth preferences.

Meanwhile, EC countries were mostly enjoying more favourable conditions with regard to living standards, inflation and the balance of payments than the UK. At the same time Britain's trade with the Commonwealth was declining. The UK therefore sought EC membership. After one application was turned down, in 1962 (effectively by the French), another was successful in 1973. Denmark and Ireland joined at the same time; Greece, Spain and Portugal subsequently, to turn the 'Six' into 'Twelve'. Control of Community matters is in the hands of:

(a) a Commission consisting of 17 members appointed by agreement among participating governments
(b) a Council comprising Ministers of the member states
(c) a Parliament to which European MPs (EMPs) are directly elected from constituencies within EC nations
(d) a Court of Justice

The political processes of the EC are beyond the scope of this book, though it should be appreciated that both the objectives and the effects of the union include political

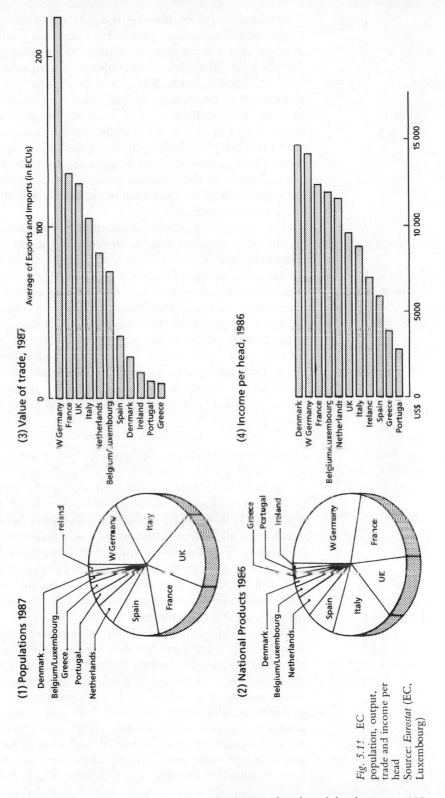

Fig. 5.11 EC population, output, trade and income per head

Source: *Eurostat* (EC, Luxembourg)

(1) Populations 1987

(2) National Products 1986

(3) Value of trade, 1987

Average of Exports and Imports (in ECUs)

(4) Income per head, 1986

matters. Economically speaking, however, the EC represents a major power grouping, with a total output approximately equal to, and a total population some 30 per cent greater than the USA. The relative importance of each member state in the EC is shown in Fig. 5.11, which focusses on four prime characteristics: population, output, trade and income per head of the population. The diagram brings out the dominance of West Germany within the EC, especially as the leading trader. If France, Italy and the UK are added to West Germany, three-quarters or more of total trade, output and population of the member countries is accounted for. In the rankings of income per head of the population, the UK holds a middle position.

Many economic and political objectives have been pursued by the EC, in such areas as agricultural policy (CAP), competition policy, the creation of a common currency unit (ECU) and a degree of exchange rate stability (EMS). The progress made has varied, and such matters are discussed elsewhere in the book. The effects of the EC with which we are most concerned in this chapter relate to international trade. Initially, attention focussed on turning the EC into a customs union with free trade internally, and a common external tariff imposed on goods imported from the rest of the world. Tariff rates were gradually lowered. As far as the UK is concerned, it was 1977 when they were finally eliminated.

The Single European Act 1992

EC development entered a new phase in 1985, when member states called on the Commission to draw up a detailed programme for what is called 'completing the common market'. A package of reforms, to be introduced by 31 December 1992, was part of the Single European Act (SEA) which came into effect in 1985 when it was approved by the parliaments in all member nations. The background to the new phase was the realisation that European integration had been limited in many ways – not least because of the concentration on tariff reductions – and that the time had come to take it a stage further.

Two kinds of restriction remained. One related to trade in services, as distinct from that in visible commodities. The UK is not the only EC country to have experienced a degree of replacement of manufacturing industry by services of one sort or another. Yet trade in services was restricted by a host of different rules which interfered with free competition among all suppliers within the EC. For example, there were financial regulations which interfered with trade in banking, insurance and other such services. There were also restrictions relating to personal qualifications, which impeded consumers in one EC country from buying the services of professionals and tradesmen resident in others.

The second kind of trade restriction relates more to goods than to services. Trade is delayed and impeded by the need to comply with frontier formalities, some based on domestic standards of safety, security, health, etc. It is hampered by national differences in laws related to such matters as patents and trade marks; in rates of taxation, e.g. on sales and profits (VAT and corporation taxes); and by practices whereby governments in their own contracts for purchases (so-called public procurement) give preferential treatment to domestic suppliers.

The eventual completion of the Single European Market involves the removal of barriers such as those mentioned above, by agreement among members to 'harmonise' if not to standardise their rules and regulations affecting economic activity. But it should not be concluded that such completion is easy, costless or even necessarily desirable. It must entail compromises, whereby some countries accept changes that they dislike in return for concessions by others, and/or financial compensation from Community funds. It is bound also to involve a degree of loss of sovereignty for national governments, in so far as they may be precluded from adopting policies that depart from EC guidelines. Some of these may be of major importance, e.g. the priority ranking of anti-inflationary and full employment goals in overall economic strategies (see pages 239 ff).

Moreover, it should not be inferred that full integration of the EC necessarily implies a free market rather than an interventionist balance in the economic systems of members. It does imply that all countries in the Community must accept the same kind of balance in their economic systems. A highly interventionist EC is as consistent with the Single Market as is an essentially free market orientation. It is up to member states through the EC institutions to determine what the balance should be.

Finally, on the question of the desirability of full integration within the Community, one should look separately at the economic and political implications (a) for EC members, and (b) for the relationship between the EC on the one hand and the rest of the world on the other. Within the EC, economic theory analyses the benefits that accrue to nations under free trade. These consist of countries specialising in the production of goods in which they have a comparative advantage, and of reaping the economies of large-scale production that were unattainable because of the limited size of domestic markets. Countervailing disadvantages may be present, but a prime consideration appears in the wider context of the EC as compared with the rest of the world. If, as some fear, 'Fortress Europe' were to become too isolationist, not only countries outside the EC but the world as a whole might be the worse off.

Trade liberalisation

Since 1945 trade liberalisation – reducing trade barriers – has operated on two bases, regional and multilateral. Regional trade liberalisation is restricted to a block of countries, such as the EC, discussed earlier in the chapter. There have been many other regional groupings, including the very recent USA–Canada Trade Agreement, which phases out tariffs over a ten-year period, starting in 1989, on the world's largest bilateral flow of trade in goods and services.

Multilateral liberalisation is world wide. The most important international institution fostering global reduction of trade barriers is the **GATT**, standing for **General Agreement on Tariffs and Trade**.

GATT

GATT acts as a forum for discussion on ways of lowering trade restrictions and for settling disputes among its members, and it has developed a number of 'codes' governing world trade and investment. GATT is, arguably, the most successful of the international organisations set up in the aftermath of the Second World War (1939–45). It presided over a major liberalisation of international trade, drastically reducing tariffs from the very high levels to which they had been pushed during the Great Depression of the 1930s.

The main mechanism for tariff reductions has been the tariff negotiating conferences organised under GATT's auspices. Countries participating in the negotiations bargain bilaterally (in pairs), but agree in advance to extend tariff concessions multilaterally to all GATT participants. Seven such meetings have been held including the first in Torquay in 1947, and two particularly successful ones in the early 1960s and late 1970s, called the 'Kennedy Round' and the 'Tokyo Round' respectively. The eighth, 'Uruguay Round', involving 105 participating nations began in 1986 and is scheduled to end in 1990 or 1991. The present round is struggling with a number of important issues, among which are an attempt to liberalise invisible trade in services, and to reach international agreement for reducing the heavy agricultural subsidies that are distorting world trade in primary products.

Economic development

One outstanding characteristic of the international economy is the inequality of the distribution of income among countries. The world's population is approaching 5 billion. Half live in countries where the income per head in 1985 was less than $400 (US) per year, compared with 1 per cent of the population in the richest countries where average per capita income exceeded $10 000 per annum.

Figure 5.12 shows the income per head of the population for a selection of countries. It is shaped like a pyramid because there are relatively few countries with high average incomes but many with low ones. It must, however, be treated with caution for a variety of reasons, some of them technical in nature. Moreover, it is important to emphasise that income per head is not by any means the same thing as 'happiness'. This is a subject beyond the boundaries of economics and involves consideration of life styles in different countries. It would be foolhardy to offer an opinion that someone in the UK watching a videorecorded colour TV programme was more or less 'happy' than an Indian listening to a local village singer.

Bearing these reservations in mind, we can examine Fig. 5.12. Clearly, some of the differences in income per head are enormous, and can hardly be due solely to statistical errors. Countries at the top of the scale enjoy per capita incomes as much as 50 to 100 times those at the bottom, which have sometimes been called LDCs (less developed countries).

The reasons why some countries have low and others high incomes per head are complex. They relate in part to the natural resources with which nations are endowed. However, per capita incomes are also affected by the size of the populations in different countries. It can hardly be an

Fig. 5.12 Average income per head (estimated GNP per capita in US$) selected countries, 1985 Source: *World Bank Atlas* 1987 (International Bank for Reconstruction and Development)

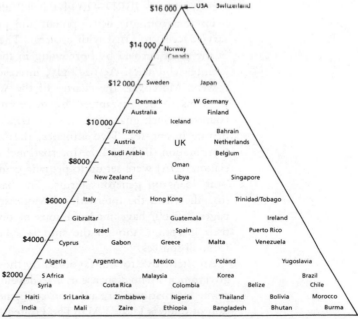

accident that many of the poorest countries are those with large populations. China and India alone have nearly 40 per cent of the total world population, double that of the whole of Europe and North America put together.

With the passage of time some countries have lifted themselves out of poverty. However, the overall inequality between rich and poor is increasing rather than diminishing. This is because rates of economic growth tend to be low for the poorest countries, many of which also have rapid population increases to cope with. Moreover, the economic health of many LDCs, especially in sub-Saharan Africa, deteriorated drastically after 1973, as a result of enormous debts they had accumulated (*see* Chapter 9 pages 262–3).

The consciences of rich countries have been pricked by the growing gap in living standards between themselves and the poor countries of the 'Third World' and by the large number of nations at the bottom of the scale. However, action to help the less developed countries of the world has not been on the massive scale that would be necessary to make a substantial impact on international income inequality. The United Nations Organisation set a target of 0.75 per cent of national income for developed countries to contribute as aid for their poorer neighbours, though few achieve that level on a regular basis.

Aid

There are a number of international agencies specifically concerned with economic development. They include the World Bank (the International Bank for Reconstruction and Development – IBRD – to give it its full title) which makes loans for economic development and provides expert field service teams to assist with projects. The funds for loans are in the main derived by borrowing in the capital markets of member countries. Accordingly, interest is charged to borrowers. Moreover, the charter of the World Bank requires its loans to be guaranteed by governments in borrowing countries. Such guarantees are not always easy to obtain for private businesses. Two affiliates, the International Finance Corporation (IFC) and the International Development Association (IDA) were set up to provide guarantees and to make 'soft' loans on generous terms. The bank and its affiliates (together with the International Monetary Fund (IMF) – *see* pages 259–60) have made billions of dollars of loans since their inception, though the sum is small compared to aid from all sources.

An alternative to aid, favoured by those who mistrust the governments who dispense it, is to develop trading links. The prime international organisation concerned with the promotion of trade is UNCTAD (The United Nations Conference on Trade and Development), established in 1964 under the auspices of the United Nations Organisation. High-sounding resolutions have been passed at UNCTAD conferences and a so-called 'north–south dialogue' has attempted to integrate the economies of some Third World countries more closely with those of the developed nations, especially in Europe. One of UNCTAD's policies was the introduction of a general system of preferences (GSP), to give the exports of manufactured goods from less developed countries preferential access to markets in developed nations.

Apart from UNCTAD, preferential treatment for less developed countries has been negotiated under GATT, and is under consideration in the current Uruguay Round. Additionally, the European Community for many years has made similar concessions, first under the Yaoundé agreements, and more recently in the 1980s under the Lomé Conventions. Lomé III, of 1986, gave some 66 states tariff preferences on exports to the EC, offered some guarantees with respect to EC imports of primary products (especially sugar), and some aid commitments. The extent of EC arrangements should not be exaggerated, but the countries that were assisted (mainly ex-colonies of France and the Netherlands and Commonwealth countries) constitute over a third of the total number of countries belonging to the United Nations itself.

Questions and exercises

For key to symbols indicating suggested sources see pages xi xii.

1   For the following countries find out the percentage change in the national product and in the volume of exports over the past ten years: USA, Japan, France, West Germany, Italy, UK. Which were the most and the least successful in raising the share of output exported? Can you suggest any reasons why? (NIFR)

2   For the latest year available find out (a) the value of imports in pounds sterling and (b) the population of the following countries:

Australia	South Africa
Belgium	Switzerland
Canada	United Kingdom
West Germany	United States of America
Greece	

Where necessary convert from local currency to pounds sterling using the current exchange rate. Calculate the value of imports per head of the population in each case. What conclusions, if any, can be drawn from your results? (WA, T, FT)

3　Calculate the percentage of the total value of United Kingdom imports accounted for by each of the following groups of commodities in the most recent year for which you have statistics:

Food, beverages and tobacco　Mineral fuels, lubricants, etc.
Machinery and equipment　　　Chemicals

Compare your results with Fig. 5.4. (AS)

4　Calculate the percentage of the total value of United Kingdom exports of manufactured goods accounted for by the following items in the most recent year for which statistics are available:

Chemicals　　　　　　　　Iron and steel
Road vehicles　　　　　　Textiles
Electrical machinery　　　Clothing

Compare your results with Fig. 5.4. (AS)

5　(a)　List for last year, three years ago and six years ago the export competitiveness of the exports of the following countries: France, West Germany, Italy, Japan, UK, USA.
　　(b)　Use the figures of the price index of their exports relative to the world average to calculate the increases for each of the three stated years compared to the previous year.
　　(c)　List the countries by rank order according to their export competitiveness for each year.

How similar or dissimilar are the lists? How do they compare with Fig. 5.10? (NIER)

6　Record the countries of origin of the goods which came from abroad that were bought by members of your family last week. What proportion came from EC countries and from the Commonwealth? Are the proportions similar to those in Fig. 5.7? (AS)

7　Prepare a table for the following EC member countries: France, West Germany, Italy and UK, showing the changes in the volume of (a) imports and (b) exports that took place over the past ten years. Place the countries in rank order.
　　Next add two more columns to the table showing the change in the general level of prices, and the change in gross output (product) over the same period.
　　Which of the last two columns do you think provides the better explanation of the changes in (a) imports; (b) exports? (NIER)

8　Prepare two historical graphs for as many of the last five years as you can obtain statistics showing:

(a)　the value and volume of UK imports
(b)　the value and volume of UK exports
(c)　the sterling-dollar exchange rate

Can you suggest reasons why the value and volume figures in *(a)* and *(b)* may or may not have moved in parallel? (*AS*)

9   Following exercise 8 above, prepare another graph showing again the value of exports and imports of the UK for the same period and the gross domestic product. Which series have moved in closest association? (*AS*)

Appendix

Table A5.1 World exports by volume
Source: *National Institute Economic Review* (November 1988)

1980 = 100

	World	US	Canada	Japan	France	West Germany	Italy	UK
1978	93	81	99	83	89	104	99	96
1979	99	91	101	83	97	104	108	99
1980	100	100	100	100	100	100	100	100
1981	98	99	104	110	104	107	105	99
1982	97	89	104	108	100	110	106	102
1983	100	86	111	116	104	109	109	104
1984	108	93	132	134	109	120	116	113
1985	112	96	137	143	111	128	125	119
1986	120	101	144	142	111	129	128	124
1987	124	116	148	142	113	132	129	131
1988*	NA	140	166	149	122	143	137	134

* First half of year.

Table A5.2 Commodity composition of UK visible trade 1977 and 1987 (£ million)
Source: *Monthly Digest of Statistics*

| | 1977 | | 1987 | |
	Exports	Imports	Exports	Imports
Food and live animals chiefly for food	1 418	5 375	3 730	8 725
Beverages and tobacco	799	562	1 861	1 433
Crude materials, inedible, except fuels	845	3 539	1 926	5 184
Mineral fuels, lubricants and related materials	2 092	5 255	8 769	6 117
Animal and vegetable oils, fats and waxes	57	281	263	427
Manufactured goods				
Chemicals and related products	3 817	2 361	10 520	8 330
Manufactured goods classified chiefly by material	6 416	6 861	11 877	16 970
Machinery and transport equipment	12 456	8 466	28 803	32 795
Miscellaneous manufactured articles	3 134	3 015	9 840	12 888
Manufactured goods total	25 824	20 703	61 040	70 984
	0,2.5	0,2.5	0,2.5	0,2.5
Miscellaneous	956	505	2 261	1 146
Totals	31 960	36 219	79 851	94 016

Table A5.3 Income per capita, selected countries (1985), Gross National Product (*see* page 187) in US dollars
Source: *1987 World Bank Atlas* (International Bank for Reconstruction and Development)

	$,US		$,US		$,US
United Arab		Panama	2020	Indonesia	530
Emirates	19 120	South Africa	2010	Yemen Arab	
United States	16 400	Portugal	1970	Republic	520
Switzerland	16 380	Hungary	1940	Lesotho	480
Kuwait	14 270	Uruguay	1660		
Norway	13 890			Liberia	470
		Brazil	1640	Bolivia	470
Canada	13 670	Syrian Arab		Mauritania	410
Sweden	11 890	Republic	1630	Zambia	400
Japan	11 330	Jordan	1560	Ghana	390
Denmark	11 240	Chile	1440		
Germany, Federal		Colombia	1320	Pakistan	380
Republic of	10 940			Senegal	370
		Costa Rica	1290	Sierra Leone	370
Finland	10 870	Guatemala	1240	Sri Lanka	370
Australia	10 840	Tunisia	1220	Haiti	350
France	9550	Ecuador	1160		
Netherlands	9180	Turkey	1130	Sudan	330
Austria	9150			Guinea	320
		Congo, People's		China	310
Saudi Arabia	8860	Republic of the	1020	Rwanda	290
Belgium	8450	Peru	960	Kenya	290
United Kindom	8390	Paraguay	940		
Libya	7500	Jamaica	940	Benin	270
Singapore	7420	Nicaragua	850	Central African	
				Republic	270
New Zealand	7310	Thailand	830	Tanzania	270
Italy	6520	Dominican Republic	810	Somalia	270
Hong Kong	6220	Cameroon	810	India	250
Israel	4920	Nigeria	760		
Puerto Rico	4850	Honduras	730	Madagascar	250
				Togo	250
Ireland	4840	Papua New Guinea	710	Burundi	240
Spain	4360	El Salvador	710	Niger	200
Greece	3550	Egypt, Arab		Burma	190
Venezuela	3110	Republic of	680		
Algeria	2530	Zimbabwe	650	Zaire	170
		Morocco	610	Malawi	170
Korea, Republic of	2180			Nepal	160
Argentina	2130	Philippines	600	Bangladesh	150
Mexico	2080	Yemen, People's		Mali	140
Yugoslavia	2070	Democratic			
Malaysia	2050	Republic of	540	Ethiopia	110

Table A5.4 Geographical distribution of UK visible trade 1977 and 1987 (£ million)
Source: *Annual Abstract of Statistics* and *Monthly Digest of Statistics*

| | 1977 | | 1987 | |
	Exports	Imports	Exports	Imports
European Community	11 849	14 160	39 416	49 557
Rest of Western Europe	4 734	5 083	7 621	12 869
North America	3 791	4 984	12 993	10 781
Other developed countries	2 089	2 846	4 046	7 282
Oil exporting countries	4 324	3 704	5 222	1 700
Other developing countries	4 201	4 259	8 514	9 286
Centrally planned economies	907	1 125	1 539	2 097

6 | Government and resource allocation

The allocation of resources in the UK is influenced by two sets of forces – those of the market, following from the interaction of supply and demand, and those induced by government intervention.[1]

The goals and tools of economic policy

We start by considering in general terms the chief goals of economic policy and the tools available to pursue them.

Goals

The government decides to intervene in the economic life of a country in pursuit of two different sets of objectives:

- macroeconomic objectives
- microeconomic objectives

Macroeconomic objectives are concerned with the *overall* performance of the economy. They relate to aggregates, especially the growth of total output, the general level of employment and unemployment and the behaviour of the average price level. These matters will be discussed in the final chapter of this book. This chapter deals with the **microeconomic goals**. These basically concern what is called the allocation of resources, i.e. how resources are used in the nation's productive activities and how many resources are devoted to producing each of the millions of goods and services that exist in the economy. There are two basic goals of policy:

- equity
- efficiency

Equity is a matter of how the national cake is divided up – the distribution of income and wealth. The government tries to change this distribution on grounds of equity or fairness. Government intervention on the grounds of efficiency, the

1 The material covered in this chapter is complementary to that covered in Lipsey and Harbury, *First Principles*, Chapters 23 and 24.

second goal, can be for one or both of two reasons:

1 The desire to ensure that outputs of goods and services are produced using the most efficient techniques and combinations of factors of production in order to minimise costs.

2 The desire to ensure that the goods and services produced are those which best satisfy the needs of the community.

There are many reasons why markets may fail to operate efficiently in the sense used here.[1] Some are due to market imperfections, as a result of which output does not best satisfy consumer demand. Others follow from the fact that consumers are not always sufficiently well informed, or otherwise capable, of deciding for themselves what goods and services benefit them most. In such cases the state may take on a paternalistic role.

Tools

A government has three main sets of tools (sometimes called instruments) with which to implement its economic policies. Two – taxation and expenditure – relate to its budget. The third is the use of rules and regulations. We start by looking at the income and expenditure of central government and of local authorities in the UK.

Government revenue and expenditure

Figure 6.1 sets out the main sources and proportions of government revenue for the UK, for the financial year 1988–89.

Changes in the government's income and expenditure are quite common. Although they may be made at any time, changes concerned with taxation are usually made when the Chancellor of the Exchequer presents the annual budget statement to Parliament in March, though since 1982 the Chancellor has also made a budget statement in the autumn.

Government revenue

By far the most important source of government income comes from taxation, as Fig. 6.1 shows. Taxes are best considered under two headings:

- taxes on income
- taxes on expenditure

Taxes on income

Taken together, taxes on the incomes of individuals and businesses account for about a third of the tax revenue of central government in the UK. Easily the most important is **income tax**, levied on part of a person's income. It is

---

1 The causes of market failure are discussed in Lipsey and Harbury, *First Principles*, pages 271–2.

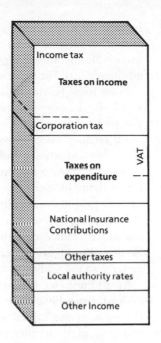

Fig. 6.1 Income of central and local government, 1988–89 Source: *Economic Progress Report*, 1988

important here to distinguish between the **tax base** and the rate of tax charged.

The tax base for a person, his/her **taxable income**, is the gross income minus certain deductible allowances. Chief among these are a personal allowance for each individual and an age allowance, but there are others such as mortgage interest on loans up to £30 000 (1988–89) for house purchases. Married couples have been eligible for larger allowances (though less than double those for two single persons), and have been taxed on their joint income. Under a new system, which should become fully operative in 1990, husbands and wives will be treated as equal with single persons as regards both allowances and taxation.

The tax base may be set in nominal terms, by stating the allowances in unchanging monetary units, or in real terms by 'indexing' the allowances. Since 1977 allowances have been indexed, although not necessarily by exactly the amount to compensate for rises in the price level. In 1988–89, the allowances were £2605 for a single person and £4095 for a married couple; in 1989–90, the allowances were £2785 and £4375 respectively.

Tax rates charged on income have been greatly simplified in recent years. A sliding scale of rising rates for different bands of taxable income was employed – at one time running from 30 per cent to 80 per cent and higher, with an additional Investment Income Surcharge levied until 1984 on such 'unearned' incomes above a threshold. Since then the rates have been lowered and the number of bands reduced.

Government and resource allocation **139**

In 1988–89 there were only two rates of income tax, a basic rate of 25 per cent and a higher one of 40 per cent applicable to taxable incomes over approximately £20 000. The government's goal for the basic rate is said to be 20 per cent.

Since some minimum amount of gross income is not taxed at all and because the rates rise as incomes become larger, the proportion of gross income paid in taxes *rises* steadily with income once gross income has passed the level of allowable deductions. Individuals with incomes less than the allowances pay no tax. Such a system is called a **progressive** tax system. In contrast, a system where the proportion of income paid in taxes *falls* as income rises is called **regressive**.

In 1944 the system known as PAYE (pay as you earn) was introduced. Since that time, tax payable by employees has been deducted at source by the employer, who pays it directly to the Collector of Taxes.

In addition to the taxes on income as conventionally defined, since 1962 taxes have also been levied on *increases* in the value of the capital assets owned by an individual. The real part of these increases is equivalent to income, since people can, if they wish, spend any gain due to a rise in the real value of their assets between the beginning and the end of a year without leaving themselves any worse off from the point of view of their accumulated wealth. A **capital gains tax**, payable on net realised gains, after the deduction of any realised losses from the sale of other assets, was levied at a flat rate of 30 per cent until 1988–89. There are exemptions for certain classes of asset, such as one private house, chattels, and in 1988–89 the first £5000 of gain for individuals and married couples. Since 1984, this exemption has been indexed, along with personal allowances under the income tax, i.e. adjusted to allow for inflation. Moreover, capital gains are no longer charged as a separate tax at a flat rate. They are incorporated into the income tax and are, therefore, payable at rates corresponding to the taxpayer's circumstances, i.e. at 25 or 40 per cent in 1988–89.

Taxes are levied on the income of companies as well as of persons. This arises as a result of treating joint stock companies as separate legal entities from their shareholders. Companies are assessed for **corporation tax** on their profits and capital gains. They also act as agents for the Inland Revenue and deduct income tax from the sums that they pay out in the form of dividends, etc. The base on which tax is calculated for companies is their **taxable profits**, a notion similar to that of taxable income for private individuals.

Companies do not, of course, qualify for personal allowances but they are permitted to deduct all expenses properly incurred in the earning of profits, and to offset sums to help provide for the depreciation of capital assets. Standard depreciation allowances are given, and deductions are permitted for investment allowances for industries and regions where the provision of such help is part of government policy. From 1976 to 1984 an important allowable deduction was for the increase in the value of stock held by *Stock Appreciation* businesses in excess of 15 per cent of their gross trading profits. This significantly reduced the corporation tax burden on many companies. Stock relief was ended in 1984, by which time the rate of inflation had substantially fallen.

The rate of corporation tax is fixed in the budget. It was 52 per cent in 1983–84, when the Chancellor of the Exchequer announced a phased reduction to a level of 35 per cent, at which it now stands. There is a reduced rate of 25 per cent for small companies. There is no difference in the rate of tax, whether profits are distributed to shareholders or retained in the firm. This may be contrasted with an earlier system which ended in 1975, whereby distributed profits were taxed more heavily. That practice (intentionally) discriminated in favour of profit retention and was introduced to encourage investment. However, it was recognised that it tended at the same time to create difficulties for new and growing companies to attract outside capital – hence the policy change.

Other taxes on income have been levied in the past and may always be introduced. For example, between 1976 and 1985 a **development land tax** was charged on the difference between the proceeds of the sale of land and its cost.

Taxes on expenditure

The difference between taxes on income and those on expenditure is that the latter are related to the goods and services bought by individuals. It is possible to avoid paying such taxes by refraining from buying taxed goods, but as the range and number of goods covered by such taxes is extremely wide this is not a seriously practicable proposition. A more important observation is that some expenditure taxes tend to be regressive, i.e. the opposite of progressive, in so far as they may take a higher proportion of the income of the poor than of the rich.

Taxes on expenditure bring in about a third of the government's revenue, about the same amount as taxes on income. The chief earners for many years have been duties on alcohol, tobacco and oil. The last of these has recently assumed increased importance with the imposition of a **petroleum revenue tax** on the profits from production (as distinct from processing) of North Sea oil. Technically, this is really a tax on income, rather than on expenditure.

There are many other goods and services subject to tax, e.g. betting, entertainment and television advertising. Licences must be bought to operate a television set, to run a motor-cycle or a car, and there are many legal documents which require the affixing of a special tax stamp.

In addition to the taxes on specific commodities mentioned in the previous paragraph, the government also levies a much more general expenditure tax. It was introduced in 1973 at the time when the UK was starting to bring taxes into line with those of other members of the European Community. **VAT (value added tax)** is levied on the amount firms add to the value of the goods they produce, i.e. on the difference between their sales revenue and the cost of purchasing intermediate goods and services from other firms. Intermediate goods and services are those inputs of the firm that are outputs of other firms. Such goods and services will, of course, already have been subjected to VAT by the firms that produced them.

VAT is essentially a tax on consumer spending and is levied in instalments at each stage in the production process. For example, the manufacturers of a starter motor for a car pay tax on their 'added value'; when they sell the motor to a car manufacturer, the price they charge reflects the tax already paid. The firm producing the car is then permitted to deduct the cost of this VAT (and VAT for other items bought) from its revenue from the sale of cars when calculating its liability for VAT.

When it was first introduced VAT was levied at a flat rate of 10 per cent on all goods and services other than certain 'essentials' (such as food, children's clothing, books and buildings), on which the rate was zero. Certain other intermediate goods, including education, health and insurance, were classified as 'exempt' from the tax, which means that traders do not have to charge it to their customers but are not entitled (as they are with zero-rated goods) to reclaim tax paid by suppliers earlier in the production process. Between 1975 and 1979 there were two VAT rates: a basic 10 per cent and a higher 25 per cent on 'luxuries', such as furs and cameras. Both were amalgamated into a new standard rate of 15 per cent.

The tax has become an important source of revenue for the government, with a yield greatly in excess of that of any single tax other than income tax, as can be seen from Fig. 6.1.

VAT replaced two taxes previously operating in Britain. One was **purchase tax**, which was a special tax on expenditure on certain luxuries and semi-luxuries; the other was **selective employment tax (SET)**. SET was a tax on all employers of labour, and may be regarded as one of a family of so-called **payroll taxes**. However, the particular form of the tax adopted in the UK was selective. One of its intentions was to favour manufacturing businesses which, it was thought at the time, might help to promote economic growth. Eligible firms in the manufacturing sector of the economy were therefore able to obtain refunds of SET. In addition, the SET system was used to help manufacturers in declining areas of the country by granting them a regional employment premium (REP), based on the numbers on their payrolls, as well as a refund of SET.

Unlike direct taxes, the majority of expenditure taxes are collected by the Board of Customs and Excise. **Customs duties** are imposed on articles imported from overseas. The remainder are known as **excise duties**. All taxes on expenditure are liable to be changed at any time, especially those fixed in money terms, such as the duty on alcohol and tobacco.

Capital taxes

Taxes on capital, as distinct from those on capital gains (*see* page 140), yield little revenue for the state. They have traditionally been less effective in this respect than they might have been, notably because of various legal devices for avoiding tax. This does not, however, mean that they are of little significance.

Estate duty, levied on the value of property left on a person's death, was in force until 1975, when **capital transfer tax** (CTT) replaced it. CTT, which lasted until 1986, introduced an important new feature in capital taxation – the extension of liability to tax of lifetime gifts in addition to death transfers (though the latter were subject to lower duty rates)

Inheritance tax (IT) replaced CTT. Rates of duty under all three systems varied with the size of estate until 1988–89, the year which saw the culmination of a process of lower rates and simplification, similar to that described in connection with the income tax (*see* page 139). In 1983 the rate bands had ranged from 30 to 75 per cent (on transfers above £2 million). In 1988–89, IT was charged at a single rate of 40 per cent regardless of the size of the transfer. There is a threshold, £110 000 in 1988–89 (£118 000 in 1989–90), which is tax exempt, so that an element of progressivity remains. Liability to IT, however, may be alleviated by taking advantage of a number of exemptions (such as for transfers between spouses, or in consideration of marriage) and specific concessions of one sort or another. One of the easiest ways of reducing IT liability is by using the seven-year cumulation period built into the tax. Lifetime gifts become tax free if the donor survives for at least seven years.

It is worth mentioning another capital tax, although it has never been levied in Britain. This is an annual **wealth tax** assessed on the total value of all the assets owned by an individual. Such a tax has been included in the proposals of past governments but has never been adopted. Rates suggested have been low. One suggestion was for 1 per cent on property worth £100 000, and between 2½ and 5 per cent on that worth over £5 million. These rates may not seem high, but a tax of 3 per cent means that someone must earn a post-income tax return on capital of at least that rate to avoid a depletion of his or her capital.

Local authorities' finances

Local authorities are responsible for spending about a third of the total budget of all government, central and local. They have also, over the years, raised a substantial proportion of their financial needs themselves, while obtaining the rest from central government. Before describing the machinery involved in local authority finance, we must explain that it is in the throes of dramatic restructuring, the full effects of which are not yet entirely clear.

The current situation, due to end in 1990 (1989 in Scotland) is that the chief source of independent income for local authorities comes from what are called **rates** levied on the owners of land and buildings, the only exception being those used in agriculture. Property is valued (by the Inland Revenue) and this is the basis for the charging of rates, as a form of property tax. The rate is usually expressed as 'poundage', i.e. pence per pound of rateable value.

The importance of rates as a source of revenue has varied considerably from district to district. The larger the amount of valuable property there is in a region, the more important is the income from rates. This is offset partly by rate support grants from central government, which are larger for authorities where there is relatively little valuable property but which have heavy needs for services, e.g. education, because of the relatively large number of children in the community.

The rating system had the effect of maintaining a considerable degree of local government financial autonomy. At the same time it had been under review for major reform for some time. Some of the reasons are as much political as economic, e.g. reflecting dissent between Labour-controlled local councils and Conservative-controlled Parliament in Whitehall. The government stressed the lack of a strong link between domestic ratepayers and recipients of services provided by local government, reflecting the fact that only about 15 million property-owning individuals paid rates, whereas about 35 million adults enjoyed the benefits that the rates were used to provide.

Several government and independent committees reviewed local government finance, and considered alternatives to the rates, such as a local income tax, used in some other countries. The Local Government Finance Act, 1988, was based on a consultative 'Green Paper' of 1986. Under its terms, rates on *domestic* dwellings are due to be replaced by a **community charge**, to be levied on local inhabitants over the age of 18 (other than those exempted on grounds of hardship), regardless of whether or not they own property previously liable to rates. Rates on business property are to remain. While local authorities will have control of the community charge, they lose control over the business rate, which is to be set nationally at a uniform level, with the proceeds distributed to the regions.

The passage of the Local Government Bill through Parliament aroused bitter controversy. Critics attacked the Bill on grounds of high expected costs of administering it, and stressed the regressive consequences of a poll tax, such as the community charge, which would benefit households with a few adult members living in expensive property (previously highly rated) at the expense of households comprising several adults living in small, low-rated, cheap dwellings. The new arrangements are due to take effect in 1990 (1989 in Scotland).

National insurance contributions

One further major source of government revenue not yet described is national insurance contributions. These are levied on employers and employees. They provide a very substantial source of income to the state – close on three quarters of the revenue from income tax. The income from these contributions goes into the National Insurance Fund and, augmented by a subsidy, is used to provide social security benefits, such as unemployment, sickness and retirement benefits related to contributions. Non-contributory benefits, such as **family credit**, for working families with children, and **income support** (formerly **supplementary benefit**) for other categories in need, are financed from general taxation.

National insurance contribution rates vary with earnings, and with whether individuals choose to 'contract out' of the state scheme and make private insurance arrangements to provide for pensions on their retirement.

Other income

The miscellaneous category shown as 'other income' in Fig. 6.1 covers many different items, including trading surpluses, royalties from North Sea oil and receipts from the European

Community. It also includes proceeds of the sales of state-owned assets in the privatisation programme (*see* pages 173–5), which can vary widely from one year to another.

The national debt

Total government income and expenditure never balance each other exactly. When expenditure exceeds income, the difference is met by borrowing.

Government borrowing has, at times, been on a very large scale, e.g. to finance wars and to pay compensation to industries taken into public ownership. The total outstanding balance is known as the **national debt**. In 1950, after the Second World War and the large nationalisation programme of the Labour Government, the debt stood at a figure of about £25 billion. Compared with the size of the national income, this was an all-time high – approximately 250 per cent. Although by 1987 the total outstanding national debt was nearer to £200 billion, it was less than half the size of the national income, having come down as a result of budget surpluses deriving partly from privatisation sales of major nationalised industries in the 1980s. The net *change* in the debt measures the amount the government needs to borrow to finance an excess of expenditure over income in any year. It is known as the **Public Sector Borrowing Requirement** (**PSBR**). When the government's revenue is greater than its expenditure, the PSBR is negative, and is known as the **PSDR** (**Public Sector Debt Repayment**). This began to occur in 1987 and 1988, when the size of the national debt was reduced slightly.

International comparisons of tax burdens

The level of taxation as a proportion of national income, as we saw in Chapter 1, has been rising considerably during the present century. It is of some interest to compare the situation in the United Kingdom with that in other countries. Figure 6.2 shows that the UK is less heavily taxed than many other western countries, though notably more so than Japan and the USA. Denmark, Sweden, Norway, France, Belgium and the Netherlands, however, are all ahead of the UK in the 'league table'.

In interpreting Fig. 6.2 it is important to remember that the lengths of the bars in the diagram indicate total taxes *and* social security contributions as proportions of national income. Countries differ greatly as to the relative importance of these components of revenue, as can be seen. Some, such as France and the Netherlands, derive high proportions of their income from social security contributions, while others, including the UK, take a much lower proportion. Countries also vary in their choice of methods used to achieve given objectives, and these can result in the figures being mislead-

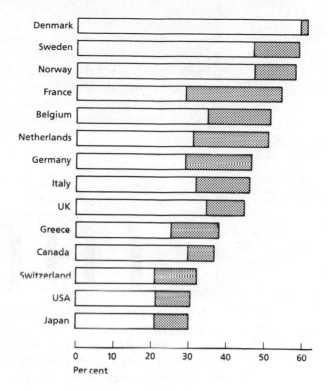

Fig. 6.2 Taxes and social security contributions as a percentage of GNP in selected countries, 1985 (shaded areas are social security contributions)
Source: *Economic Trends*, 1988

ing. For example, help can be given to people through the tax system, by giving tax deductions for families, or via the expenditure side of the account, through a system of allowances. Lastly, it must be borne in mind that similar overall average tax burdens can conceal quite different tax treatments for particular groups.

Government expenditure

Total government expenditure, as we saw in Chapter 1 (*see* page 19), has been equal to about 40 per cent of national income in the UK since the end of the Second World War. The principal categories of total government expenditure, i.e. both central and local, are shown in Fig. 6.3. There are several ways of classifying them; the method used here is based on specific programmes, i.e. for defence, social security, etc.

The social services are by far the largest category if the term is used to include health, education, housing and social security benefits provided out of national insurance contributions and taxation. Much of the expenditure on education and housing is paid for by local authorities. Defence is an important category, taking about one-eighth of the government budget according to plans for 1990. The other items of expenditure are of a varied kind. About a tenth of the total is used to provide services in Scotland, Wales and Northern Ireland. The rest is used for such things as law and order, the construction and maintenance of roads, overseas aid, support for industry and agriculture (including both private sector and nationalised industries) and interest on the national debt, which varies both with the amount outstanding and the rate of interest payable on it.

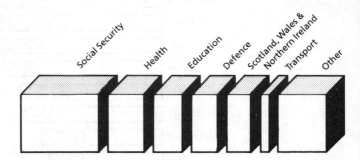

As previously stated, the method used for classifying items of government expenditure for Fig. 6.3 is not the only one possible. We could alternatively distinguish between **current expenditure**, such as retirement pensions and drugs for use in hospitals, and **capital expenditure**, such as the provision of new schools or prisons. The former is concerned with immediate effects on the distribution of income or resources. Capital expenditure, on the other hand, has lasting effects.

A third classification could be based on a distinction between what are known as **transfer payments** and **exhaustive expenditures**. Exhaustive expenditures are those on goods and services, such as roads and hospitals, where the state decides directly how the money should be spent. In contrast transfer payments, which include personal grants such as pensions and income support, permit individual recipients to allocate the proceeds as they wish. Transfer payments have grown greatly relative to exhaustive expenditures in recent years.

A fourth and final classification could be between goods and services which benefit the community generally, as distinct from those that are provided for individuals. The former are referred to as **public goods** and include roads, courts of law and environmental services. The latter comprise all transfers, as well as hospital beds specifically for the sick and schools for the young. It has to be admitted, however, that many if not most classes of government expenditure have something of a public nature about them. For example, it is usually claimed that education benefits society generally, as well as the individuals who take personal advantage of it.

We now know enough about the government's budget to look at some of the ways in which it has been employed to pursue certain specific economic policy goals. It must be understood that virtually all the tools of policy have implications for both equity and efficiency. For example, taxation policy designed to redistribute income can affect resource allocation and growth; or competition policy (*see* pages 160–4) directed at monopolies almost certainly influences also the distribution of income.

Income redistribution

Both sides of the government's budget, as well as rules and regulations, are used to try to bring about a distribution of income which society regards as in some sense fair. Many of these devices do not imply a search for simple equality between everybody, but instead involve questions of equity between the sexes, between different ethnic groups, allowances for varying needs, etc. Moreover, it is usual to accept that a degree of inequality, commensurate with the reward of effort, is desirable, so that a compromise distribution is sought, even on equity grounds.

The most obvious, though quantitatively not the most important, policy tool is taxation. Certain taxes are designed expressly to bear more heavily on higher income groups than on lower ones. Of outstanding significance in this connection is the progressive income tax. Figure 6.4 shows the progressiveness of income tax in 1988–89, by expressing the total tax burden as a proportion of total income for different income classes. It is important to emphasise that the diagram shows the situation for a single person who enjoys only the

Fig. 6.4 Income tax for a single person as a percentage of gross income, 1988–89

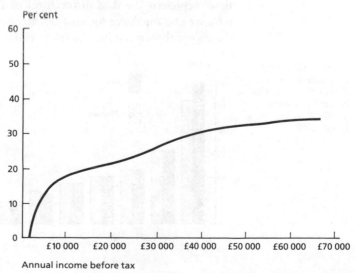

Per cent

Annual income before tax

minimum allowances of £2605 (1988–89). A different diagram could be drawn for any individual or family with
different circumstances. For example, the tax burden would
be lower for a married couple, or for someone buying a
house on a mortgage, because of other tax allowances to
which they would be entitled.

The picture which emerges from Fig. 6.4 is, nevertheless,
reasonably representative of the progressiveness of income
tax in Britain. It can be seen that the proportion of income
paid in tax rises with income. It is zero until all allowances
have been used, but rises to a figure of 30 per cent at an
income of about £40 000 per annum. The progressiveness is
due to the existence of the exemption limit, below which no
tax is paid, and to the fact that the marginal rate of tax rises
from the basic 25 per cent to 40 per cent on taxable incomes
in excess of £19 300 (1988–89).

The general effect of income tax at the present time is to
reduce the inequality of post-tax income compared to that
before tax. Quantitatively, this impact is not very great, as
can be seen from Fig. 6.5, which shows the shares in total
income, pre- and post-tax, of different income groups. (The
groups are in ranges of 10 per cent, known as *deciles*; i.e. the
richest 10 per cent of persons, the next richest decile and so
on.)

The shares of the richest 20 per cent of the population are
less when measured after income tax is deducted; those of
the lower income groups are larger post-income tax than
before tax. However, only in the case of the top decile (the
richest 10 per cent) is the difference significant. Their share
declines from 29.5 per cent to 26.5 per cent of the total. The
share of the poorest decile rises only from 2.3 to 2.7 per cent.
If we represent the data in the form of Lorenz curves (Fig.
6.6), we find the curve for post-tax income lies slightly nearer
the diagonal representing complete equality.

Fig. 6.5 Distribution
of income before and
after income tax, 1984–
85 (decile shares)
Source: *Economic
Trends*, 1987

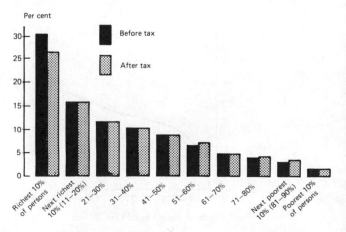

There are two reasons why income tax is not a very powerful redistributive tool. The first is that its progressiveness arises largely from the deductible allowances rather than from rising tax rates. The allowances do not vary with income, though they do mean that the *average* tax paid rises as income rises. There is but a single tax rate above the basic 25 per cent. It comes into play only at high incomes and therefore affects only a very small proportion of taxpayers, the vast majority of whom pay at the same standard rate.

The second reason for the relative ineffectiveness of income tax as a redistributive tool is that there are substantial numbers of individuals too poor to be liable to income tax at all. Their incomes are, by definition, the same both pre- and post-tax.

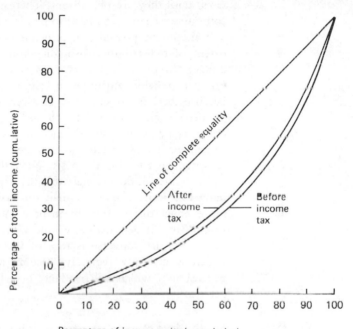

Fig. 6.6 Income distribution, Lorenz curves before and after income tax, 1985–86
Source: *Economic Trends*, 1987

Income redistribution and the government's budget

Even a neutral tax (which is neither progressive nor regressive) can be used to finance spending in a way that involves redistribution. There are a good many items on the expenditure side of the account of the UK government that fall into this category. Benefits are provided in cash and in kind, both of which have redistributive effects. Cash benefits include retirement and other pensions, unemployment and sickness benefits, family credit and income support. Benefits in kind are, for example, those from state-provided education, the National Health Service, and subsidies on housing and public transport.

A controversial question arises, especially with cash

benefits (e.g. for children) as to whether they should be *targetted*, i.e. given only to those in need, or *universal*, i.e. given to everyone with families in order to ensure a minimum floor below which no such families should fall. Those in favour of targeting stress the clear efficiency advantage in terms of cost to the taxpayer. Those against it point to the low take-up of benefits that are available only on application by the poor, who are put through the indignity of means-testing. The choice between targeting and universality has, of course, strong political connotations.

Finally, account must be taken of taxes other than income tax that are paid by people. The chief taxes on expenditure are: VAT; duties on alcohol, tobacco and fuel oil; and local rates, until they are phased out. Thereafter, the poll tax, or community charge will have to be included.

It should be possible, in principle, to determine the full extent of redistribution brought about by the whole state budget. In practice, however, it is extremely difficult to produce reliable quantitative estimates. This is mainly because there is no sure way of ascertaining precisely how the benefits and burdens of each category in the accounts fall on different individuals and income groups. There are also some benefits, like defence and the police, which can only be allocated on an arbitrary basis. Nevertheless, we can with considerable confidence state that the expenditure side of the budget is more important than the tax side in effecting a more equal distribution of income. While income tax is progressive, if perhaps more mildly so than you may have suspected, the converse is true of the community charge, which is certainly regressive, as are also some taxes on expenditure, which fall relatively heavily on lower income groups.

Non-budgetary redistribution

Finally, it is essential to point out that there are many state acts which expressly, or by implication, affect the distribution of income. They include all interventions in the market place, such as price controls, import duties, regulations affecting the regional distribution of industry, etc. We cannot deal with them all here. However two kinds of measure specifically aimed at income redistribution are too important to ignore.

The first set of measures is directed towards the removal of inequalities due to sex or ethnic origin. We saw earlier (*see* page 96) that women tend to earn between half and two-thirds as much as men in industry. In an attempt to reduce this differential, two Acts of Parliament were passed. One, the Equal Pay Act of 1976, stipulated that men and women doing the same work should receive equal pay for doing so. It reinforced the Sex Discrimination Act of 1975 which forbade discrimination in employment between the sexes.

There is little doubt that the Equal Pay Act had some effect. Before the legislation, in 1970 for example, average weekly earnings for full-time female manual workers stood at barely more than 50 per cent of the comparable male earnings. By the end of the decade the female comparable earnings for the same group had risen to 62 per cent, at which level they appear to have settled.

The main reasons why women are less well paid than men were pointed out in Chapter 4 (*see* pages 96–7). They relate to the concentration of women in certain industries and occupational groups, their lower trade union membership and tendency to work shorter hours. It must also be realised that women are on the whole less well qualified than men. A smaller proportion of them move into higher education after they reach the statutory minimum school-leaving age, and less is spent on their job-training by employers. To the extent that male/female differentials are influenced by any of the forces just mentioned, they cannot be said to be due to simple sex discrimination.

Finally we must consider wage settlements as an important determinant of income distribution. We saw in Chapter 4 that in many industries these settlements are the result of collective bargaining between trade unions and employers' organisations. However, the public claims an interest as well as the parties involved, to ensure that negotiations are conducted in a reasonable manner and that the resulting settlements are fair. Government intervention in the field of industrial relations has several aspects. Those directed at the avoidance of strikes are discussed in the final chapter of this book, but we should refer here to bodies known as wages councils which were set up to fix minimum wages in industries where negotiating machinery was regarded as inadequate. There are over 20 wages councils in industries such as retail distribution and clothing, with similar arrangements for agriculture. The influence of wages councils was reduced, however, in 1986, since when they have ceased to consider wages for workers under the age of 21, and since when the powers of each council have been limited to setting a single minimum hourly (and overtime) rate. Review bodies have been formed for assistance in the settlement of pay negotiations, mainly of professional workers and employees in the public sector, e.g. for members of the armed forces, doctors and dentists and those earning so-called 'top salaries' (senior civil servants, judges, chairmen of the boards of nationalised industries, etc.). For a brief period there was even a standing Commission on Pay Comparability, set up by a Labour government in 1979 and abolished by a Conservative one in 1980. At the national level, governments have from time to time set up pay boards and issued 'guidelines' for wage settlements as part of their anti-inflation policies. Discussion of these is deferred to Chapter 9.

Trends in the size distribution of income

Most of the previous discussion has been focussed on the current distribution of income. However, we must also consider how it has been changing as a result of government action.

Comparisons of income distribution are difficult to make, especially over longish periods. The subject is, however, important, and the government set up by a Royal Commission (the Diamond Commission) in 1974 to report on the facts of the situation. Its reports on long-term trends recognised a decline in the share of the highest income groups in the period between the late 1940s and the 1970s. Those in the top percentile, i.e. with incomes which put them in the top 1 per cent of the population, suffered a virtual halving of their share of income, from about 11 per cent to about 5½ per cent of the total. Those in the top 10 per cent (including, of course, the top 1 per cent) suffered a fall in their share from about a third to a quarter of total income.

If the highest income classes lost, other groups must have gained and it seems clear that the chief beneficiaries were the middle income groups. Within the top half of income earners those lower down the scale gained approximately as much as the top 10 per cent lost, so that the share of the top half of income earners remained virtually unchanged (at about three-quarters of total income). On balance, the lowest half of the population neither gained nor lost over this long period –both at the beginning and at the end they were receiving about a quarter of total income.

Let it be clear that these are long-term trends. In the short term, the experience has been different over some years. Recent data relating to the period since the Diamond Commission was disbanded, 1979–80 to 1984–85, show a clear reversal of the trend for the higher income classes. The top 1 per cent of income distribution then increased its share from 5.3 to 6.4 per cent, a rise of a fifth; while the top 10 per cent of the distribution (including, of course, the top 1 per cent) increased its share by more than 10 per cent. These gains accruing to the richest income groups were at the expense of the rest of the distribution, among whom the losses were fairly evenly spread.

The bottom 20 per cent of the income distribution suffered

only a marginal drop in their share of the pre-tax total, to 2.3 per cent in 1984–85. However, this group deserves attention as being close to what one thinks of as poverty (arbitrary though any definition of that word has to be), and because its composition has changed since the 1970s. Roughly a third of those in this bottom 20 per cent consist of persons of working age, and nearly another quarter of single-parent families. This division may be compared with that obtaining at the beginning of the 1970s, when over half of this lowest income group was made up of pensioners. That should not lead to the inference that there has necessarily been an improvement in the living standards of those in retirement, so much as that it reflects higher unemployment in the 1980s and larger numbers of one-parent families in the population.

It is important to point out that the changing shares described in the preceding paragraphs relate to pre-tax income. When looking for explanations of trends, therefore, we must look at such matters as the determinants of factor shares and the distribution of earnings (see pages 83–4). Thus, trends in the supply of and demand for labour with different skills, and the overall state of the economy, including the general level of unemployment, are likely to be important. We should also recognise the relevance of the social and demographic structure of the population in this connection. In so far as income is related to age and education, for example, changes in the proportion of the population engaged in full-time education, or over retirement age, will be likely to have an effect on the size distribution of income. Finally, we have to take account of the fact that income is partly derived from the ownership of capital assets which bring in income, and that this, too, is liable to change over time.

Turning to post-tax shares in income distribution, which reflect changes in the degree of progessivity of the income tax, these were generally in the same direction as the changes in pre-tax shares, both in the long run and more recently. Indeed, the period 1979–80 to 1984–85 saw the top 1 per cent of incomes raise their share even slightly more post-tax than pre-tax (from 3.9 per cent to 4.9 per cent). More recently, since 1984–85, the reductions made by the government in rates of tax have been especially great for the top income brackets – with the abolition of the investment income surcharge, and the telescoping of the higher rates of tax of 45 per cent, 50 per cent, 55 per cent and 60 per cent into a single 40 per cent rate – at the same time as the basic rate was cut from 30 per cent to 25 per cent. It is too early for these tax rate changes to affect the published distributions of income, but there can be little doubt that they will show a rise in the share of those in the top income brackets, due to a lessening of the progressivity of the income tax.

Income distribution and price changes

One influence on the distribution of income that is not often discussed is that of changes in relative prices. Movements in the *average* level of prices are usually measured by what is called the **Index of Retail Prices (RPI)**, published monthly by the government. This index shows what is happening to the cost of living as represented by the prices of a typical 'basket' of goods and services bought by the average household. In the basket are the goods most commonly consumed, with 'weights' attached to them representing their relative importance in the average household budget.

Index of Retail Prices

Movements in the RPI record changes in the cost of living between two dates for an average family. Such a family spends nearly 20 per cent of its income on food, about 15 per cent on housing, and on transport and vehicles, 12 per cent on alcohol and tobacco, and 6–7 per cent on each of clothing, fuel and light, and durable household goods. The average family is, of course, a statistical artefact. For any individuals or groups the index may not accurately portray *their* cost of living. That will depend on their own expenditure pattern because all prices do not move in line together.

Figure 6.7 shows price level changes for different commod-

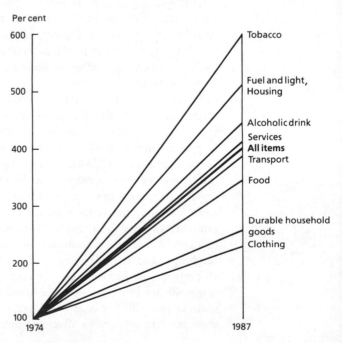

Fig. 6.7 Index of retail prices (percentage increase of major classes of goods and services in 1987 compared with 1974) Source: *Monthly Digest of Statistics*

ity groups between 1974 and 1987. During this period the index number for the *average* price level (RPI) was about 400 on the base of 1974. However, as can be seen, the price index for tobacco was around 600 and that for fuel and light and housing around 500, while those for durable household goods and clothing were both under 300.

The effect of these wide variations in the rate of inflation for different commodity groups on the distribution of real income depends, of course, on the relative importance of each of these items in household budgets. Figure 6.8, by way of illustration, shows how households at three different income levels were affected. We can see that the three classes of goods which rose most in price between 1974 and 1986 (fuel and light, tobacco, and housing) were relatively more important in the budget of low income groups than of high ones. At the same time, the two classes of goods which rose least in price during the same period (clothing and durable household goods) were relatively more important in the budget of high income groups.

One should be careful before concluding from the information in Figures 6.7 and 6.8 that relative price changes have had an inegalitarian influence, though a careful study of the distributional effects of inflation during the part of that period when the price level roughly tripled, 1974–82, concluded that there were sizeable differences in its effect on households, with greater cost of living increases being

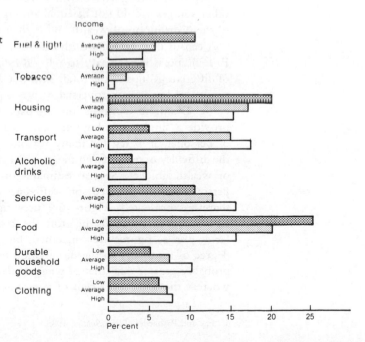

Fig. 6.8 Household expenditure at different income levels (percentage of total expenditure on commodity groups) 1986
Source: *Family Expenditure Survey 1986*, Department of Employment (1988)

experienced by the less well off.[1] That is not to say that these results would necessarily hold good for different periods.

Furthermore, redistribution should not be considered only from the point of view of different groups of persons distinguished by their income levels. Consumption patterns are affected by many other considerations, of which family size and age are among the most important. The government publishes regular indices of the cost of living for pensioner households, as well as the more general RPI. The pensioner price indices give greater weight to items such as food and fuel and less to motoring, alcoholic drink and tobacco and other classes of expenditure which feature less in the budget of the average pensioner. Over the 15 years ending in 1988, the RPI rose by a factor of 391 compared with 397 for pensioner households. Hence there might be said to have been a very slight worsening of the purchasing power of the pound for pensioners compared with the population as a whole, but the difference was marginal – about one-third of 1 per cent per annum on average.

The distribution of wealth

One explanation of why some people are rich and others poor is that relatively few individuals receive a disproportionately high share of income derived from the ownership of capital. The top 1 per cent of recipients of income derive 14 per cent of their total income in the form of income from investment – double the percentage contribution for the average income recipient. Hence, even if *earned* incomes were evenly distributed, *total* incomes from employment and all other sources would not be equal among individuals because of the distribution of wealth. What then are the facts?

A census of personal wealth has not been taken in modern Britain and it is necessary to rely on estimates of the shares of different groups in the total. This is a difficult exercise and results tend to be controversial. It was one of the tasks given to the Diamond Commission (*see* page 154), who failed to provide a single unambiguous statement on the ownership of personal property for many reasons, not the least being the difficulty of quantifying the property of the lowest groups of wealth holders. Several estimates of the distribution of personal wealth, based on different assumptions, were therefore presented. Figure 6.9 uses figures chosen from among them. It should, therefore, be treated with caution as far as precise figures are concerned, but it suggests that the degree of inequality in the distribution of personal wealth is probably greater than that of personal income. For example, whereas the top 10 per cent of *income units* receive about 30

---

1 Fry and Pashardes, *Fiscal Studies*, 1985.

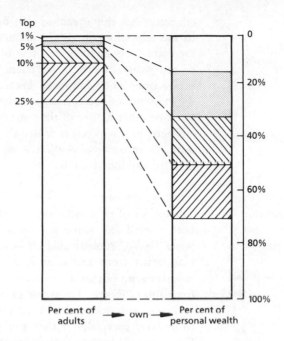

Fig. 6.9 Distribution of marketable personal wealth 1985 Source: *Inland Revenue Statistics*

per cent of total income (*see* page 150), the share of the top 10 per cent of wealth holders in marketable wealth is half as much again.

The concentration of personal wealth in relatively few hands is no new feature of society. It results from many factors, of which inheritance and the tendency for people to accumulate wealth during their working lives, and decumulate it after retirement, are the most important. The distribution is liable to change as the prices of the different assets comprising wealth alter over time. Chief among them are land, houses, shares and other securities, which are held in different proportions by rich and poor. Year-to-year fluctuations in the distribution of wealth can be very considerable, but one can discern a long-term reduction in the degree of inequality, as measured by a substantially declining share of the top 1 per cent of wealth holders in total wealth during the present century. To the extent that this is partly offset by an increasing share of other wealth holders within the top 20 per cent, it may indicate a spread of wealth within families rather than a more general redistribution.

Government and economic efficiency[1]

The term efficiency as used in economics has a wider connotation than in everyday speech, where it usually means simply that production is at minimum cost. In economics,

1 The meaning of efficiency is discussed in Lipsey and Harbury, *First Principles*, pages 270–71.

efficiency has this meaning too, but it extends also to refer to the allocation of goods and services itself. Cases where there are thought to be too few of some goods and services or too many of others are taken as evidence of inefficient production. They can occur because of lack of competition, the existence of social costs or benefits differing from private ones, or other failure of the market system.

There are many areas where the state intervenes to try to improve resource allocation – we can only illustrate them here by looking at a few.

Competition policy

The extent of concentration of industry in large enterprises, both overall and some sectors is, as we saw in Chapter 3 pages 68–70, considerable. It is clear, too, that the power that stems from the control of a high proportion of an industry's output in a few large businesses can be a matter for public concern. Firms, or groups of firms, which attain such positions are said to have a degree of monopoly power. Moreover, especially if they can prevent the entry of new firms into the industry, they are able to fix prices and act in other ways that may be damaging to consumers.

Barriers to entry can take many forms. Some are man-made, such as the patenting of products and the deliberate restriction of entry to an industry by large firms or groups of firms acting in collusion. Some are technologically dictated, such as substantial economies of large-scale production that leave room in an industry for only one or a few firms operating at an efficient scale of output.

Government may choose from a range of possible policies to control monopolies. An industry may be nationalised, or pricing and investment policies may be regulated. Competition may be encouraged from overseas by lowering barriers to international trade (*see* pages 127–8). Alternatively, the state can make a set of institutional arrangements to deal with certain aspects of competition policy, which has happened in the UK. The chief components of such a policy, which is mainly operated by the **Office of the Director General of Fair Trading (DGFT)** and the appropriate minister, the Secretary of State for Trade and Industry, may be considered under the following heads:

- monopolies
- restrictive practices
- mergers

Monopolies

The first step was taken forty years ago, with the creation of a Monopolies Commission, later renamed the **Monopolies and Mergers Commission (MMC)** (*see* page 162). This body is required to investigate monopoly situations (defined as where an enterprise controls at least 25 per cent of the market) referred to it by the DGFT or the minister.

Where the MMC finds a monopoly does exist, it reports on how the public interest is affected. The Commission is given only broad guidelines on how to interpret the public interest, e.g. how the enterprise's activities affect competition, consumers, innovation, the distribution of industry and of employment, and international trade.

In the years since it was set up, the Commission has made about two hundred reports – recently investigating, for example, the BBC, British Airports Authority and British Rail. The Commission's reports include the products of a very wide range of industries, such as electric lamps, cigarettes, beer, breakfast cereals, insulin, contraceptives, ice cream, greyhound racing, package holidays and salt. In a great many cases, it found practices operating against the public interest, especially price-fixing and measures to prevent the entry of new firms.

A further step in the government's monopoly policy was taken by the Competition Act 1980, which gave the DGFT powers to deal with what are called 'anti-competitive practices', without the need for a full reference to the MMC. These were broadly defined to include such behaviour as the refusal of a firm to supply another, such as a discount store which might sell its products at 'cut' (i.e. low) prices, and the tying of sales of one product to those of another. But not a great deal of use has been made of this legislation.

Restrictive practices The second aspect of competition policy is concerned not so much with monopolies as with restrictive practices by *groups of firms acting together*, e.g. to fix prices. Collusive agreements (with some exceptions, for instance affecting patents) have to be registered with the DGFT, who can take proceedings against them to a Restrictive Practices Court. The presumption of the law is that all such agreements are contrary to the public interest unless special circumstances can be shown to exist (so-called 'gateways') which provide a substantial net benefit to the public. About 4500 agreements have been registered, although the vast majority were abandoned voluntarily and only a tiny proportion were contested before the Court. Of these about a third were allowed to continue. The majority were found to be against the public interest and declared void.

One especially pervasive practice was treated separately. The Resale Prices Act, 1964, prohibited agreements, even by individual manufacturers, to fix in advance minimum resale prices of their goods by retailers, unless granted exemption by the Restrictive Practices Court. This piece of legislation was particularly effective. As a result of the Act the previously widespread practice of fixed prices for goods in all shops virtually disappeared from Britain; the two exceptions being books and pharmaceuticals, though one major bookseller (Pentos which owns the Dillons chain of shops) announced in January 1989 that it would start discounting books below manufacturers' stipulated retail prices in defiance of the Net Book Agreement.

Mergers

A third strand in competition policy focusses on mergers. As we saw in Chapter 3 (pages 73–4), merger waves have characterised recent British economic history, as they have throughout the industrialised world, and are estimated to have been responsible for at least half of the increase in concentration that occurred after 1960.

The Monopolies and Mergers Commission was given extended powers in 1965, when 'Mergers' was added to its name. The Secretary of State for Trade and Industry has the power to refer any merger proposals to the Commission if it is thought they might create a monopoly market share (i.e. over 25%) or involve the take–over of assets above a threshold (£30 million in 1988).

Investigating merger proposals has occupied an increasing amount of the time of the MMC. Recent mergers on which the view of the Commission was sought included those between British Airways and British Caledonian, GEC and Plessey, P & O and European Ferries, Elders IXL and Allied Lyons, and Trusthouse Forte and establishments belonging to Hanson Trust. In practice, however, the great majority of technically referable mergers have not been sent to the MMC, because the public interest was not thought to be seriously threatened. On any merger which is given to it, the Commision must make recommendations within six months to the Secretary of State, who then decides whether to allow the merger, with or without conditions, or prohibit it. In response to allegations that some mergers were referred on nationalistic grounds, the government has, since 1984, been at pains to stress that only the effect on competition would be considered. The refusal of the Secretary of State to refer the Nestlé bid for Rowntree in 1988 is evidence that this policy is being pursued.

The future of competition policy

Seen as a whole, British competition policy as it has developed represents a distinctive approach to the problems arising from the existence of monopoly power in the private sector of industry. In contrast to policy in other countries, particularly that in the USA, the underlying philosophy, especially for monopolies and mergers, has been to adopt a case-by-case approach, with potential benefits and detriments to the public interest being weighed against each other. Each case is judged on its merits before an overall assessment is made.

One consequence of this approach is that it tends to work slowly. Other criticisms have been made. The findings of the MMC do not have to stand up to public enquiry as do those of the Restrictive Practices Court. For another thing, the government of the day has not always accepted the recommendations of the Commission, and in most cases reliance has been placed on voluntary assurances from businesses after the publication of reports, rather than on formal orders from the government for implementation. At the same time, mergers policy has been accused of being too weak, because the onus of proof is on the MMC to show that a merger is against the public interest, rather than on the parties to show that it is not so. Policy on restrictive practices has been attacked as slow, inflexible, lacking effective monitoring and enforcing mechanisms, and costly in so far as processing of many harmless mergers is concerned.

An official review of aspects of competition policy was published in 1988, as a result of which some major changes may take place. The review committee's main proposals for reform lie in the area of restrictive practices, where it recommends:

(a) a change in approach stressing the effects on competition rather than the legal form of restrictive agreements
(b) the establishment of a new competition authority with stronger enforcement powers and stiff legal penalties for breaches of the law

Mergers policy, in contrast to restrictive practices, is not seen as being in need of drastic changes so much as of methods of speeding up processes by prenotification of mergers and by granting conditional permission for mergers without full reference to the MMC. However, in the light of very recent developments, especially of mega-mergers involving international businesses (*see* pages 75–6), it may be that this aspect of competition policy will also be thought in need of more reform.

Competition policy of the EC
UK competition policy has to work within the context of the European Community, a matter likely to assume increasing importance as the 'single market' of 1992 approaches (*see* pages 125–6). EC competition policy is based on Articles 85 and 86 of the Treaty of Rome, and applies where trade between member states is concerned.

Article 85 deals with restrictive practices which reduce competition and must be notified to the Commission. Article 86 concerns market dominance, i.e. the abuse of monopoly power. In addition, mergers were judged by the European Court of Justice to fall within the ambit of EC competition policy – effectively as an ultimate kind of restrictive agreement covered by Article 85. Increasingly EC rules and regulations have influenced UK policy in recent years. In 1988, for example, the Commission insisted that, in the interests of competition, conditions should be attached to the take-over of British Caledonian by British Airways, which the UK government had been prepared to allow.

Regional policy

As we saw in Chapter 3, industries are not evenly spread over the country but tend to concentrate in particular areas. Heavy dependence on one or more failing industries caused serious local pockets of unemployment in the interwar years and government action was taken to alleviate this problem. The first step was taken in 1934 when certain 'Special Areas' were scheduled as depressed and commissioners were appointed to try to attract new industry to them. Postwar Distribution of Industry Acts reinforced this policy, giving powers to the government. These included building factories for letting in the areas (renamed **Development Areas**) and making loans and grants to encourage individual firms to go there. At the same time a policy of creating **new towns** was started in more prosperous regions.

In a negative way, too, the government's control over factory location was materially strengthened by legislation whereby new factories required planning permission from the local authority, and larger factories also required the granting of an **industrial development certificate**. The government was therefore able to influence industrial location by granting or withholding these certificates – a powerful weapon.

Outside Northern Ireland, which is treated separately, the areas of Great Britain which qualify for assistance fall into two categories (*see* Fig. 6.10):

- Development Areas
- Intermediate Areas

Development Areas are those which are judged to have the greatest needs. The help available includes grants for new investment for small firms under Regional Selective Assistance (which replaced Regional Development Grants in 1988), and grants towards the cost of business consultancy schemes. Mention might also be made of the old Regional

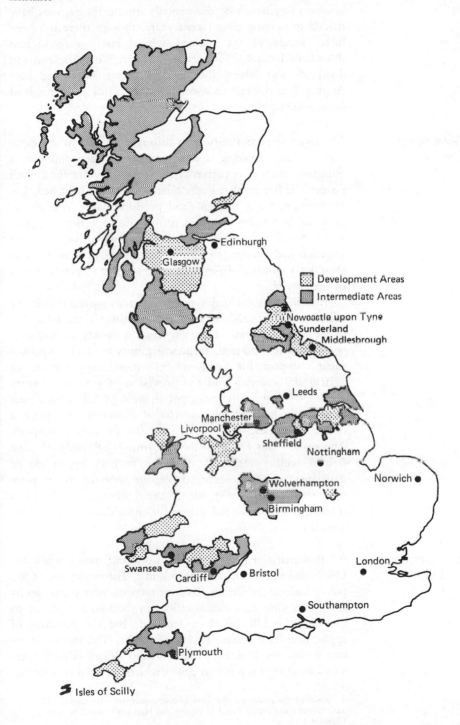

Fig. 6.10 Location of
industry policy, 1988 –
areas entitled to
assistance

Development Areas
Intermediate Areas

Edinburgh
Glasgow

Newcastle upon Tyne
Sunderland
Middlesbrough

Leeds
Manchester
Liverpool
Sheffield
Nottingham
Norwich
Wolverhampton
Birmingham

Swansea
Cardiff
Bristol
London

Southampton

Plymouth

Isles of Scilly

Employment Premium of 1967–77 (*see* page 143), which related aid to numbers of employees, since it tended to favour labour-intensive rather than capital-intensive industries.

Unemployment rate differentials among the regions have tended to narrow over recent years, though there has been little change in the regions whose rates were highest (Northern Ireland, Northern and North West England and Scotland) and lowest (South East, South West and East Anglia). It is difficult to know how much this is the result of government policy.

Government and agriculture[1]

The farming community goes through difficult times, especially when harvests are at bumper levels and prices plummet, such as occurred in the interwar years for British farmers. It is true that every year was not equally bad, but competition from foreign food producers was intense and even the best years were less prosperous in agriculture than in many other industries. By the beginning of the 1930s the situation had become so serious that the government began to adopt a number of piecemeal measures to improve the lot of the farmer.

After the war the major political parties agreed that every effort should be made to prevent agriculture from returning to its depressed state. Over the years a variety of measures were therefore enacted, including grants for land improvement, support for farm amalgamations, sponsorship of agricultural research and the provision of a farm advisory service. However, the principal element of UK agricultural policy, which lasted for a quarter of a century after the end of the war, took the form of subsidies for British farmers. The system was based on the free import of foodstuffs into Britain while subsidising domestic farmers by means of deficiency payments, representing the shortfall in the price they received from the sale of their produce on the open market, and guaranteed prices for individual products, set annually.

Agriculture and the EC

All this changed (except for potatoes and wool) when the UK joined the European Community. The objectives of EC policy include stabilising farm incomes at 'reasonable' levels and promoting agricultural efficiency, and so are similar to those of the UK which it replaced, but the methods of application have certain basic differences. The most important is that the **Common Agricultural Policy (CAP)** operates a system of minimum prices which apply in all member

1 Some of the problems that arise in connection with policies designed to assist agriculture are analysed in Lipsey and Harbury, *First Principles*, Chapter 10.

states. The prices themselves are set by the Council of Ministers on the recommendations of the Commission and are maintained through purchases made by EC agencies and by import levies on products entering the Community from outside.

It is beyond the scope of this book to describe the complexities of the CAP, which include grants for farm modernisation, and a system of artificial, so-called 'green' exchange rates for the conversion into local currencies of support prices set in ECUs (*see* page 126). The scope for disagreement among member countries on the level of support for individual products and the method of financing it is tremendous, not least because about three-quarters of the entire EC budget is spent on agriculture. Moreover, the level of support has been so high as to generate enormous surpluses of some commodities – 'mountains' of butter and sugar, and 'lakes' of wine and milk, as they have been called.

The severity of the problems of the CAP led, around 1984, to a serious search for solutions acceptable to member states with very different interests, e.g. those of relatively poor countries with substantial agricultural sectors, such as Greece and Portugal, and others, such as France, West Germany and the UK, where the political power of the farming community varies.

Three types of solution have received support. First, setting quotas on output (introduced for milk in 1984); second, 'set aside' measures providing compensation for farmers who move out of production of commodities in surplus; third, narrowing the margin between the world market price in the outside world and the support price in the EC, by lowering the latter. So called 'stabilisers', which cut the support price as output passes predetermined levels, and favoured by the UK government, have been agreed for cereals. This occurred after hard bargaining by heads of state at a summit meeting in 1988. It may be readily appreciated that the key to the effects of such solutions depends critically on the level at which the threshold is set, as well as on the principle behind it.

Community agricultural policy affects not only member states but also the world at large, which finds itself discriminated against, compared with trade among EC countries. The USA, in particular, has been in conflict with the EC in recent years as a result of its exports coming under pressure with expansion of the Community. Minor trade wars have occurred, with the USA seeking retaliatory measures, e.g. raising duty rates on imports of products from the EC.

There are several areas where the government intervenes by directly providing goods and services, as well as attempting to influence the private sector of the market. Three important areas where this takes place are housing, education and health.

Housing

Both the supply and the allocation of existing houses are regarded by some people as proper targets for social policy. The reason is a feeling that a minimum standard of housing should be available for all families, regardless of income, especially where there are children in the household. A relevant distinctive feature of houses is that their cost is high – it is extremely rate that anyone can buy a house outright out of current income. Furthermore, it has often been thought reasonable that those living in rented accommodation should enjoy a certain security of tenure.

State intervention in the housing market occurs through both sides of the government accounts as well as by means of rules and regulations. On the expenditure side of the budget there are rent subsidies for persons on low incomes and the provision of council housing by local authorities. Council housing is allocated to persons on waiting lists according to criteria decided locally, but they usually take into account such things as family size, current housing conditions, length of residence in the area, etc. Rents charged to council house tenants vary from one authority to another, but are almost always below – sometimes well below – those of the free market. Since the Housing Act of 1980 council house tenants of at least three years' standing have been given the right to buy the property at a discount related to the length of time that they have lived in it. Approximately a million houses, representing a third of the total, were sold at an average discount of some 50 per cent in the ten years from 1979 to 1988. The proportion of families living in council accommodation has, accordingly, fallen from about a third to a quarter of the total (*see* Fig. 6.11).

On the revenue side of the account there is the important provision that mortgage interest payments on loans of up to £30 000, together with other allowances, are deductible from gross income before tax is calculated. This policy has been under attack, as being largely responsible for house prices having risen a great deal more than they otherwise would have done. Hence mortgage interest relief may not have benefited *new* purchasers of houses. Removal of the tax concession is, nonetheless, politically difficult; though the *real* relief has been kept down by failing to raise the maximum house purchase loan on which the concession is allowed so as to bring this in line with inflation, as has occurred with

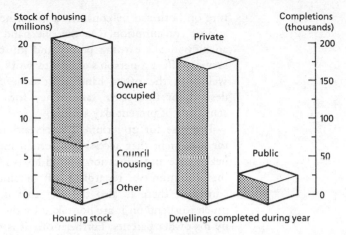

Fig. 6.11 Dwellings (stock of houses and flats at end 1986, and dwellings completed during year 1986) Source: *Annual Abstract of Statistics*

other tax allowances (*see* page 139).

The majority of the regulations affecting housing are related to health standards, environmental issues and town planning, but there is one area of special importance to economists – control of rents in the private sector.[1] **Rent control was introduced as an emergency measure in 1915** during the First World War! Landlords of unfurnished flats and houses at the lower end of the market were prohibited from raising rents above those charged in August 1914 unless improvements had been made (or rates increased). Tenants were also given security from eviction. The measure had been intended as a temporary one but it was in fact continued after the end of the war and has persisted to the present day. As a result, by 1939, in spite of some relaxation of the rules, about a third of all privately rented houses and flats were subject to restrictions.

Since the end of the Second World War there have been several pieces of legislation extending, reducing or varying the scope of rent control. The most important Rent Acts in recent years have been those of 1974 and 1980. The former brought unfurnished tenancies into the network, while the latter introduced the notion of 'shorthold' lettings, reducing the security of tenants against eviction from security for life to a shorter period of 1–5 years by agreement. Partly as a result of long-standing rent control legislation, which makes the provision of rented accommodation unattractive for private investors, the supply of private rented accommodation today accounts for only about 10 per cent of the total number of dwellings.

Education and health

Education and health services have certain similarities which form the basis for state intervention in the market. Expendi-

1 The effects of maximum price controls are analysed in Lipsey and Harbury, *First Principles*, Chapter 10.

ture on both can be considered investment in human capital and/or consumption. On the one hand education increases an individual's earning power and job choice, while health services affect a person's ability to work, or at least to work well. On the other hand both education and health are desired for their own sake. They form part of the living standards of present-day society.

The case for government intervention is partly based on the argument that access to a certain minimum standard of health care and education should be available to everyone in the community, regardless of income. In the case of education there is also the fact that decisions about how much to spend on it are not taken by the individual child but by his or her parents. Furthermore, it is widely believed that society, as well as the individual, benefits from having its members healthy and well educated. This is obvious in the case of, say, infectious and contagious diseases, but of wider importance is the beneficial effect on economic growth and, more vaguely perhaps, social cohesion.

The tools of intervention in health and education are both budgetary and via rules and regulations. Health and education each absorb about 10 per cent of total government expenditure, nearly half that percentage of national output (see Fig. 6.3). For those who choose to opt out of state education or health there are no provisions for tax deductions in the UK as there are in some other countries, partly because the public sector is so very large (about 90 per cent of children attend state schools, for example). Most expenditure on education is financed out of general taxation, though there are some user charges, e.g. for school meals and income-based parental contributions to the maintenance grants of students undergoing higher education, due to be supplemented by the introduction of loans to students in the 1990s.

Most of the cost of running the **National Health Service** comes from general taxation, a part coming from the national insurance fund (see page 145) and an increasing proportion from charges for such items as drugs, spectacles and dental treatment. In spite of the large public provision, the UK spends a lower proportion of its total income on health (about 6 per cent) than several other countries (e.g. USA 11 per cent; France and West Germany 9 per cent). The Conservative Government of Mrs Thatcher has been considering ways of encouraging more private sector provision of health services.

Regulations are used to maintain standards of quality in both services. In the case of education the rule of compulsion was first introduced in 1876, but the minimum school leaving age has, of course, been raised since then. Compulsory health insurance was brought in by the Lloyd George Government in 1912, well before the advent of the national health service (1948). A more recent example of the use of rules is that for the compulsory wearing of seat belts in cars (1983).

Miscellaneous measures

There is not enough space in this book to list, let alone describe in any detail, the multifarious measures that governments have used, and still do, to influence economic activity and resource allocation in the UK. Some idea of their range and diversity may be gleaned from mentioning a few. In the area of the quality of products, there is legislation on safety standards and on misleading trade descriptions. The Office of the Director General of Fair Trading has responsibilities for consumer protection, as does a special National Consumer Council. In the area of industrial co-operation there is a National Economic Development Council (known as 'Neddy') on which serve senior members of industry, trade unions and government. This meets under the chairmanship of the Chancellor of the Exchequer to discuss matters such as investment, productivity, training and economic growth. In the area of investment protection, there are bodies set up under the Financial Services Act 1986, and in a wide range of other areas there are the initiatives of the Department of Trade and Industry, which relaunched itself as the 'Department of Enterprise' in 1988.

Nationalised industries

One final option for state intervention in the economy is for the government to own industries and to run them more or less as commercial enterprises. The organisation and control of the nationalised industries were described in some detail in Chapter 2 (*see* pages 44–7), where the extent to which they were in the course of transfer back to the private sector was also covered.

By 1988, the industries remaining nationalised (apart from water and electricity due for privatisation the next year) were coal, the railways and the Post Office. Coal had, in fact, been the first important industry to be nationalised by the Labour Government in 1947. It then employed three-quarters of a million workers, compared with barely more than 100 000 today on the payroll of the British Coal Corporation (formerly the National Coal Board). Nationalisation of the railways took place the same year as that of coal, when a massive and complex British Transport Commission was set up to run the bulk of road passenger and freight transportation as well. The Post Office was not nationalised in the sense of being a private industry bought up by the state. Postal services, together with telecommunications, were run directly as a department of the central government until 1969. In 1981 the telecommunications and postal services were separated, the former being sold to the private sector in 1984.

The record of the nationalised industries in comparison with private enterprise is not easily assessed. One basis for comparison might be relative profitability, which economists often use as a yardstick for measuring efficiency. However, this approach is not always appropriate for nationalised industries, for two basic reasons. In the first place, they may be asked to fulfil social obligations which may not be profitable. For example, they may be expected to prevent unemployment in a depressed area; they may have to provide transport for people living in isolated parts of the country; they may need to maintain national prestige, e.g. airlines; they may be told to keep their prices low as part of an anti-inflation policy, e.g. gas. Despite the guidelines of the White Papers of the 1960s and 1970s (*see* pages 46–7) to separate social and commercial activities, the problems remain of relying on profitability to measure efficiency.

The second reason for caution in relying on profitability experience by which to judge the nationalised industries' performance is that several of them have possessed degrees of monopoly power which would allow them to make large profits without being very efficient.[1] There is plenty of evidence that profitability in such circumstances can be manipulated. This is to be found in the history of recent sales of shares in privatised companies, where a prime objective of the operation was to make the share issue a success. For example, the sale of British Gas in 1986 as a single monopoly supplier, rather than being split into separate competing divisions (as several economists proposed).

An alternative measure of comparative efficiency that has been used in some studies is labour productivity. This measure is not without difficulties of a different kind, because labour productivity can be affected by inputs of factors of production other than labour, especially of capital. For what it is worth, however, careful studies have been made on the comparative performance of public and private enterprise since 1960. The results are inconclusive, but interesting in so far as they suggest that the nationalised industries performed at least as well as the private sec-

---

1 See Lipsey and Harbury, *First Principles*, pages 209–216 for analysis of efficiency and monopoly.

tor in the 1960s, substantially less well in the 1970s, and as well again thereafter.

Privatisation

The term 'privatisation' has been used in this book to describe certain kinds of policy associated with Conservative Governments in the 1980s, including the transfer of some publicly-owned assets to the private sector. However, the term 'privatisation' means more than simply denationalisation, though there is no universal agreement on what it does cover. This is not really surprising, since an integrated specific privatisation policy was not so much thought out in advance as developed as circumstances evolved. It may be useful to identify the goals of privatisation and the main mechanisms (instruments) for achieving them.

Objectives and instruments of privatisation

Three sets of goals can be distinguished. The first set relates to economic efficiency and is associated with the philosophy of the Conservative Government of the day that market forces should play a stronger part in deciding resource allocation. The second set of goals relates to equity, including the distribution of income and wealth, and a desire to foster 'popular capitalism' by raising the proportion of the population owning shares in joint stock companies. The third set of goals relates to uses for the revenues raised from sales of state-owned assets. Two stand out to be mentioned. One overlaps with the goal of equity in so far as the proceeds of privatisation share issues can be used to cut tax rates. The second concerns macroeconomic rather than microeconomic policy goals – especially the control of inflation. We consider this in Chapter 9.

The goals of the privatisation programme have been pursued by various means, some more prominent than others, including assets transfers, deregulation, subcontracting/franchising, and charging for state-provided services which were previously free (or subsidised).

The chief asset transfers involving nationalised industries were listed in Chapter 2 (*see* page 48), but the sale of a million council houses to tenants should also be regarded as a privatisation measure. Together these provided the Chancellor of the Exchequer with an unprecedented revenue which could help finance tax cuts.

The issues of shares in newly privatised companies proved immensely popular, both with employees and with the general public, since many of the largest were offered at heavily discounted prices, yielding immediate capital gains. Critics, not surprisingly, have stressed the consequent cost to the taxpayer (called 'giving away the family silver' by former Prime Minister, the late Harold Macmillan, Earl of Stockton). Share ownership was certainly widened, but, as a recent survey showed, over half of all shareholders own shares in only a single company. The strongest criticism of the denationalisation measures, however, has been that increasing competition has not been a sufficiently prominent component of the arrangements for asset transfers. Some people see this as a consequence of the whole privatisation programme having too many goals, some of which are at times conflicting. For example, in order to make the share issues as successful as possible, British Telecom and British Gas were sold as single going concerns with significant degrees of monopoly power, rather than being broken down into separate competing components, which would not have appeared as attractive propositions for prospective purchasers.

Regulating the
natural monopolies

New-style regulatory machinery has been developed to monitor and control the activities of the now privately-owned public utilities. Additionally, in the case of three-quarters of the privatised corporations, the government retained possession of a single share with unique rights (commonly called 'golden shares') which gave it a veto in the event of 'undesirable' take-over bids from a foreign, or indeed any, large 'predator'.

The machinery is run by new specialised agencies, e.g. the Office of Telecommunications (OFTEL) and, for gas, OFGAS. One of the objectives of the regulatory bodies is to monitor quality, e.g. the number of telephone boxes out of order. Another is to control prices in order to protect the consuming public from exploitation of monopoly powers. The price control system is called RPI–X, because allowable price changes are linked to the rate of inflation (as measured by movements in the Retail Price Index), with X being set by the regulatory agency to encourage efficiency and cost cutting.

Outside straight denationalisation, the privatisation programme has used several ways of strengthening the power and influence of market forces, including deregulation, sub-contracting/franchising, and introducing charges for state services previously provided free or at less than cost.

Deregulation means removing restrictions on competition. The ending of legal monopolies for qualified opticians in the sale of spectacles and of solicitors in conveyancing of house property are examples of the deregulation measures of the 1980s. Another is the repeal of the legislation limiting competition among the operators of road passenger transport, i.e. buses and coaches.

Sub-contracting, or franchising, introduces competition in the provision of state-financed services by allowing outside contractors to tender for the right to do the actual supplying. It has been used by some local authorities for refuse collection and by hospitals for some services, e.g. cleaning.

A final aspect of government policy, which could be regarded as part of the privatisation programme in the widest sense of strengthening market forces, concerns the introduction or raising of charges for some state-provided benefits, e.g. for dental treatment under the National Health Service. The principle here is that the beneficiaries from expenditure should pay for it. There has also been discussion about introducing a kind of charging for education by the issue of vouchers which could be used only to buy schooling, but the idea has yet to be implemented.

Questions and exercises

For key to symbols indicating suggested sources *see* pages xi–xii.

1 Refer to one of the 'serious' national newspapers for details of the last budget presented to Parliament. Identify a change in taxation, if you think there is one, which fits each of the following categories:

(a) redistributes income more equally
(b) encourages personal saving
(c) stimulates people to work harder
(d) promotes business investment
(e) serves a purpose other than (a) to (d) above

Give reasons for each answer (not more than 150 words for each). If you cannot identify a change in any of these cases, propose a tax change yourself which would fit the requirement. (*T, FT, FPR*)

2 Prepare a graph for the last ten years showing the proportion of total public revenue of central and local government derived from taxes on incomes and taxes on expenditure. Have the proportions changed? (*AS, F*)

3 What is the maximum sum your parents could give you without incurring any liability to inheritance tax this year? Suppose they were generous and gave you (a) double or (b) six times the maximum. What would be the average tax rate on the gift in the two cases? Do your results throw light on whether inheritance tax is progressive or regressive? (*WA*)

4 Find out the size of each of the main items of central government expenditure in both a recent year and one five years previously. Mark each *E* (exhaustive) or *T* (transfers). Calculate also the percentages of the totals for the two years, and pick out any significant changes which may have taken place. (*AS*)

5   The Inland Revenue's statistics of the distribution of income give numbers of incomes in about 15 size classes of income, together with the total income in each class. Collect the data for a recent year and collapse the number of size classes into eight. Calculate for pre-tax income:

(a) the percentage of the *total number of incomes*, and
(b) the percentage of *total income* in each of the eight groups.

Plot the eight pairs of percentages on a graph similar to Fig. 6.6, to yield a Lorenz curve. Repeat the exercise for *either* post-tax income for the same year *or* pre-tax income for an earlier year. How different is the new Lorenz curve from the old? Does comparing the two curves have any implications for the progressiveness of income tax? (*AS*)

6   Prepare a table containing statistics of the size of the national debt (debt of the public sector) for a recent year, and two others — five years and ten years previously.
   In the next row, write in the total population in the UK in each of the three years.
   In the new row, insert the amount of the GDP (Gross Domestic Product) for each of the three years.
   In the next row, insert the total government expenditure in each of the three years.
   Now calculate the debt, *(a)* per head of the population; *(b)* as a percentage of GDP; and *(c)* as a proportion of total government expenditure in each of the three years. Comment on the changes, suggesting both causes and consequences. (*AS*)

7   Draw a graph showing the year-to-year changes over the past ten years in the RPI (Retail Price Index), and of the following sub-groups of commodity prices included in the RPI:

(a) food;
(b) fuel;
(c) durable household goods;
(d) services.

Compare the changes for each sub-group with the RPI, and consider the effects on the following sets of people, as compared with the effects on the whole population:

(a) high income groups;
(b) old persons;
(c) large families. (*AS*)

8   Using the index to *The Times*, find references to reports by the Monopolies and Mergers Commission in the last year or so. From the press coverage of the reports list in each case:

(a)   whether the report was : *(1)* on a proposed merger; or
       (2) on a monopoly;

(b) in cases of *(1)*, whether the merger was approved or not, and why;

(c) in cases of *(2)*, whether the monopoly was confirmed and, if so, what, if anything, was found to act against the public interest.

Do your findings fit the general picture of the operation of UK competition policy in the past? (*T*)

9 Using the information contained in Fig. 2.4 on page 48, find the share price of any six of the privatised companies in the table: *(a)* in the year when they were sold to the private sector; *(b)* this year. Calculate the change in the share price. List the companies in order of improvement in the share price. Can you offer any explanations for such differences as you have found? Do you wish you had bought *(1)* all of the companies; *(2)* the four best performers? Check the changes in the *Financial Times* index of share prices before answering. (*T, FT*)

Appendix

Table A6.1 UK government current income and expenditure, 1977 and 1987 (£ million)
Source: *UK National Accounts*

Income	1977	1987
Taxes on income	20 490	55 601
Taxes on expenditure	19 834	67 980
Social security contributions	9 503	28 449
Gross trading surplus	183	– 177
Rent, etc.	2 256	4 313
Interest, dividends, etc.	2 687	5 859
Miscellaneous	1 181	3 049
Total current income	56 134	165 074

Expenditure		
Goods and services	28 424	83 040
Non-trading capital consumption	1 045	2 732
Subsidies	3 386	5 762
Grants to persons	15 031	52 478
Grants paid abroad (net)	1 083	3 287
Debt interest	6 288	17 667
Total current expenditure	55 257	164 966
Balance (current surplus)	877	108

Table A6.2 Distribution of personal income 1978–79 and 1984–85 (before and after income tax)
Source: *Economic Trends* (November 1987)

Percentage Group	Before tax		After tax	
	1978–79	1984–85	1978–79	1984–85
	%	%	%	%
Top 1 per cent	5.3	6.4	3.9	4.9
2–5 per cent	10.7	12.1	9.8	11.1
6–10 per cent	10.1	10.9	9.7	10.5
Top 10 per cent	26.1	29.5	23.4	26.5
11–20 per cent	16.5	16.8	16.3	16.6
21–30 per cent	13.5	13.0	13.5	13.0
31–40 per cent	11.2	10.3	11.3	10.4
41–50 per cent	9.2	8.2	9.3	8.6
51–60 per cent	7.3	6.6	7.7	7.1
61–70 per cent	5.8	5.4	6.4	6.0
71–80 per cent	4.5	4.4	5.1	4.9
81–90 per cent	3.5	3.5	4.1	4.2
91–100 per cent	2.4	2.3	2.9	2.7

Table A6.3 Public expenditure by the UK government 1988–89 and 1991–92 (£ million)
Source: *Economic Progress Report* (December 1988)

	1988–89 outturn	1991–92 plans
Defence	19 300	22 090
Foreign Office (including aid)	2 230	2 540
European Community	950	1 580
Agriculture, fisheries, food and forestry	1 860	2 350
Trade, industry, energy and employment	6 150	5 800
Arts and libraries	980	1 050
Transport	4 810	5 660
Housing	2 050	2 380
Other environmental services	4 380	4 700
Home Office and law	7 240	8 630
Education and science	18 440	20 770
Health and personal social services	21 740	25 390
Social security	47 600	58 700
Other departments	4 030	4 860
Scotland	8 720	9 680
Wales	3 600	4 010
Northern Ireland	5 160	5 910
Reserve	—	10 500
Privatisation proceeds	−6 000	−5 000
Adjustment	360	—
Planning total	153 600	191 600

Table A6.4 Retail prices and house prices 1978–88
Source: *National Institute Economic Review* (November 1988)

	All items	Food	Housing	Nationalised industries, goods and services	Other	House prices
	1985 = 100					
1978	52.9	60.6	38.3	47.5	55.0	49.2
1979	59.9	67.9	46.2	51.5	61.2	63.2
1980	70.6	76.1	59.6	64.3	72.2	73.8
1981	79.1	82.5	70.3	76.8	80.7	76.9
1982	85.8	88.9	79.2	87.2	86.4	77.1
1983	89.7	91.8	81.2	92.0	90.9	85.3
1984	94.3	97.0	88.7	95.0	95.1	93.0
1985	100.0	100.0	100.0	100.0	100.0	100.0
1986	103.4	103.3	105.8	103.7	103.1	115.7
1987	107.7	106.4	114.8	105.8	106.7	133.5
1988★	112.3	110.1	121.9	111.2	110.7	161.7

★ First half of year.

7 | National income and the balance of payments

In this chapter we pass from a consideration of the allocation of resources between industries and sectors to look at the economy as a whole. We begin with the sum total of all outputs – what is known generally as the national income. Later in the chapter we consider the balance of payments – the record of transactions between residents and non-residents.

National income[1]

The national income is a measure of all goods and services produced in the economy during some period of time (usually a year) and valued in money terms. It can be estimated in any one of three ways by summing:

- incomes
- outputs
- expenditures

In principle all three of these methods will give the same answer. This is because the value of output produced is equal to the value of expenditure needed to purchase it and to the income claims generated by its production (because all value produced must belong to someone). Figure 7.1 shows the breakdown of national income estimated in each of the three ways listed above.

Expenditure-based measure of national income

There are three major components of national expenditure:

- consumption
- investment
- government

1 National income accounts are discussed in Lipsey and Harbury, *First Principles*, Chapters 26, 30 and 32.

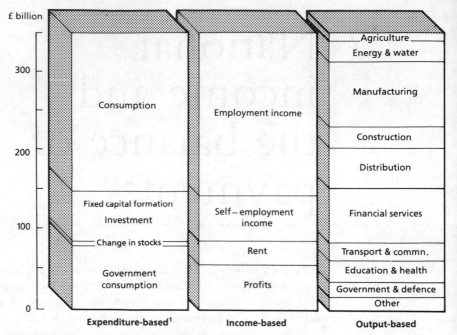

£ billion

| | Expenditure-based[1] | Income-based | Output-based |

Consumption / Employment income

Fixed capital formation
Investment / Self–employment income

Change in stocks

Rent

Government consumption / Profits

Agriculture
Energy & water
Manufacturing
Construction
Distribution
Financial services
Transport & commn.
Education & health
Government & defence
Other

300

200

100

0

Fig. 7.1 Gross
Domestic Product 1987
Source: *UK National
Accounts*

and a fourth of relatively small magnitude:

● net exports

Consumption

Private consumption expenditure is the largest category. As can be seen from Fig. 7.2 much consumer expenditure is on regular needs for food, fuel, clothing and household goods, etc., and does not fluctuate greatly. The proportion of income which is spent on consumption can be relied on to be fairly stable most of the time.

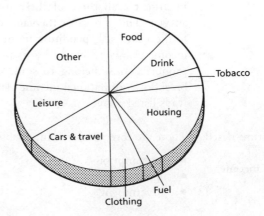

Food
Other
Drink
Tobacco
Leisure
Housing
Cars & travel
Clothing
Fuel

Fig. 7.2 Consumer
expenditure 1987
Source: *UK National
Accounts*

1 Net exports are not shown because in 1987 exports and imports were approximately equal; hence net exports were zero.

182 An Introduction to the UK Economy

The second component of national expenditure, investment, tends to be more volatile than consumption. Investment is of two kinds:

- **fixed capital formation** in plant, machinery, equipment and housing
- **change in stocks of goods** at different stages in the production process

Figure 7.3 shows the composition of fixed capital formation in 1987. About three-quarters of the total is invested in the private sector, the remainder in the public sector. All the items, with the exception of dwellings, raise the productive potential of the economy and, given favourable circumstances, can lead to economic growth. Excluding dwellings, **gross fixed investment** has averaged 16–17 per cent of gross domestic expenditure in the 1980s, having fallen, compared with the 1970s, in common with other countries such as France, West Germany and Japan.

Fig. 7.3 Gross domestic fixed capital formation 1987 Source: UK National Accounts

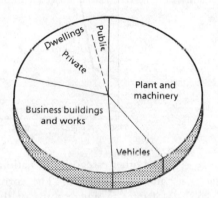

The relative volatility of total national investment expenditure mentioned earlier is not traceable to fixed capital formation but to the second component of investment – changes in stocks (or inventories) of goods and materials held by businesses. They are considered in economics as part of investment and play a key role in economic theory.[1] Although the size of stocks is to a certain extent decided upon by firms, it is also liable to change *involuntarily* as a result of unexpected alterations in levels of sales. Figure 7.4 shows the annual movements in the changes in stocks between the start and end of each year for 1980–1987.

1   See Lipsey and Harbury, *First Principles*, pages 342–3.

National income and the balance of payments   **183**

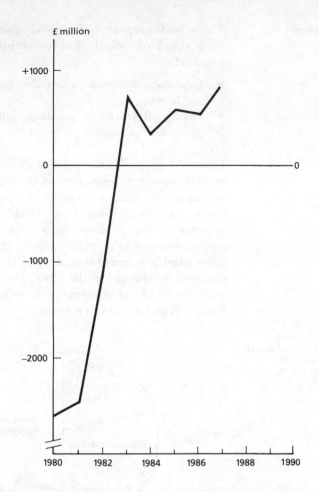

Fig. 7.4 Change in value of stocks (at 1985 prices)
Source: *UK National Accounts*

£ million

+1000

0

−1000

−2000

1980   1982   1984   1986   1988   1990

Government expenditure and exports

The other categories of national expenditure are government and (net) exports. The former constituted the subject of Chapter 6, where some of the determinants of government expenditure were discussed. Somewhat surprisingly, perhaps, it fluctuates remarkably little in the short-term, mainly because much of it is the result of long-term commitments which are procedurally difficult to alter.

Finally, net purchases of goods by foreigners (exports net of imports) are a part of national expenditure. They are discussed in the second part of this chapter. However, we should explain why net exports are not shown in the left-hand section of Fig. 7.1. The reason is simply that in 1987, the year to which the diagram relates, they were approximately zero, because exports and imports were of about equal value.

Income-based measure of national income

The second column in Fig. 7.1 on page 182 shows the main categories of national *income*. They were discussed in Chapter 4 when we were looking at the distribution of income among factors of production (*see* pages 84–5 and Fig. 4.2). Only two matters need further attention. In the first place, we should emphasise that the only incomes included are *factor* incomes. i.e. incomes earned by supplying factor services for current production. As we know from Chapter 6 on government policy, some individuals receive incomes from the state, e.g. retirement pensions, unemployment benefits, etc. These are *transfer incomes.* They are paid by taxing some people and then using the proceeds to pay state benefits. Since we are interested in measuring the income derived from contributions to production by factors of production, we do *not* include these transfer payments.

For some purposes we want to know how much people have to spend. This is called **disposable income**. To calculate it, we take total factor and transfer incomes to persons, and deduct income taxes and national insurance contributions.

Savings

One of the key variables in national income analysis is savings, which is closely related to **personal disposable income**. Personal savings do not appear in Fig. 7.1 because they are, by definition, income *not spent* on consumption. They can, however, be estimated and Fig. 7.5 shows the course of personal savings expressed as a percentage of personal disposable income between 1977 and 1987.

Fig. 7.5 Savings as a percentage of personal disposable income 1977 to 1987
Source: *UK National Accounts*

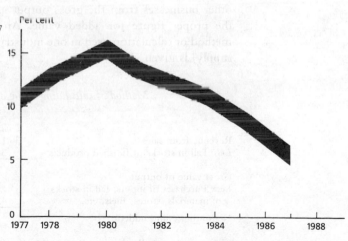

The diagram shows an upward trend in the **savings ratio** (the proportion of personal income saved) during the second half of the 1970s, and a prolonged decline since 1980. There is no simple explanation of these trends, since the ratio tends to rise in booms, and to fall in slumps. One would, however, expect the savings ratio to be correlated with the inflation rate, indicating more stability in real than in nominal terms (*see* pages 193–4). But it should be appreciated that a substantial portion of personal savings are contractual and to an extent invariable, e.g. life assurance premiums and mortgage repayments on house purchase loans.

It would be dangerous to read too much into the meaning of trends in the savings ratio, which is one national income statistic known with particularly little degree of precision. Past figures have been subject to large revisions as time passes (*see* pages 187–90). This is why we drew the line on the graph in Fig. 7.5 with a thick pen. It has been suggested, too, that the recent decline in the savings ratio may well have been exaggerated by the statistics.

Output-based measure of national income

This measure of national output was encountered in Chapter 3, which described the structure of British industry (*see* pages 55–6 and Fig. 3.1). There is, however, one aspect that requires explanation here. The value of the output of each of the main sectors in the economy is known as a **net output**, or **value added**. Since we want to know the value of final output, we must not count the total value of sales every time a good changes hands. If we added together the gross sales revenues of all businesses this would involve a considerable amount of **double counting**, as the outputs of some firms are the inputs of others. Hence, when calculating national output, we deduct the purchases of inputs by firms from other businesses from the gross output in order to arrive at the proper figure for added value. An illustration of the method of calculation used in one industry (energy and water supply) is given in this table.

Method of calculating value added

	£ million	£ million
Revenue from sales	36 127	
Less: Fall in stocks of finished products	313	
Gross value of output		35 814
Less: Purchases of inputs, fall in stocks of materials, stores, fuels, etc.	427	20 762
Net output (value added)		15 052

Source: Census of Production; *Business Monitor*, PA 1002 (1988) (figures relate to Energy and Water Supply 1986)

The national accounts

In a complex economy like the UK, where there is a large government sector and many international transactions, the national income is estimated annually and published in the national accounts – the so-called 'Blue Book', *UK National Accounts.*

There are several standard forms in which the accounts may be used in economic analysis. The relationship between them is shown in Fig. 7.6.

Foreign trade

The top row in Fig. 7.6 shows total *domestic* expenditure, broken down in the manner to which we have become accustomed, i.e. into consumption, investment and government sectors. However, we need to take account of exports and imports. To derive *total* expenditure on UK products, it is necessary to add expenditure by non-residents on UK exports to domestic expenditure. This gives **total final expenditure (TFE)**. To obtain a measure of total UK *output*, it is necessary to deduct expenditure on imports. This total is known as **gross domestic product (GDP)**.

Taxes and subsidies on expenditure

It will be noticed that the wording in the bar in the third row of Fig. 7.6 is: **GDP at market prices.** This, however, reflects taxes on expenditure (e.g. on tobacco) and subsidies (e.g. on housing). Taxes cause market values to exceed factor earnings, while subsidies allow market values to be less than earnings. To convert GDP at market prices to GDP at factor cost, these taxes must be subtracted, while the subsidies are added. The item shown in the national accounts is usually the net effect of these two and reads 'deduct net taxes'. This yields **GDP at factor cost.**

Property income from abroad

The national income of the residents of the UK must take account of receipts (net) of income derived from the ownership of property overseas. This is added to the GDP to yield **gross national product (GNP)** in the fifth row of Fig. 7.6.

Capital consumption

All measures of national income or output dealt with so far have been termed *gross*. This is because they are calculated before any allowance has been made for the depreciation that takes place in the value of the national capital as a result of age and market forces. Very roughly, 15 per cent of the gross value of output is needed to make good such depreciation. When this is deducted from GNP it gives the **net national product** (or **national income**) in the final row of Fig. 7.6.

The reliability of national income statistics

Figures of national income in official statistics appear to have a high degree of numerical precision. However, one should not be misled by their apparent accuracy. It is no simple task to estimate all the elements needed to compute

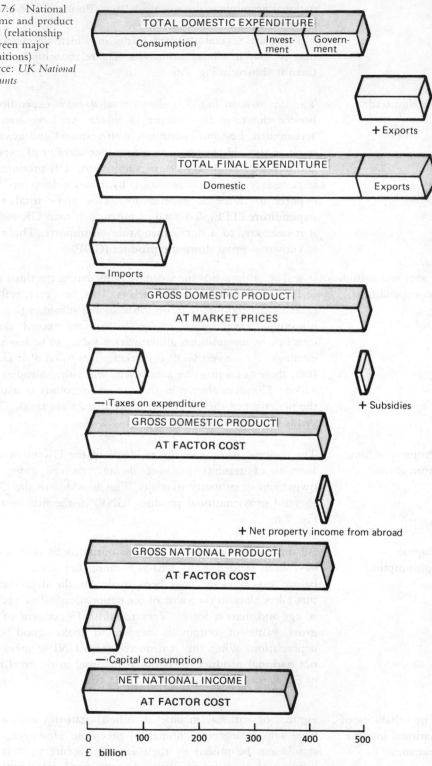

Fig. 7.6 National income and product 1987 (relationship between major definitions)
Source: *UK National Accounts*

TOTAL DOMESTIC EXPENDITURE

| Consumption | Invest-ment | Govern-ment |

+ Exports

TOTAL FINAL EXPENDITURE

| Domestic | Exports |

− Imports

GROSS DOMESTIC PRODUCT

AT MARKET PRICES

−Taxes on expenditure   **+ Subsidies**

GROSS DOMESTIC PRODUCT

AT FACTOR COST

+ Net property income from abroad

GROSS NATIONAL PRODUCT

AT FACTOR COST

−Capital consumption

NET NATIONAL INCOME

AT FACTOR COST

| 0 | 100 | 200 | 300 | 400 | 500 |

£ billion

the national income. Of course, some of the data are more reliable than others – unfortunately not always those most important for economic analysis. The level of personal savings, revised annually, is a good example. Consider, for example, the reported value of savings for one particular year – 1973. When the figure was first published, in the 'Blue Book' for 1973, it appeared as £4711 million. Subsequent annual editions showed revised figures. The Blue Book current at the time we were writing the previous edition of this book (that for 1984) gave the figure for personal savings in 1973 as £6321 million – 34 per cent greater than the statistic originally reported. We then wrote that the more recent revised figure was 'presumably more accurate', but we cannot say that again. The 1988 edition of the Blue Book reports the re-revised figure for personal savings in 1973 as £5435 million – which is nearer to the first guesstimate! Small wonder that commentators are sceptical of interpreting trends in the reported savings ratio (see pages 185–6). We should take it as a warning of the degree of (un)reliability that attaches to some of the statistics in the UK national accounts, though the example we chose to illustrate that point is one of the most dubious of all the series in the Blue Book. Others are less unreliable, but all should be treated with caution.

When the national income is estimated by each of the three methods, the answer should, as we have seen, be the same. An indication of the minimum errors involved is shown by the differences in the figures arising out of each method. To reconcile them the Blue Book gives a 'residual error' which must be included to make the income data add up to the same total as the expenditure data. The discrepancy varies between ½ per cent and 2 per cent of the total.

Errors of 1 to 2 per cent are bothersome when calculating totals, but they are extremely serious when calculating annual growth rates, which are usually based on changes in GDP of no more than 3 to 4 per cent per year, i.e. the error in the estimated GDP can be up to half, or even more, of the growth rate being measured. For this reason, although trends in the growth rate over several years can be significant, not too much should be read into changes in the measured growth rate from one year to the next. Figure 7.7 illustrates this point. It shows the range between the highest and lowest estimates of the year-to-year growth rate of Gross Domestic Product for some recent years. Although all three methods of measuring GDP are supposed to come up with the same answer, the range between them varies. Sometimes they can be close, e.g. GDP in 1985 was between 3.8 per cent to 4.1 per cent higher than in 1984. At other times

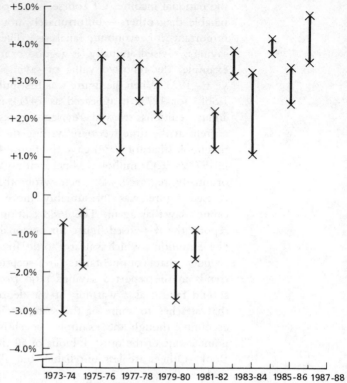

Fig. 7.7 Estimated year-to-year changes in Gross Domestic Product 1973–74 to 1986–87 (the length of the vertical bars shows the range between the highest and lowest estimates of the GDP growth rate for each year)
Source: *UK National Accounts*

they can be far apart, e.g. in 1983–84 the output-based estimate of the growth rate was 3.3 per cent, whereas the income-based estimate was a mere 1.1 per cent.

Living standards and the national income

We now know national income to be a measure of the goods and services produced in a country. It would not be unreasonable to infer that it is, therefore, a good indicator of the standard of living there. If we divide the national income, or product, by the number of people living in a country we obtain a figure of income per head of the population, and it is true that this is fairly closely related to living standards. However, they are *not* the same thing.

The national income does not measure *everything* that contributes to living standards. There are many differences between the two concepts and we can do no more than mention some of the most important here. Nearly all arise from the fact that the goods and services included in the national income total are those that are bought and sold in the market place or provided by the state (in which case, incidentally, they are mostly valued at cost). Among things excluded, therefore, are the beauty of the environment, the pleasures of a good climate and all the cultural legacies inherited from the past. A different type of exclusion is the leisure that is enjoyed. For example, if people decide to produce fewer goods and services and to spend more time at home or on holiday, their living standards may be considered to have risen while the national income will have fallen.

We must also consider various exclusions that are simply due to the nature of economic organisation in the country. Some services, for example, are performed without any money transactions taking place, while others, which may be equally important, go unrecorded. Principal among the former are the services of housewives, as distinct from those of paid housekeepers, the do-it-yourself jobs undertaken by men and women rather than paying for the work to be done, and illegal unrecorded transactions, e.g. in drugs and work done 'for cash only' by individuals who wish to evade paying tax, in what is called the 'black economy'. These cash-only transactions are a commonplace of economic life today. No one knows precisely how much all these would add up to if they could be counted, valued and added into the national income. Estimates of the size of the black economy put it at anything up to 7½ per cent of GDP, but none are very reliable.

A further, final, exclusion which is relevant to comparisons of national income over time is the inability of the statistics to make full allowance for changes in the *quality* of products. The switch from black-and-white to colour television, for example, was widely regarded as raising the quality of satisfaction derived from watching TV, but it is not automatically catered for in the national accounts. Again, the price of personal computers has come down (because of economies of large-scale production) but this component of output has not really fallen in one sense, although as conventionally measured it has.

The only conclusion that can be drawn is that there are substantial differences between the measured national income and what goes to make up the standard of living of the population. We must therefore treat the statistics with caution.

One last consideration deserves comment. The matters mentioned so far tend to suggest that living standards may be higher than would be indicated by the size of the national income. There are, however, some reasons why the opposite may be true. The most important is the existence of what have rather unfortunately been called economic 'bads' (the use of the word 'bads' is analogous to that of the word 'goods' – both imply value judgments on the part of society). These are things like pollution and spoliation of the environment that have sometimes been observed to accompany rapid economic growth. They can lower the standard of living even when the national income appears to be rising.

The distribution of national income

The previous section concerned the living standards of a country taken as a whole. We discussed the meaning of *average* national per capita income. Such a figure, however, can be extremely misleading since income is not evenly divided among all the population. Some people are better off than others.

We discussed the distribution of income in an international perspective in Chapter 5, when examining the range of incomes per capita among countries at different stages of economic development (*see* Fig. 5.12 page 129). We can also put the concept of average income per head in a national context. Figure 7.8 shows the extent of regional variation within the UK. In the diagram, each region's per capita income is shown in *relative terms*, i.e. as a percentage of the average for the UK as a whole. The spread is seen to be considerable. The South East is well ahead of the field, and Northern Ireland well behind, reflecting the fact that GDP per capita in the South East is 50 per cent more than that in Northern Ireland.

Fig. 7.8 Regional GDP per head 1986 (each region is shown as a percentage of the UK average; standard regions are shown in Fig. 3.7b)
Source: *Economic Trends* 1988

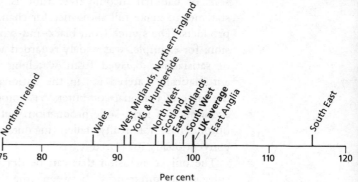

Even these figures are themselves averages, concealing more variability within regions. For example, within the South West, where per capita income is close to the national average, lies Cornwall, 20 per cent below, and Wiltshire, 7 per cent above the average; and within the South East, where income per head is 16 per cent above the UK average, lies Greater London where it is 44 per cent above that.

Explanations of such regional differences are complex, but include reasons why levels of economic activity and of wages and salaries differ around the country, reflecting, among other things, the effects of market forces.[1] It should not be

1 For an explanation of the causes of income differences, see Lipsey and Harbury, *First Principles*, pages 250–1.

inferred, of course, that living standards necessarily vary as greatly as do incomes per head. This is because there may well be offsetting living costs, such as expensive travel and housing in high income regions, and compensating non-pecuniary advantages of living in a rural setting (*see* pages 97–8).

Real and nominal national income

GDP measures the total *money* value of final goods produced during a year. Thus it has a price and a quantity component; a particular change in GDP can be caused by many different combinations of price and quantity changes. A 10 per cent rise in GDP might, for example, have been caused by a 10 per cent rise in prices, all quantities remaining unchanged; or by a 10 per cent rise in quantities, all prices remaining unchanged; or by any appropriate changes in both prices and quantities. For some purposes the money value of national income is just the measure required. This is not always the case, however. Sometimes we wish to know what is happening to the actual quantity of output, in which case we need to separate changes in GDP caused by variations in market prices from changes caused by variations in the quantities of output.

To estimate the physical change in GDP, output is valued in **constant prices**. Each year the total quantities of output are determined. Instead of being valued at current prices, however, they are valued at a set of prices that ruled at some time in the past, called the **base year**. When current GDP is valued in constant 1980 prices, for example, we measure what the total value of output would have been if prices had not changed since 1980. The change in the GDP valued at constant prices is a measure of the pure quantity change. Thus, if GDP at constant prices is 30 per cent higher than 1980, this means that physical output has increased by 30 per cent since 1980, in the sense that price changes have not been allowed to affect these figures.

Figure 7.9 shows the experience of national income measured in money terms at current prices, known as **nominal** national income, and **real** national income measured at constant prices, since 1966. It can easily be seen how far apart the two series have moved. Money income in 1987 was ten times its level of twenty or so years earlier, but real income, allowing for the rise in the general level of prices, was up by only about 50 per cent. The difference between the two series is the result of inflation, which is considered in detail in Chapter 9 pages 233 ff. One should add, perhaps, that the population of the UK grew by about 4 per cent over the period, so that real income *per head* rose by rather less than 50 per cent.

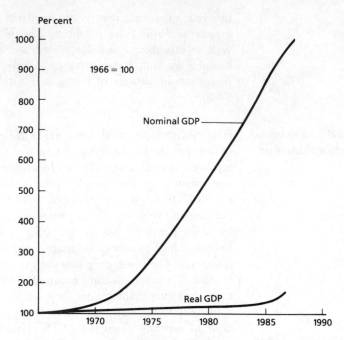

Fig. 7.9 Gross Domestic Product 1966–1987
Source: *UK National Accounts*

Per cent

1966 = 100

Nominal GDP

Real GDP

The balance of payments[1]

The influence of transactions between residents and non-residents of the UK on the calculation of the national income has been described earlier in this chapter. There is, however, a separate account involving such flows of expenditure. It is known as the **balance of payments**, and is a record of all payments and receipts between residents and non-residents over a period of time, usually a year.

Current and capital transactions

The balance of payments is usually divided into two sections:

- the current account
- the capital account

The **current account** records all payments and receipts involving purchases and sales of goods and services. The **capital account** lists flows of capital items, or **transactions in external assets and liabilities** as the account is now officially known. Included here are transactions made by the Bank of England on behalf of the UK government (*see* pages 221–3), previously listed separately in an account called Official Financing.

Taken together the two sections of the balance of payments must always balance. The balance of payments is an accounting concept, so this is true by definition. Thus, a deficit on current account must be offset by a surplus of exactly the same amount on the capital account, and vice versa.

1 The balance of payments is discussed in Lipsey and Harbury, *First Principles*, Chapter 32.

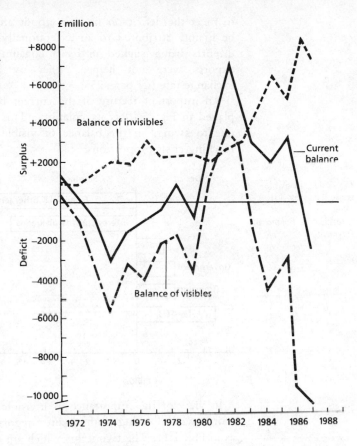

Fig. 7.10 Current account balance of payments since 1971
Source: *Annual Abstract of Statistics*

£ million

Balance of invisibles

Current balance

Balance of visibles

Surplus

Deficit

+8000
+6000
+4000
+2000
0
−2000
−4000
−6000
−8000
−10 000

1972   1974   1976   1978   1980   1982   1984   1986   1988

The current account

Two sets of items are contained in the current account:

- transactions involving goods, called **visible trade**
- transactions involving services, known as **invisibles**

Figure 7.10 shows the history of the current account balance of payments since 1971. The UK has traditionally recorded a surplus of receipts over payments on its current account as far back as the 19th century. This has been the result of surpluses of invisible earnings being more than enough to offset deficits on trade in visible goods.

Recent history has been a little different, as Fig. 7.10 shows. In the early part of the 1970s, the current account moved into debit, as UK exports continued to lose ground to competitors and the quadrupling of the price of oil by the action of the OPEC group of countries in 1973 pushed up the price of imports. Then, in the late 1970s and into the 1980s, the exploitation of North Sea oil came to the rescue. Exports of oil exceeded imports for the first time in 1980, and for three years even the visible balance went into surplus. Since then the traditional pattern has begun to reassert itself, though invisible earnings became insufficient to meet the deficit on trade in goods after 1986. This can be mainly attributed to an exceptionally large quantity of imports being sucked in by a consumer boom, though exports were not helped either by a strong sterling exchange rate (*see* page 255).

An important feature of the current balance record displayed in Fig. 7.10 is its volatility. This is almost entirely due to swings in the balance of visible trade, sometimes reaching crisis proportions.

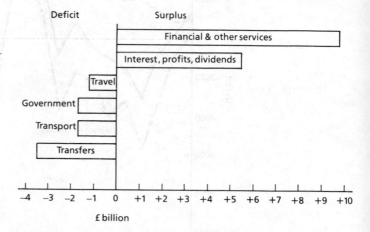

Fig. 7.11 Invisible trade balances, UK 1987
Source: *UK Balance of Payments*

In view of the importance of invisible transactions, it is worth while looking at the main categories in more detail, as in Fig. 7.11. The two items which are responsible for the overall net credit balance are: *(a)* interest, profits and dividends; and *(b)* financial and other services. The latter is the larger of the two, and includes banking, insurance, financial services and royalties. Interest, profits and dividends result from past investments by British and foreign investors. The credit balance can fluctuate quite a lot, but has been especially favourable for the UK in the 1980s, reflecting growing overseas assets owned by UK residents.

The net debit items are travel, transport, government, and transfers. Foreign travel payments and receipts cover spending by tourists and people travelling on business. This was a net credit item in the 1970s, but the upward trend in holidays abroad turned it into a net debit in the 1980s. The sea transport account used to be a substantial source of net income, but the decline in Britain's merchant fleet made it into a net outflow from the late 1970s. Civil aviation's story is similar, though the reversal into debit occurred more recently, in the second half of the 1980s. The drain among invisibles due to the government includes that from military and diplomatic expenditure abroad, aid to developing countries, and contributions to membership of international organisations, such as the EC. Finally, the traditionally unfavourable item, called transfers, comprises mainly personal transactions involving gifts and asset transfers by migrants.

The capital account The capital account records movements of capital funds between residents and non-residents, lending to and borrowing from the rest of the world, both on short and long terms.

Foreign investment can take one of two main forms:

- **direct investment** in overseas subsidiaries of home-owned companies
- **portfolio investment**, involving merely the purchase of foreign securities or shares in foreign-owned companies

These transactions appear in the capital account of the balance of payments, but it is exceedingly difficult to know, especially with portfolio investment, which are really long-term. Once a person or a company has bought shares in a foreign company they may be held indefinitely, perhaps resulting in the acquisition of a controlling interest. Alternatively, they may be sold the week after they are bought. Moreover, a great deal of international investment is done by multinational corporations (see pages 75–7) which switch funds among their subsidiaries in different countries, and the accounting practices they employ sometimes make it difficult to identify all the international investment that takes place.

These difficulties do not, of course, mean that we have no idea at all about what is going on. Figure 7.12 traces the recent history of UK investment overseas (outflows of capital), and investment in the UK by non-residents (inflows of capital). It can be seen that the sums involved are very large. The exceptional £36 billion total capital outflow in 1986, for example, is not far short of half the bill for all visible imports in that year.

The diagram distinguishes direct foreign investment by the UK from the total, which includes portfolio investment. The trend in direct investment appears a good deal steadier than that in the total, portfolio investment being much more volatile. Much of the outflow represented by the large portfolio component in 1985 and 1986 was by banks and other financial institutions located in the UK.

The gross value of the accumulated overseas assets owned by UK residents (persons, corporations and government) is around £750 billion, or roughly half the value of the nation's total domestic capital assets (see pages 7–8). However, accumulated liabilities reduce the *net* asset position of the UK on overseas account to something around £100 billion, which is still one of the highest figures of any country in the world.

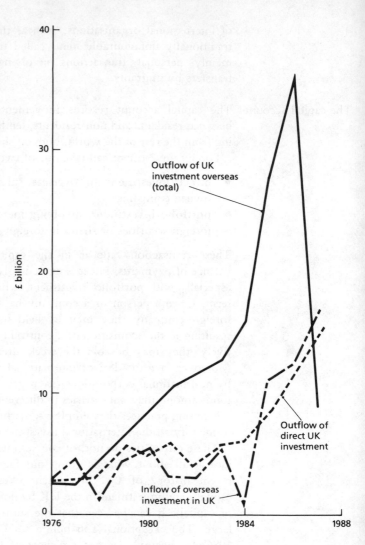

Fig. 7.12 Private investment outflows and inflows since 1975
Source: *Annual Abstract of Statistics*

Outflow of UK investment overseas (total)

Outflow of direct UK investment

Inflow of overseas investment in UK

£ billion

How the balance of payments balances

As previously stated, the balance of payments is a record of all payments made by and to residents from non-residents. Since the sum of all credit items must be matched by an equivalent sum of debit items, it follows that the balance of payments must itself balance. This may be explained with reference to the balance of payments of the UK in 1987. Figure 7.13 traces the inward and outward flows of all kinds.

The best way to understand Fig. 7.13 is to proceed row by row starting from the top. Row 1 shows the balance of current account transactions. Referring back to Fig. 7.10, we note that the current balance was in deficit by £2.5 billion. The first line in the diagram moves, therefore, left from the zero mark on the scale to − £2.5 bn.

This sum would, of necessity, have to be covered either by borrowing or by using up reserves of gold or foreign

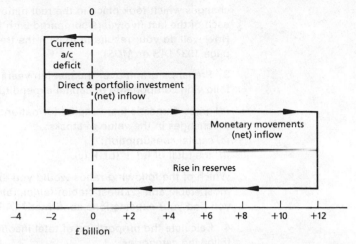

Fig. 7.13 Balance of payments, UK 1987
Source: *Annual Abstract of Statistics*

exchange. Indeed, if no borrowing or lending had taken place, the reserves would have fallen by £2.5 bn.

What actually happened is shown in the next three lines in the diagram. The UK did borrow. We know from Fig. 7.12 that there was a net inflow of funds from direct and portfolio investment of £7.8 bn. This is £5.3 bn more than is necessary to cover the current account deficit of £2.5 bn. Hence the second line in the figure moves to the right, to + £5.3 bn.

Had there been no other monetary movements, the reserves would have risen by exactly £5.3 bn. However, there were other monetary transactions which, on balance, also resulted in an inflow of funds – of another £6.7 bn. This is represented in Fig. 7.13 by a further movement in the third line to the right, to + £12 bn. (+ £6.7 + £7.8 – £2.5 = + £12). Hence the reserves ought to have risen by exactly £12 bn, which they did, and which takes the fourth line in the diagram back to the zero mark on the scale. It takes us to zero because the sum of all the items in the balance of payments is zero, because the balance of payments balances.

Questions and exercises

For key to symbols indicating suggested sources *see* pages xi–xii.

1 Trace Fig. 7.6 on page 188. For the most recent year that you can find statistics, insert numbers of pounds (billions) for each segment of the diagram. If you were going to redraw the diagram for the year you have chosen, which segments would require changing the least, and which the most. (*AS, BB*)

2 How much did the national income increase last year *(a)* in nominal terms, and *(b)* in real terms? Calculate the

National income and the balance of payments 199

changes which took place in the real national product for each of the last five years compared with the previous year. How well do your results fit in with the trends mentioned on page 193? (*AS* or *MDS*)

3   Prepare a graph over the last ten years showing the following components of capital expenditure in the UK:

(a) gross domestic fixed capital formation;
(b) changes in the value of stocks;
(c) capital consumption;
(d) the total of (a) + (b) + (c).

Which of the following ratios would you expect to find *(1)* most stable and *(2)* least stable: (a)/(c), (a)/(d), and (b)/(d)? Do you find your expectations confirmed? (*AS, BB*)

4   Calculate the proportions of total income falling into the following categories:

(a) employment income,
(b) self-employment income,
(c) rent,
(d) profits,

for the most recent year for which you can find statistics.
    Compare your results with those in the middle section of Fig. 7.1. Have they changed? If so, why? If not, can you suggest some economic event which would make any one component larger, and some other event which would make any other component smaller? (*AS, BB*)

5   Construct a table to show the percentage which personal savings took of personal disposable income for the year 1983:

(a) as it was reported in 1983;
(b) as it was revised and reported in 1984, in 1985 and all subsequent years to the present.

(Your table, remember, tells you only what the percentage was in a single year, 1983, as officially estimated over the run of years.)
    Do the annual revisions give you confidence that the later figures are getting progressively more accurate? If so, how many years does it seem to take for them to be more reliable?
    Repeat the exercise for 1984. Do you reach a similar conclusion?
    (Note that you will need to use a run of *Annual Abstracts of Statistics* or *UK National Accounts*.) (*AS, BB*)

6   What is the value of GDP in £s per head of the population at the present time? Try to make some sort of estimate of how the figure would change in the following circumstances (very rough estimates will suffice):

(a) Defence expenditure is excluded from the national accounts.

(b) Ten million married women keeping house for their families go out to work for their next door neighbours and are paid the average earnings of female workers for the work.

(c) The number of men in the labour force who were unemployed rises by 25 per cent. (AS, BB)

7   On a piece of graph paper, mark off scales on the two axes to allow for consumption expenditure and for GDP to be measured on each. (Use the vertical scale for consumption.)

Now plot ten points, each corresponding to the relationship between consumption and GDP for the *same* year. Join the points in a line.

Repeat the exercise using the same consumption figures but related to the GDP of the *previous* year. Join the second set of points with a line in red. Do you prefer the first or second line as an illustration of the relationship between income and consumption? (AS, BB)

8   Prepare a table for the UK balance of payments for the past ten years showing:

(a) total imports;
(b) *net* balance of services;
(c) *net* receipts of interest, profits and dividends;
(d) reserves of gold and foreign exchange.

Calculate the percentages: (b)/(a), (c)/(a) and (d)/(a). What inferences can be drawn from the percentages which you calculated? (AS, DD)

9   Construct graphs to show: (a) the relationship between the volume of UK exports and relative unit labour costs in the UK; and (b) the volume of imports and import price competitiveness. Do either, or both, of the graphs show the relationships to be reasonably consistent? Why should they? Why might they not be consistent? (NIER)

Appendix

Table A7.1   UK National Product 1977 and 1987 (£ million)
Source: *UK National Accounts,* 1988 edition

	1977	1987
At market prices:		
Consumers' expenditure	86 887	258 431
General government final consumption	29 469	85 773
of which: Central government	17 824	51 689
Local authorities	11 645	34 083
Gross domestic fixed capital formation	27 036	70 767
Value of physical increase in stocks and work in progress	1 824	627
Total domestic expenditure	145 216	415 597
Exports of goods and services	43 305	107 506
Total final expenditure	188 521	523 103
less imports of goods and services	–42 592	–112 030
Gross domestic product at market prices	145 386	414 455
Net property income from abroad	265	5 523
Gross national product at market prices	145 651	419 978
Factor cost adjustment:		
Taxes on expenditure	19 834	67 980
Subsidies	3 386	5 762
Taxes *less* subsidies	16 448	62 218
Gross national product at factor cost	129 203	357 760
less Capital consumption	–16 501	–48 238
Net national product at factor cost	112 702	309 522

Table A7.2 UK Gross Domestic Product, Consumption and Investment, volumes 1977–87 (1985 = 100)
Source: *UK National Accounts*

	Gross Domestic Product at constant factor cost			Expenditure at constant market prices	
	Based on expenditure data	Based on income data	Based on output data	Consumption	Gross fixed capital formation
1977	88.2	87.4	87.2	81.8	88.4
1978	90.9	89.7	90.2	86.4	91.1
1979	92.8	92.3	92.9	90.0	93.6
1980	91.1	90.3	90.2	90.0	88.6
1981	90.3	89.5	89.0	90.0	80.1
1982	91.4	91.5	90.9	90.8	84.5
1983	95.0	95.0	94.0	94.9	88.7
1984	96.2	96.1	96.6	96.6	96.3
1985	100.0	100.0	100.0	100.0	100.0
1986	102.8	103.4	102.9	105.4	100.9
1987	106.5	107.9	107.7	110.8	106.5

Table A7.3 UK balance of payments on current account – selected years, 1946–87 (£ million)
Source: *Economic Trends* and *Monthly Digest of Statistics*

	Exports	Imports	Balance (visibles)	Invisible credits	Invisible debits	Balance (invisibles)	Balance (current account)
1946	960	1 063	– 103	885	1 012	– 127	– 230
1950	2 261	2 312	– 51	1 383	1 025	+ 358	+ 307
1960	3 737	4 138	– 401	2 207	2 034	+ 173	– 228
1970	8 150	8 184	– 34	5 126	4 269	+ 857	+ 823
1980	47 422	45 909	+ 1 513	25 934	23 818	+ 2116	+ 3 629
1985	77 988	80 334	– 2 346	80 662	74 979	+ 5 683	+ 3 337
1986	72 678	81 394	– 8 716	77 249	68 732	+ 8517	– 199
1987	79 422	89 584	– 10 162	80 010	72 352	+ 7 658	– 2 504

Table A7.4 UK balance of payments on capital account, 1985–87
(£ million)
Source: *Monthly Digest of Statistics*

	1985	1986	1987
Lending by UK			
UK investment overseas			
Direct	8 653	11 525	15 372
Portfolio	19 440	25 243	6 463
Lending by UK banks	21 971	53 975	50 264
Other lending	730	893	3 112
Borrowing by UK			
Overseas investment in UK			
Direct	4 213	4 176	5 953
Portfolio	7 121	8 447	10 805
Borrowing by UK banks	29 461	63 721	52 789
Other borrowing	3 390	4 313	2 985
UK Government			
Reserves (increase)	1 758	2 891	12 012
Other transactions★	– 707	– 332	726

★ – signifies UK assets increase/liabilities decrease

8 | Money and banking

Aside from a brief reference in Chapter 1 to money, this book has been written as if the 'filthy lucre', as the New Testament called it, did not exist. A visitor from space, reading the previous chapters might well think that money, per se, was of insufficient importance to merit much attention. This would, of course, be wrong. Although we have concentrated almost exclusively on the *real* side of the economy – on the supply of real resources, goods and services – we have valued them always in money terms. Indeed, in Chapter 7 on the national income we used money values to add together production of various kinds, this being the only economically relevant way to add such diverse things as aerospace equipment, bread, cinema tickets and dwellings. It is time to look at the nature of money and at financial institutions in the UK.[1]

Functions of money[2]

Money, however, has more functions than merely to act as a unit of account – it is also a medium of exchange and a store of value. Its existence is of immense help in lubricating the complex economic system of a country like the UK, although it can cause major problems too – those arising from inflation, when the value of money falls.

Forms of money

People have employed a variety of objects to perform the functions of money, from seashells and cattle in primitive societies to cigarettes in prisoner-of-war camps. Although we do not use such primitive currencies nowadays, there are more types of money in use than we might at first imagine.

Coins

The kind of money most commonly used to make small payments is coins. Gold and silver used to circulate in Britain before the First World War. Today coins are made of bronze or of alloys of copper and nickel. They are manufactured by

1 The subject matter of this chapter is covered in Lipsey and Harbury, *First Principles*, Chapters 33–37.

2 Money is dealt with in Lipsey and Harbury, *First Principles*, Chapters 33–34.

the Royal Mint and are only legally acceptable up to certain amounts, known as 'legal tender'. This term means that the money must be accepted if you offer it to someone in payment of a debt. Pound coins have unlimited validity as legal tender; 50p and 20p coins are legal tender up to £10, and 10p and 5p coins up to £5.

Notes

For somewhat larger payments, where coins would be unsuitable, debts may be settled in notes. Bank notes, or paper money as it is sometimes called, have an interesting origin. In the 17th century the most general form of money was the gold coin. Rather than keep a large quantity of gold at home, people used to take it for safe keeping to local goldsmiths, who were early bankers. In return for the gold the goldsmith issued a receipt, on which was stated a promise by the goldsmith to pay on demand to the holder of the receipt the amount of gold mentioned. Following upon this, the custom grew for individuals to accept such receipts, or notes, in payment for debts since, with the signature of a reputable goldsmith, and later a banker, they were 'as good as gold'.

Today, bank notes are the principal form of paper currency, although it is no longer open to any banker or goldsmith to issue them. In England and Wales this right is now exclusively reserved for the Bank of England. Bank notes, however, still retain their original form. If you look at a £10 note you will still find printed there a statement, which no longer has any real meaning (since gold is no longer obtainable on demand in exchange for notes), but which is signed by the Chief Cashier on behalf of the Bank of England and reads 'I promise to pay the bearer on demand the sum of ten pounds'. Bank notes are legal tender without limit.

Small debts are most frequently settled by using currency (notes and coin). There are, however, many alternative instruments, such as IOUs, promissory notes and – of ever-growing importance – credit cards; there is also a National Giro, which is run by the Post Office.

Finally, we should point out that currencies other than sterling are capable of performing the functions of money. Of particular importance in this respect is the ECU, the use of which has been increasing lately. ECU stands for European Currency Unit. It is a 'basket' of currencies, the value of which is calculated by reference to the values of the currencies of the EC member states which make it up. The ECU performs a specific function for the European Monetary System (EMS, *see* pages 261–2), but is also used as a unit of account in the Community's budget, and e.g. for price-setting within the Common Agricultural Policy (*see* pages 166–7). The SDR, the currency unit of the International Monetary Fund (*see* page 260), can play a similar role.

Bank deposits

By far the most important means of settling debts in modern Britain is carried out with the assistance of banks, and usually involves the drawing of cheques. Cheques originated at roughly the same time as bank notes. After depositing gold in a local bank or with a goldsmith, it became common for people to write a letter to their bankers instructing them to pay a sum of money to a named person. The letter was then given to the person to whom the money was owed. This person would then dispatch it to their banker, who would arrange to collect the cash for them. Quite soon this form of settling debts became so important that it was unnecessary to write a special letter every time one wanted to make a payment, as the banks themselves began to print letter forms, known as cheques. These need only the insertion of the amount, the date, the name of the payee and the signature of the person making the payment. Today banks issue books containing such cheques to their customers, although there are other means of transferring money in bank accounts.

The advantages of making payments through banks are simplicity and safety, especially when the sum involved is large. All businesses use banks, as do many private individuals. The importance of bank deposits in comparison with the volume of notes and coin in circulation is shown in Fig. 8.1.

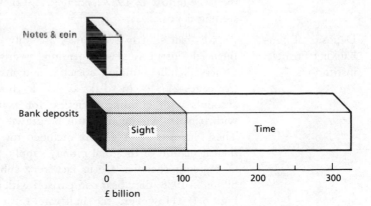

Fig. 8.1 Sterling money stock, end October 1988 Source: *Financial Statistics*

It must be understood that Fig. 8.1 is a simplification of the stock of money in existence. There is no single statistic that can be regarded as *the* measure of the supply of money. Several are available, based on different definitions and all have their uses.

| *Sight and time* | As Fig. 8.1 shows, there are two kinds of bank deposits: |
| *deposits* | |

- **sight deposits**, kept in current accounts
- **time deposits**, kept in deposit accounts

Sight deposits are withdrawable on demand and without notice, merely by presenting a cheque. Traditionally they used not to earn interest, but, mainly to counter competition from building societies (*see* pages 217–8) banks began recently to pay interest on money held in some current accounts. Banks usually charge customers for the work involved in running such accounts, especially small ones.

Most businesses do not keep all their money on current account, so they put some of it in a deposit account. Here it earns interest, but seven days' notice is required for its withdrawal. In practice, however, banks seldom object if customers make transfers of reasonable amounts from deposit to current account for immediate payments. Indeed, the distinction between time and sight deposits is in the process of breaking down. As we shall see, some definitions of the money supply include both types of deposits.

Non-sterling deposits Figure 8.1 includes only bank deposits held in sterling. However, businesses and individuals may choose to hold some of their cash balances in foreign currencies, either to make purchases overseas or to convert them into sterling when circumstances are favourable.

The size of these non-sterling deposits can vary enormously, reflecting balance of payments inflows and outflows of capital in search of high interest rates (*see* page 197). After the large inflow in 1987 (*see* Fig. 7.13) they were larger than sterling deposits.

Deposits of non-banking financial institutions

As we shall shortly see, banks are only one of a range of financial institutions performing overlapping functions. Others include building societies and insurance companies (*see* pages 217–9). In so far as people choose to keep credit accounts with building societies, for example, rather than with banks, their deposits can be drawn on to settle debts. These deposits are therefore included for some purposes in the calculation of the total money supply. The total deposits of building societies are in fact very substantial – at £160 billion in 1988, they bear comparison with those of banks (*see* Fig. 8.1). However, the bulk are regarded as long-term investments, and only a relatively small proportion of them are used to settle current transactions.

Definitions of the money supply

Economic theorists like to define an abstraction called money that is clearly distinct from all other financial assets. In the real world, however, there is a whole spectrum of assets which have some or all of the characteristics of money. Thus there is no clear and obvious dividing line between what is and is not money. The line can be drawn finely to exclude everything but currency, which performs money's function of being a medium of exchange. However, a better definition of the money supply fulfilling that function would include also sight deposits. If we wanted to estimate the money supply from the viewpoint of financial assets which were held as a store of value as well as a medium of exchange, we should include deposits in building societies, which are speedily convertible at a fixed rate of one for one. For example, you cannot pay your bills with a time deposit but in practice you can easily transfer it into a sight deposit on a pound-for-pound basis. This makes a time deposit almost as good as money.

Official statistics of several **monetary aggregates**, as they are called, are available. They are used in connection with the monetary policy of the government (*see* Chapter 9, pages 242–4), and are not at all easy to keep track of. Old measures are replaced by new, sometimes only slightly different, and others have their names changed. The spectrum of monetary assets which make up one or other of the official statistics of the money supply include notes, coin, sight and time deposits with banks, deposits with building societies, Treasury bills and negotiable certificates of deposit (*see* pages 214 and 213).

Each measure of the money supply focusses on a particular point in the spectrum and includes, as a group to measure, everything up to that point. When the Bank of England decides to change the measures of the money supply, this leaves the spectrum of assets unaltered, but changes the specific groupings being measured. Very probably, between the time of our writing and your reading this book, the Bank will have chosen to measure some new groupings and to stop measuring some existing groupings.

It is common to divide the various measures into two classes, called **narrow money** and **broad money**. Narrow money is associated with a high degree of liquidity, in that it is readily available to finance spending in fulfilment of money's function as a medium of exchange.

The definitions in use in the UK in 1987–88 are set out below. (The three most recently dropped are printed in italic type. They may be resurrected.)

Narrow money

M0 | M0 is the narrowest measure of the money supply, most nearly corresponding to the concept of 'high-powered money' used in economic theory. M0 is almost entirely made up of notes and coin held by the public and the banks. The small residue consists of working balances held by the commercial banks with the Bank of England (*see* page 222).

M1 | *M1 comprises notes and coin* plus *the sterling sight deposits of the private sector with banks.*

M2 | *M2 consists of notes and coin* plus *non-interest-bearing sterling sight bank deposits,* plus *certain interest-bearing sterling deposits of banks and building societies.*

Broad money

M3 | M3 comprises M0 *plus* private sector sterling bank sight and time deposits. This measure was known as Sterling M3 until 1987.

M3c | *M3c consists of M3 plus private sector holdings of foreign currency bank deposits. This measure was known as M3 until 1987.*

M4 | M4 consists of M3 *plus* shares and deposits of building societies (net of their holdings of other components of M3).

M5 | M5 consists of M4 *plus* private sector holdings of certain other financial assets, including bills of exchange and Treasury bills and some national savings. This measure was known as PSL2 until 1987.

The magnitudes of the four measures of the money supply in current use are shown in Fig. 8.2. They can be useful in examining the operation of the government's monetary policy, to be explained in the next chapter. It is important to have an idea of their relative magnitudes and to appreciate how each measure is defined. All are stated at their current values but changes in the money supply can be adjusted to allow for inflation, thus yielding the *real* money supply (in

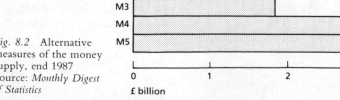

Fig. 8.2 Alternative measures of the money supply, end 1987 Source: *Monthly Digest of Statistics*

£ billion

a fashion similar to that used to derive real income from nominal income – *see* page 193).

All the above are measures of the stock of money and should not be confused with a measure of *changes* in the stock called DCE, standing for Domestic Credit Expansion, which was at one time in use in the UK.

The banking system[1]

The importance of banks has already been mentioned in connection with the supply of money. Now we must examine them in more detail. This can best be done under three heads:

- commercial (or deposit) banks
- investment banks
- the Bank of England

Commercial/ deposit banks

For well over 100 years the principal type of banking institution for the conduct of everyday business has been a commercial enterprise, formed as a joint stock company. However, this has not always been the case; previously the joint stock form of organisation had been prohibited to banks, leaving the business in the hands of a multitude of small private partnerships and the Bank of England, the latter being founded by Royal Charter (*see* pages 221–3). It took a year of financial crises in 1825 to bring about a change in the law.

Bank mergers in the 19th century, during the First World War and in the 1970s brought the number of banks down to the present level. Four large banks – Barclays, Lloyds, Midland and the National Westminster (NatWest) – now account for well over 90 per cent of the total business of the London clearing banks (see below).

Bank clearing

The major commercial banks in Britain are known as clearing banks. Here is why.

Every time someone draws a cheque in favour of another person it is necessary to transfer a sum of money. If both persons have accounts at the same bank it is a simple matter; the bank makes entries in the two customers' accounts, debiting one and crediting another. If they have accounts at different banks, however, this procedure is not possible. One solution would be for the bank of the person making the payment to transfer cash to the other bank, which is what happened in the past. However, the bank clerks who used to travel around the City of London transferring sums of cash soon realised that their work would be minimised if they all met to sort out the payments that were due, particularly as

1 The banking system is dealt with in Lipsey and Harbury, *First Principles*, Chapter 35.

it often happened that a clerk from bank A was collecting from bank B, while his counterpart from bank B was collecting from bank A. Obviously if the sums involved were identical there was no need for either clerk to be collecting. Even if the amounts were not equal the smaller could be offset against the larger and the clerk from the latter bank could collect the difference, thus halving the work.

The essential requirement for the successful working of this system of offsetting claims against one another, known as **clearing**, was that the clerks should meet. In the 18th century they organised this themselves, but there is now a bankers' clearing house in the City, where computerised data on the transfer of sums between different bank accounts is reconciled and the subsequent differences between the banks settled.

Assets and liabilities of commercial/deposit banks

Commercial banks are in business to make a profit. They are essentially borrowing and lending institutions, i.e. they borrow from one set of people and lend to others at a profit. How is it possible for a bank to 'lend other people's money' which it is supposed to be keeping in safe custody? What happens if the people who have deposited their money in the bank demand payment and the banks are unable to satisfy them?

The answers to these questions cannot be provided in full here. However, they depend on a fact which the earliest goldsmith–bankers did not take long to grasp, namely that it is extremely rare for any signficant fraction of their customers (let alone all of them) to wish to withdraw their money *at the same time*. The banker therefore needs to hold only enough cash to meet the needs of those that do make demands.

Bankers can keep their cash reserve low by holding also some financial assets which are, so to speak, 'near money' in the sense of being speedily and easily exchangeable into cash. So protected, the bankers can make loans which earn interest. The best proportions of cash and **liquid assets** (as money and near-money assets are called) to deposits have evolved in the light of experience. Traditionally a figure of about 8 per cent was preferred. In modern times, however, the freedom of the banks to decide how to allocate their assets in different forms is subject to some control by the government, acting through the Bank of England. We shall consider these matters in Chapter 9.

Figure 8.3 shows the two sides of the business of the London clearing banks, as depicted by their balance sheet accounts of assets and liabilities.

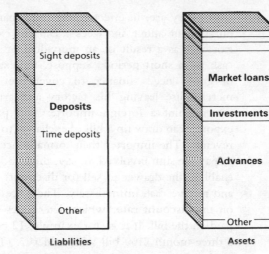

Fig. 8.3 Sterling liabilities and assets of UK banks, end October 1988 Source: *Financial Statistics*

Liabilities / Assets

Notes & coin
Balances at Bank of England
Bills
Market loans
Investments
Advances
Other

Sight deposits
Deposits
Time deposits
Other

Liabilities

The liabilities, which we have already mentioned, consist almost wholly of current and deposit accounts standing to the credit of the banks' customers. The difference between these has been explained earlier (*see* page 208).

There are two sets of liabilities included in the 'other' category of Fig. 8.3. One consists of liabilities to the banks' shareholders, while the other is **certificates of deposit**. These are notes (receipts) issued by the banks and which are in circulation in the money market; they have to be paid when presented by a holder at the maturity date.

Assets

The asset side of the balance sheet of the clearing banks may best be examined using the concepts of profitability and liquidity, the latter referring to the speed and ease with which an asset may be turned into cash.

Notes and coin held in the vaults are the banks' first line of reserve – they are perfectly liquid and earn no return at all.

Accounts at the Bank of England are the credit balances of the clearing banks at the Bank of England, which, among other things, acts as the 'bankers' bank'. The deposits kept there by the clearing banks may be of two basic kinds. The first are the balances which the banks freely decide to hold at the Bank of England for their own convenience. The second are balances which the banks may be forced to hold if so instructed by the Bank of England, acting for the government and forming part of monetary policy, which we discuss in Chapter 9. Such required holdings at the Bank have taken several forms, known as Special Deposits, Supplementary Deposits (the 'Corset') and Cash Ratio Deposits (*see* page 245).

Bills of exchange and **Treasury bills** are fairly liquid assets; they are, in effect, short-term loans with an average duration of about six weeks. Bills of exchange come into existence as a result of an individual or institution needing cash for a short period. Suppose, for example, an exporter of goods needs finance to cover the time between the merchandise leaving his factory and arriving overseas, at which point a foreign importer will pay for them. The exporter can draw up a bill of exchange to cover the expected revenue. The importer then formally accepts the obligation to pay the sum involved in, say, three months' time, thereby enabling the drawer to sell (or **discount**) the bill in the City and receive cash immediately. The price of the bill depends on the **discount rate**, which determines the rate of interest paid on the bill. If it is, for example, 12 per cent per annum, a three-month £100 bill will yield £97. (The discount rate is almost, but not quite, the rate of interest. Thus a £100 three-month bill sold for £97 carries a 3 per cent quarterly discount rate, although the borrower pays £3 interest and gets £97 which implies an interest rate of 3/97 per cent, i.e. approximately 3.09 per cent.)

Treasury bills are similar to bills of exchange; they are promises by the government to pay sums of money in the future, which are sold at a discount which determines the rate of interest that they yield. The Treasury issues them from week to week to finance current government expenditure (*see* discount houses pages 216–7).

Market loans are assets with a high degree of liquidity comprising short-term loans to city financial institutions, including the discount houses.

Investments are longer-term securities, mainly issued by the government. The liquidity of the banks' portfolio of securities depends on how long the securities have to run to maturity. Those which are almost due for redemption are highly liquid, whilst those with longer periods of time to run are less so. Securities can, of course, be sold at any time at the prevailing market price, but this varies from day to day as market interest rates change; the liquidity of the securities being related to the certainty of the sum realisable on sale.

Advances to customers are the largest group of assets held by the banks. They are both the least liquid assets and the most profitable. Such advances may be made on **overdraft**, with permission for borrowers to overdraw their accounts up to stated limits, or as straightforward loans. The overdraft system is particularly convenient for borrowers whose needs fluctuate, as interest is paid only on the amount actually borrowed. Sometimes the banks require **collateral** security, e.g. businesses may be required to deposit share certificates, but loans are often made to businesses on the strength of trade prospects. The rates of interest charged vary from time to time, with the riskiness of the project for which the loan is to be used, and with the credit standing of the borrower. Banks publish **base lending rates**, to which charges to borrowers are usually linked.

The distribution of loans and advances among the main classes of UK borrowers is shown in Fig. 8.4. It is a very different distribution from that of ten and more years ago. In the mid-1970s the production industries accounted for over half of all bank advances, with loans to persons and financial institutions taking only around 20 per cent. The expansion of the personal sector to become the largest single category is partly the result of the banks competing with the building societies (*see* pages 217–8) in the provision of loans for house purchase. Now loans to persons and financial institutions together absorb more than half of the banks' total lending.

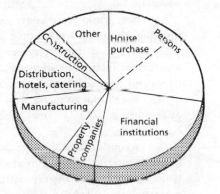

Fig 8.4 Loans and advances to UK residents (amounts outstanding end August 1988) Source: *Financial Statistics*

We conclude this section on the clearing banks with a general comment. All the ways in which banks choose to use their resources (except only holding cash) involve the sacrifice of ready money for some asset which will bring in a larger sum at a future date. As a general principle it may be said that the longer the wait and the greater the risk, the more profitable the loan will be. To sacrifice all for the chance of large profits, however, could soon lead to the collapse of a bank, and it is the maintenance of a portfolio which shows a nice balance between profitability and liquidity which is the art of banking.

Investment banking

The transformation of the banking system mentioned in the previous paragraph from one which engaged in taking deposits from persons and lending to industry is not the only major change that has taken place. A second has been the integration of distinctive types of banking institution.

Previously one could identify two sets of banking institution. On the one hand there were the deposit banks, which we have already described (included here we would count the branches of overseas banks that have been established in increasing numbers in recent years). On the other hand there were the merchant banks, or **accepting houses** as they were also known.

The term sprang originally from the role played by financial houses, with well-known names such as Baring, Hambros, Lazard and Rothschild, in guaranteeing bills of exchange (*see* pages 213–4). By maintaining agents in the major trading centres of the world, they were able to check on the financial standing of traders. In return for a commission, they would add their name to that of the original acceptors (or accept the bill themselves), thereby assuring the British exporters that they would be paid in full for their goods, when the bill of exchange became due for payment.

Merchant banks have continued to perform this accepting function, though it has become a small part of their business. They diversified their activities in several directions, taking a particular interest in advising companies on mergers, take-overs and financial reconstructions. Another growing activity has been **underwriting** new capital issues of shares, i.e. guaranteeing to buy any unsold stock, in return for a commission.

The second major change in the structure of the UK banking system, referred to at the beginning of this section, is the virtual end of the separation of deposit banking and of what is now called **investment banking**, i.e. the functions performed previously by merchant bankers. The integration of the two branches has come about as a result of all large British and overseas deposit banks having acquired an existing merchant bank, or having entered the field independently from scratch.

| Non-banking financial institutions | Outside the banking sector as defined in the previous section are certain other distinctive financial institutions, of which the most important are discount houses, building societies, insurance companies and pension funds. |

| Discount houses | As their names implies, these institutions are involved in discounting bills of exchange and Treasury bills in what is sometimes called the money market. When they do so, either for the government or for a private trader, they must, of course, have a supply of cash. This they finance by short-term borrowing from the banks, who lend at relatively low rates of interest. The discount houses are able to make a |

profit by charging a rate for discounting slightly above the rate which they have to pay for this accommodation.

Although the bills which they discount usually become due for payment only after anything from two to six months, and the money which they borrow is repayable at shorter notice, the discount houses are not normally left short of funds. This is because it generally happens that when one bank is calling in its loans another is offering more to the discount market. Even if this is not the case the discount houses can always turn to the Bank of England which, as we shall see, acts as a **lender of last resort**. If they are forced to borrow from the Bank, they are likely to have to do so on unfavourable terms. Hence, they will probably show a loss on such transactions, which they naturally try to avoid. The frequency with which the discount houses are forced 'into the Bank' depends upon the general financial state of the country and the monetary policy of the government.

The discount houses hold a considerable number of the bills which they discount, but they also rediscount some with the banks which, as we have seen, like to keep a proportion of their assets in this form. When bills are rediscounted with the banks, they are sold to the banks by the discount houses at a price which represents the rediscount rate. In fairly recent times discount houses have also become quite important dealers in other government securities which are approaching maturity. The freedom of action of the discount houses has been limited since 1981, when they became subject to controls similar to those imposed on banks in the government's monetary policy (see page 243).

Building societies   In terms of sheer size the largest category of non banking financial institutions is building societies. Their total accumulated funds at the end of 1987 amounted to £160 billion – a figure comparable with the sterling deposits of the banks (see Fig. 8.1).

Building societies have a history going back to the 18th century, when many were founded by small groups of people to finance the building of their own homes. Today there are fewer than 150 building societies, as the number has been decreasing, with smaller societies being absorbed by larger ones. Two of the largest, Halifax and Nationwide Anglia, in fact hold about one-third of the total deposits of all societies.

The prime function of building societies is not the building of houses but the lending of money to borrowers for house purchase – this accounts for about 80 per cent of the societies' funds. The remainder is held in short- and long-term securities. The method of borrowing money from a building society is known as obtaining a **mortgage**. An individual wanting to buy a house obtains a loan by surrendering to the society the title to the property and paying interest on the loan at a rate varying with conditions in the market. For suitable houses in first-class condition societies are, in normal times, prepared to lend about 90 per cent of the value of the house. The borrower then has to find the balance elsewhere and to pay off the mortgage over a period of 15 to 20 years, or even longer.

Building societies obtain the money they lend by borrowing from the general public at a lower rate of interest than that charged when they lend, and they have been assisted by a concession which makes them liable to income tax at a reduced rate. Money is lent to borrowers either on deposit or in return for shares in the society. The distinction between these two is close to that between the two types of deposit of the clearing banks, i.e. sight and time deposits. Withdrawal of funds in the form of shares may require formal notice, but shareholders, like deposit account-holders at the commercial banks, can normally make withdrawals much more quickly. Indeed, as mentioned earlier, people have come to treat accounts with building societies as highly liquid assets, with the effect that the societies have themselves taken on some of the characteristics of deposit banks.

The Building Societies Act 1986 freed building societies from many restrictions on their activities, opening the way for them to offer a range of financial services previously denied them. Many of these, e.g. money transmission, investment, insurance and pension fund management, were operated by the banks. Hence the building societies are being led to compete with the banks at the same time as the banks are competing with the building societies in their traditional speciality – the provision of loans for house purchase (*see* page 220). Increasingly, too, building societies are offering chequing accounts, credit cards and other facilities previously associated with banks. The decision, in early 1989, by the second largest building society (Abbey National) to change its status to become a public joint stock company is further evidence that the distinction between banks and building societies is likely to continue to diminish.

Insurance companies
The business of insurance companies is to take over from individuals specific risks in return for a payment known as a **premium**. They can do this because, although a risk is uncertain for an individual, it is not so for a company which specialises in risks of a particular type. A business can have no idea whether its factory will be damaged by fire next year, nor can individual motorists know whether they will

meet with an accident. However, an insurance company, dealing with thousands of similar risks, is in a different position, as the law of averages works with large numbers.

On the basis of claims experience and detailed statistical analyses, insurers are able to assess risks, the essential principle of insurance being the pooling of risks and their proper classification into groups. For example, the premium payable to insure family cars used for social and domestic purposes is very different from that to insure high-performance cars for youthful drivers.

There are several types of insurance to be distinguished. Marine insurance covers ships and cargoes for maritime perils. (Much of this insurance is done through the institution known as Lloyd's, where the risks involved with single vessels are spread among a number of **underwriters**.) Fire insurance covers material loss to buildings and contents from fire and kindred perils. Accident insurance means what it says, the principal class being cover for motor vehicles.

By far the most important single category of insurance from the viewpoint of sources of finance is **life assurance**. This differs from the other types in an important respect. Whereas in the case of fire or accident there is uncertainty as to whether an incident *will* take place, in the case of life assurance there is no doubt as to whether a person will die. The uncertainty is *when* the unfortunate event will take place. Life assurance enables individuals to provide for their relatives on their death, or for a lump sum at a fixed future date, such as when they expect to retire. The life assurance companies have data on the risk of death for various classes of individual. For example, they know that the risk varies with age and premiums rise accordingly – the older a person is when he or she takes out a life assurance policy, the higher the rate of premium.

The great importance of insurance funds arises from the fact that they are accumulated over long periods and are invested in ways which allow for claims to be met and profits to be earned. The Life Offices have the largest sums to invest but the total accumulated funds of all insurance companies stood at £160 billion at the end of 1986. The relative importance of the different classes of asset held is shown in Fig. 8.5. Government securities used to be the largest category, but, increasingly, insurance companies have turned to investing in industrial and commercial corporations, mainly buying ordinary shares, which give them the role in controlling such companies mentioned in Chapter 2 (*see* page 40). By the end of 1986, about half of the assets of insurance companies were held as company securities, as shown in Fig. 8.5.

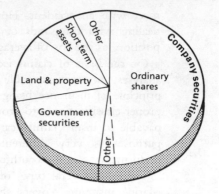

Fig. 8.5 Assets of
insurance companies,
end 1986
Source: *Financial
Statistics*

Land & property

Short term assets

Other

Company securities

Ordinary shares

Government securities

Other

Pension funds

Employers in the public sector and many privately owned companies provide their employees with pensions on retirement, as do some trade unions. In certain pension schemes employees make contributions as well as employers. Pension (or superannuation) funds accumulate from the contributions made during the working life of employees. They are used to purchase securities and shares which earn interest and dividends that are exempt from income and capital gains taxes. Pension funds may be self-administered or handled by insurance companies or banks.

Pension funds began to take off in the 1960s. By the end of 1987 the amount of the accumulated funds was approaching £200 billion, having overtaken the insurance funds. Moreover, nearly two-thirds of the assets held by pension funds consist of ordinary shares in joint stock companies. The managers of pension funds therefore play a role in the ownership of British industry similar to that of their counterparts in insurance companies.

The changing financial system

Our description of the UK financial system has shown that it does not comprise clearly distinct types of institution, each with its own function. Such was not too far from the case in the past. However, the last 25 years or so have seen certain important changes in the nature of the financial system. Concentration in fewer and fewer firms has been accompanied by diversification and the extention of international links, so that the dividing lines between the different types of institution have become blurred.

We explained how banks and building societies are becoming more and more similar; how previously separate deposit banks and merchant banks have become linked within single institutions, competing over a wide range of activities; how concentration in fewer and fewer firms has resulted from mergers of building societies and other institutions. It needs only to be added that all these tendencies are widespread, as the entire financial system is in the process of profound structural change. This is occurring within a framework that is becoming increasingly international, as overseas banks, stockbrokers, insurance companies, etc., move into the UK to join the development of a new structure, which is, perhaps, best characterised by the term 'despecialisation'.

The Bank of England[1]

We have left until last the major financial institution that stands apart from the rest – the Bank of England. Whilst all the important institutions mentioned so far are privately owned commercial bodies, the Bank of England is not. It is the **central bank** of the UK – a nationalised industry operated on behalf of the government.

The history of the Bank of England goes back to 1694 when it was founded by Royal Charter. Originally a private concern owned by its shareholders, its great importance led to nationalisation in 1946, when the shares were taken over by the government. A few relics of ordinary banking business remain, but today the Bank is on an entirely different footing from the commercial banks, over which it exercises a profound influence. The Bank of England controls the currency and acts as banker both to the government and to the commercial banks. It also plays a key role in the government's monetary policy. Its activities are discussed below under the headings of the two main departments into which it was divided by the Bank Charter Act of 1844.

The Issue Department

The Bank of England has a monopoly of the note issue in England and Wales, though certain banks in Scotland and Northern Ireland have limited issuing rights. The balance sheet of the Bank's Issue Department, shown below, lists its assets and liabilities.

At one time the Bank's notes had to be backed by gold. Today, they are covered by government and other securities in the **fiduciary issue** (from the Latin *fiducia* meaning trust).

Bank of England
Issue Department: 16 November 1988 (£ million)

Liabilities		Assets	
Notes in circulation	14 364	Government securities	10 467
Notes in Banking Dept	6	Other securities	3 903
	14 370		14 370

Source: *Financial Statistics*

1 The Bank of England is dealt with in Lipsey and Harbury, *First Principles*, Chapter 27.

The Banking
Department

The more important, as well as the more interesting, of the Bank of England's activities concern the Banking Department. It is here that the Bank functions as the government's bank and the bankers' bank.

The chief classes of assets and liabilities of the Banking Department of the Bank of England are shown in Fig. 8.6, which bears a similarity to Fig. 8.3 on page 213 which displayed the balance sheet of the London clearing banks. This is more apparent than real because of the totally different functions of these institutions.

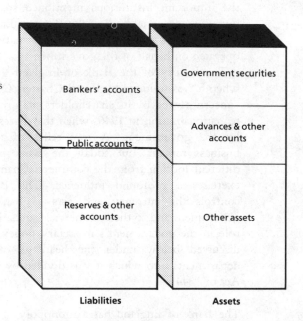

Fig. 8.6 Bank of England (Banking Department) liabilities and assets, 16 November 1988 Source: *Financial Statistics*

Liabilities

Bankers' accounts relate to the Bank of England's function as the bankers' bank. They are the credits standing on deposit in favour of the clearing banks and discount houses, i.e. assets to them, but liabilities to the Bank of England. There are two types of such deposits. One, operational deposits, are freely chosen by the banks and discount houses. They are available for any purpose, e.g. for settling debts among the banks themselves. The second type of deposit comprises funds which the banks may be required to hold at the Bank of England. They may be told to do this by the Bank, acting for the government. The banks may not use the second type of deposit freely; their control is part of monetary policy (*see* Chapter 9, page 243).

Public accounts relate to the Bank's function as banker to the government. It is under the title of public accounts that the government banks its money. The size of the public accounts reflects the current state of official finances – the flow of tax receipts and public expenditure – although the government tries to keep a low balance here to avoid unnecessary costs.

Reserves and other accounts include the small amount of ordinary banking business in which the Bank of England still engages. The private customers are overseas banks and other City institutions, the total also covering liabilities to overseas central banks.

Assets

The assets side of the Bank's activities shows a marked difference from that resulting from the search for profitable lending of the commercial banks. There are three principal groups of assets.

Government securities (including Treasury bills) are not purchased by the Bank of England for the interest they carry, nor for liquidity purposes, as is the case with the commercial banks. The Bank of England engages in the purchase and sale of securities in order to influence the liquidity of the commercial banks, as will be explained in Chapter 9.

Advances and other accounts include those made to its ordinary customers. However, the most significant advances are those made to banks, discount houses and other financial institutions. As has been stated earlier (*see* page 217), the Bank of England is always prepared to act as lender of last resort, to make advances to such institutions if they are temporarily in need of cash. It does this by rediscounting bills of exchange and Treasury bills, although in doing so it may charge a rate of interest which is penal, i.e. in excess of the current market rate. Such loans are regarded by borrowers as temporary expedients, to be avoided if possible.

Other assets include premises and equipment, other securities (including bills of exchange) and notes and coin. The last of these are the carry-over of the note issue from the Issue Department, and are available for release at any time, as required.

The ways in which the Bank of England operates in the course of implementing the government's monetary policy and the exchange rate will be examined in Chapter 9.

Questions and exercises

For key to symbols indicating suggested sources *see* pages xi–xii.

1 Prepare a table showing for the last ten years:

(a) total currency (notes and coin) in circulation
(b) total of sterling bank deposits
(c) total of bank deposits in sterling and other currencies
(d) GDP (Gross Domestic Product)

Calculate the ratios *(a)/(d)*, *(b)/(d)* and *(c)/(d)*, and comment on the trends. (*AS, FS*)

2　Prepare a graph showing the course of the following over the past five or more years:

M0
M3
M4
RPI (retail price index)

Can you tell which of the measures of the money supply is best correlated with the rate of inflation? (*NIER, MDS, FS*)

3　Ask at the local branch of one of the large banks for a copy of their last balance sheet. Group the items into categories corresponding to those used in Fig. 8.3. Construct a diagram for the bank similar to Fig. 8.3. Are any differences you might find more likely to be due to your bank being non-representative of banks in general, or because the date you are using it later than 1988?

4　Imagine that you want to borrow money in the London money market:

(a) to discount a two-month Treasury bill to the value of £10 000 issued today
(b) to discount a six-month trade bill for £1000 issued three months ago
(c) to discount with the Bank of England a three-month prime bank bill for £5000 issued today
(d) to borrow £10 000 overnight

How much would you have to pay in interest at current market rates in each case? (*T, FT*)

5　Prepare a table with statistics for a recent year and another five or more years previously, containing details of bank lending to the following groups:

(a) persons, for all purposes;
(b) persons for house purchases;
(c) the financial sector;
(d) total of all sectors not included in *(a)*, *(b)* and *(c)*.

Calculate the proportions of *(a)* to *(b)*, *(a)* to *(c)* and *(b)* to *(c)*. What do any changes you find suggest for changes in the role of UK banks? (*AS*)

6　Make a list of all building societies whose assets exceed *(a)* £2 billion *(b)* £10 billion. Then calculate the percentage of total assets and the total number of societies represented by *(a)* and *(b)*. (*WA*)

7　Prepare a table showing *(1)* total liabilities, *(2)* total assets, held in the form of shares in joint stock companies by the following financial institutions in a recent year:

(a) banks
(b) building societies
(c) insurance companies
(d) pension funds

Repeat the exercise for a year at least five years previously. Which of any changes have the greatest implications for: *(i)* the UK money supply; *(ii)* control of British industry? *(AS)*

8   Prepare a graph showing the trends in the following interest rates over the last three years for:

(a) banks' base rate
(b) the average yield on industrial ordinary shares
(c) the average yield on long-dated British government securities

Are the series associated in any way? *(AS)*

9   Using a recent weekly return of the Bank of England, prepare a chart on the lines of Fig. 8.6 showing the size of the various liabilities and assets in the Banking Department. Compare your chart with that in the book, and explain any differences you find. If the two charts are very similar, can you suggest an event which would have had the effect of altering your chart (at least for a short while) so it was different from the one in the book? *(FS, or the Quarterly Bulletin of the Bank of England)*

Appendix

Table A8.1 Monetary aggregates, UK. Amounts outstanding at end-years, 1981–87 (£ million)
Source: *Monthly Digest of Statistics*

Money Supply measure	1981	1982	1983	1984	1985	1986	1987
M0	11 931	12 343	13 082	13 835	14 412	15 194	15 847
M3	83 115	92 115	102 311	112 564	127 642	151 704	186 241
M4	138 481	155 575	176 214	200 006	225 959	261 747	304 480
M5	148 370	166 378	187 682	212 559	239 676	276 873	319 638

Note: for definitions *see* page 210.

Table A8.2 Banks: liabilities and assets of reporting institutions, end October 1988 (£ million)
Source: *Financial Statistics*

Liabilities		Assets	
Notes outstanding	1 246	**Sterling assets**	
		Notes and coin	2 454
Sterling deposits: total	422 326		
		Balances with Bank of England:	
Sight deposits		Cash ratio deposits	1 124
UK monetary sector	9 907	Other	214
UK Public sector	2 233	Market loans	
UK Private sector	91 791	London Discount Market	9 137
Overseas	10 872	Monetary sector – other	67 249
Time deposits		Certificates of deposit	12 914
UK monetary sector	62 827	Overseas	25 549
UK Public sector	6 238	Other	3 108
UK Private sector	94 113	Bills	
Overseas	49 576	Treasury bills	1 231
Certificates of deposit	39 569	Other	7 886
Other currency deposits: total	558 159	Advances	
		UK Private sector	228 369
Sight and time deposits		UK Public sector	1 907
UK monetary sector	83 967	Overseas	13 367
Other United Kingdom	31 527	Investments	
Overseas	375 994	British government stocks	6 299
Certificates of deposit	66 670	Other	14 793
		Other currency assets	
		Market loans	
		UK	139 899
		Overseas	394 702
		Bills	3 131
		Acceptances	21 184
		Advances	127 715
		Investments	37 671

Table A8.3 Bank of England, balance sheet, end October 1988 (£ million)
Source: *Financial Statistics*

Issue Department

Liabilities:		*Assets:*	
Notes in circulation	14 285	Government securities	9 110
Notes in Banking Department	5	Other securities	5 180
	14 290		14 290

Banking Department

Liabilities:		*Assets:*	
Public deposits	89	Government securities	712
Special deposits	—	Advances and other accounts	651
Bankers deposits	1 293	Premises, equipment and other securities	1 850
Reserves and other accounts	1 821	Notes and coin	5
Other	15		
Total	3 218	Total	3 218

9 Growth and stabilisation policy

Chapter 6 dealt with government policies in pursuit of two objectives related to the allocation of resources – efficiency and equity. These goals were described as microeconomic, in contrast to **macroeconomic** targets. This chapter now considers government policy aimed at such macroeconomic objectives as the promotion of growth and the stabilisation of the economy as a whole.[1]

Economic fluctuations

The long-term rate of growth of real output in the UK since the beginning of the present century has averaged about 2 per cent per annum. If you look closely at year-to-year changes, rather than at long-term trends, you will find that economic activity proceeds on an irregular path, with forward sprints interrupted by pauses and even relapses. These short-term fluctuations are commonly known as the **trade cycle**, or **business cycle**.

Trade cycles are characterised by four fairly distinct phases:

- a **boom** when output and employment are at high levels
- a **recession** when output and employment are falling
- a **slump** when output and employment are at low levels. (A severe slump is called a **depression**)
- a **recovery** when output and employment are rising

In addition two distinct points are sometimes noted

- the **upper turning point** when the recession begins
- the **lower turning point** when the recovery begins

Trade cycles have been observed well back into the 19th century, when their duration was reasonably regular, lasting 8 to 10 years, and there were no prolonged periods of boom or slump (*see* Fig. 9.1). The experience in the present century,

1 This chapter deals with material discussed in Lipsey and Harbury, *First Principles*, Chapters 37–45.

Fig. 9.1 Percentage
unemployment since
1875 (figures for 1860–
1926 relate to the
unionised labour force;
for 1926–1982 relate to
the total registered
working population;
for 1982–88 relate to
unemployed claimants)
Sources: *Abstract of
British Historical
Statistics*, B R Mitchell
and P Deane
(Cambridge University
Press, 1962), *Annual
Abstract of Statistics* and
*Monthly Digest of
Statistics*

however, has been rather different. For Britain, the period between the two World Wars was one of lengthy depression, lasting for the greater part of 20 years. It culminated in the Great Depression of the 1930s, which was unparalleled in its severity and was international in that very few countries escaped it. (Although no part of the world escaped the Great Depression, the 1920s were a period of boom for much of the rest of the world.)

During the Second World War unemployment fell to an extremely low level. For the first 25 years following the war unemployment still fluctuated, but the fluctuations were over a much narrower range than in any comparable period, as Fig. 9.1 shows. Even with all possible allowances for changes in the definitions of the unemployment statistics, that period was one where the average level of unemployment was exceptionally low.

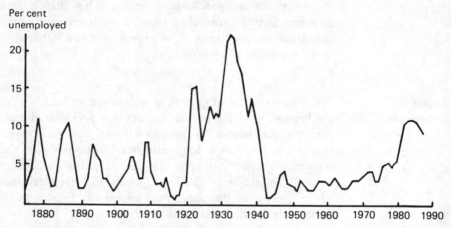

In the early 1970s the pattern changed yet again. Fig. 9.2 shows that an upswing was in progress at the start of the decade. Then, in 1974, the UK and the rest of the world slipped into recession, which bottomed out in 1975. The following recovery was short-lived, however, and in 1979 the economy was in the midst of a new recession, the worst since the 1930s. This too came to an end and 1981 saw the beginning of a new upswing in real output.

The decade of the 1970s was different in another extremely important respect from previous experience. In the typical cycle of earlier years the tendency was for inflation to be associated only with booms, while slumps were periods of relatively stable, or even falling, prices. Between 1971 and 1982, however, the price level rose substantially every year. The lowest inflation rate was 7 per cent and the highest 24 per cent (1974–75), while the average rate was over 12 per cent per annum. Moreover, the rate of increase in the general level of prices, as noted above, no longer followed its traditional pattern of falling off during recessions. For the first time high unemployment and high rates of inflation existed simultaneously, giving rise to a new phenomenon which came to be called **stagflation**.

Fig. 9.2 Fluctuations in output, prices and unemployment since 1971 (percentage unemployment and year-to-year changes in prices and output) Sources: *Annual Abstract of Statistics* and *Monthly Digest of Statistics*

The goals of macroeconomic policy

Three primary goals of macroeconomic policy can be identified as:

- a high rate of economic growth
- a relatively stable price level
- a low and stable level of unemployment

In addition, a fourth goal related to the balance of payments and the exchange rate may be distinguished. It is, however, secondary in nature, in the sense that there is no immediate or lasting advantage to a country from having a favourable balance of payments position, *per se*. An unsatisfactory balance of payments position may, however, inhibit attainment of one or more of the three primary goals. Each goal will be discussed in turn, though in an international perspective. Towards the end of the chapter, we deal with balance of payments problems and ways of trying to overcome them.

Economic growth[1]

There is no need to elaborate on the reasons why economic growth is a desirable objective of policy – it is the major cause of rising living standards. Moreover, as we explained earlier (*see* page 15), even quite small differences in growth rates can lead to large differences in income per head because of the power of compound interest. This is exactly what happened after the Second World War.

1 Economic growth is covered in Lipsey and Harbury, *First Principles*, Chapter 39.

As can be seen in Fig. 9.3, during the 1960s and 1970s the UK's growth rate lagged far behind that of other major developed countries. During the decade of the 1980s, economic growth slowed down on a world scale. The UK's performance over the decade was, in consequence, relatively better (and even absolutely better in the most recent years) than some other countries such as France and West Germany.

Despite this late rally, the long-term result was that income per head in the UK, which had been well above the average of EC countries in 1960, had fallen in 1986 to only about two-thirds that of West Germany, three-quarters that of France, and a little ahead of Italy, a country which 25 years earlier had had a per capita income only half that of the UK. (*See* Fig. 5.11 (d) page 126.)

Fig. 9.3 Comparative rates of growth of GDP, selected countries, 1960s, 1970s and 1980s (1980–87) Source: *International Financial Statistics*

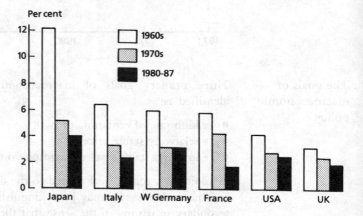

The reasons for international differences in growth rates are complex. Growth depends, ultimately, on the quantity and quality of the factors of production available and on the efficiency with which they are combined.

Some observers have laid the blame for the UK's poor performance on its relatively low proportion of national income devoted to investment (and correspondingly high proportion devoted to consumption). It is certainly the case that the country at the top of the economic growth 'league table', Japan, has consistently maintained a ratio of investment to GDP well above that of other major industrialised countries. The differences between the UK, on the one hand, and countries such as France, West Germany and the USA on the other, have been much smaller, as well as declining. Moreover, the correlation between high investment and high growth rates is not perfect; it is clear that other forces are also at work. It is important also to remember that high growth is only one of several policy goals. When others, such as quality of life and reduction of pollution, come into conflict with the goal of high growth, some compromise has to be reached.

Price stability[1]

Fig. 9.4 Price index of consumables in southern England 1275–1980 (the cost of living index has been used to extend the series beyond 1959; the shaded areas indicate periods of unreversed inflation)
Source: *Lloyds Bank Review*

The second macroeconomic goal is that of stability of the general level of prices. This target must be distinguished from the stability of each and every price, which is not possible, let alone desirable. Changes in *relative* prices are important signals of changing costs or demand, and they can activate appropriate changes in the allocation of resources.

The price stability which is the aim of macroeconomic policy is stability in the *general* level of prices, i.e. the prevention, or moderation, of inflation. Fig. 9.4 shows changes in the prices of the basic items – food, clothing and fuel – in a worker's budget in southern England since 1275, based on calculations made by Professor Henry Phelps Brown for the period ending in 1959 and extended to 1988.

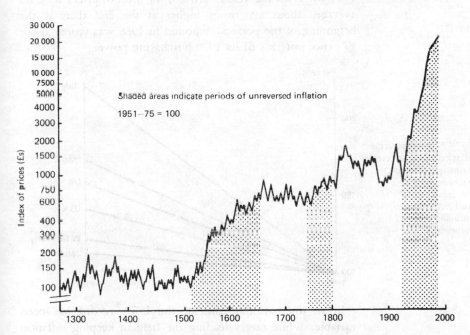

Shaded areas indicate periods of unreversed inflation

1951–75 = 100

The average rate of increase of prices over the whole period was about 0.5 per cent per year. The data also show that our current inflationary era is not unique. Although there have always been substantial short-term year-to-year ups and downs, 700 years of price level history is divided between periods of a stable price level, on average, and periods when the trend in the level has been sharply rising.

1 Price stability and inflation are covered in Lipsey and Harbury, *First Principles*, Chapter 41.

The overall long-term trend, though, has been upwards, and only in the 19th century was there any appreciable period of a slightly falling trend in prices.

Experience in more recent years is better known. In the 1950s the price level rose relatively moderately, by about 3 to 5 per cent per annum. In the 1960s the inflation rate rose a little, prices being about 50 per cent higher by the end of the decade. The 1970s then witnessed a significant upsurge in the rate of inflation, especially after the oil price rise of 1973–74 (*see* page 195), though certainly not just because of it. So-called double digit inflation, i.e. 10 per cent per annum or more, first occurred in 1974, and the rate subsequently accelerated, reaching 24 per cent the following year. Over the decade of the 1970s prices rose on average by 250 per cent. Inflation continued into the 1980s, though the rate fell back to the single digit level in 1982, dropping to 3½ per cent in 1986, before climbing back to 6 per cent and upwards in 1988–89. Over the years 1970–88, the level of prices was, on average, about six times higher at the end than at the beginning of the period. A pound in 1988 was worth about 17 pence in terms of its 1970 purchasing power.

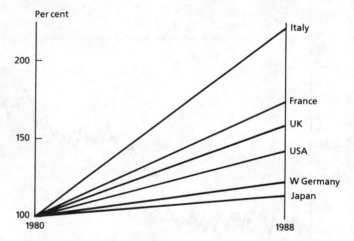

Fig. 9.5 Comparative inflation rates, selected countries (consumer prices in 1988 as a percentage of 1980) Source: *National Institute Economic Review*

In an international context, the UK's record has been variable. While rarely leading the field in keeping inflation low, neither has the UK been a candidate for a booby prize. Figure 9.5, which covers the period 1980–88, shows the UK in a middle position, with prices having risen less than in Italy and France, but more than in Japan, West Germany and the United States.

The effects of inflation

Inflation has many consequences. It distorts the allocation of resources, for example by making 'investment' in 'collectables', e.g. works of art and postage stamps, more attractive than investment in 'real' productive activities, as individuals seek 'hedges' for their savings which at least keep pace with the general level of prices. Inflation, especially at an unpredictable and variable rate, makes it difficult for businesses and private individuals to plan with confidence for the future and it may affect the balance of payments (*see* page 254).

However, one of the main effects of inflation is redistributive. It penalises those whose incomes are fixed in money terms, e.g. holders of annuities, while favouring those whose incomes rise faster than the rate of inflation itself. Chapter 4 showed something of the way in which different groups of workers manage to increase their relative earnings (*see* pages 94 ff), and it is important to recognise that the relative strength of trade unions in various occupations and industries may have been influential in combating the effects of inflation on their members. We also saw, in Chapter 6 (pages 156–8), how unevenly inflation fell on different categories of expenditure, with differential effects on persons in various income groups.

Full employment[1]

There is no need to elaborate on why a high level of employment is regarded as a desirable target. Unemployment causes economic waste and human suffering, especially if it is heavy and prolonged. The experience of the interwar years, when unemployment never fell below 10 per cent per annum, and exceeded 20 per cent in the Great Depression, was dramatic. During the Second World War the two main political parties in the then coalition government made a statement accepting 'as one of their primary aims and responsibilities the maintenance of a high and stable level of employment after the war'[2]. This was a policy accepted by succeeding postwar governments and continued to the present day, though other, at times conflicting, objectives have interfered with its achievement.

Fig. 9.6 Comparative unemployment rates (standardised), selected countries, 1988
Source: *National Institute Economic Review*

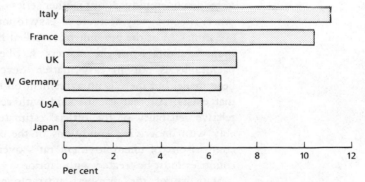

1 Full employment is covered in Lipsey and Harbury, *First Principles*, Chapter 40.
2 *Employment Policy*, Cmd 6527, 1944.

Short- and long-run trends in unemployment have been charted in several places in this book (*see* Figures 1.15, 9.1 and 9.2), to which we now add Fig. 9.6, which puts the UK in an international context. Again, our record has been variable. In the period up to 1980, UK unemployment rates were often below those of other major industrial countries, such as the USA. In the early 1980s the UK record tended to be of relatively high unemployment rates, but in the latest year, 1988, on which Fig. 9.6 is based, the UK is in a middle position.

Unemployment rates, as measured in official statistics, are very sensitive to definitions, both of who is to be counted as unemployed and of who is to be included in the totals on which the percentage rates are calculated. Unless the conventions are broadly similar, or standardised, international comparisons can be very misleading. Trends in the UK unemployment rate in the 1980s have been particularly difficult to interpret because of frequent changes in the ways in which the statistics are prepared. Since all but one of the changes had the effect of reducing the apparent level of unemployment, some observers (not all of whom have political axes to grind) have been suspicious that the changes, justifiable though they may be on other grounds, may have been in part politically motivated.

The most important innovation was a redefining of who was to count as unemployed. Prior to 1982, the basis had been one of *registering for work*. The new basis substituted *claiming benefit*. Its use resulted in an immediate drop of nearly a quarter of a million in the numbers officially jobless. Although disabled unemployed are counted for the first time, the main difference between the new and the old bases relates to those (mainly married women) who do not claim benefit on losing their jobs because they are not entitled to it. The probable effect of the change has been to increase the number of hidden unemployed, but neither series of statistics (nor any other) is completely accurate or easy to interpret.

Estimation of the amount of so-called **hidden unemployment** resulting from the matters decribed in the previous paragraphs is not an easy matter. Several attempts have been made, but there is no agreement on the precise amount that exists. All that can be said with certainty is that the relative reliability of the official estimates varies considerably with underlying conditions of the economy, and that comparisons of unemployment rates over time and among countries must be treated with caution.

Statistics of the numbers unemployed expressed as a percentage of the labour force can, if taken by themselves, be misleading for two additional reasons:

- they ignore the distribution of unemployment
- they need to be considered in the light of jobs available

The distribution of unemployment

When unemployment strikes, its impact does not fall evenly among the population as a whole, but bears much more heavily on some groups than on others, as we saw in Chapter 4.

You may like to refer back to pages 90–3 on this matter, but we remind you of the main conclusions, which were that unemployment varies regionally, with race, age and occupation. Characteristics favouring low unemployment are living in the South East, East Anglia and the South West, being white, age group 45 to retirement, and in a non-manual occupation. Characteristics favouring high unemployment are living in Northern Ireland, Scotland, North and North West England and Wales, being non-white, in the 16–24 age group and having a manual occupation. An additional social matter of relevance is that some 45 per cent of unemployed men and 30 per cent of unemployed women were out of work for more than a year.

Job vacancies (U–V ratio)

Comparisons of the number of unemployed with the number of job vacancies is shown in Fig. 9.7. The relationship between these two variables is sometimes referred to as the **U–V ratio**. When the number of unemployed is equal to the number of vacancies (U=V), as it was approximately in the 1950s and 1960s, there is a job available of some kind for every person looking for one. In the aggregate, the demand for labour is then equal to its supply, so that unemployment is not due to deficient aggregate demand. When U−V the unemployed can be regarded either as **frictionally unemployed** (those moving between jobs) or **structurally unemployed**, or both. Structural unemployment is caused by a mismatch between the skill and regional components of labour demand and supply, e.g. a vacancy existing for a plasterer in Perth when there is an unemployed carpenter in Cardiff. A boom is associated with V being greater than U, i.e. there is an excess demand for labour compared with the supply of people seeking jobs. In contrast, a slump is associated with U being greater than V, i.e. there are more people seeking jobs than there are jobs available.

The Phillips curve

Thirty years ago Professor A W Phillips, then of the London School of Economics, published a paper showing a relationship between unemployment and the rate of change of money wages in the UK over the preceding century. This paper became famous and the relationship subsequently came to be known as the **Phillips curve**.

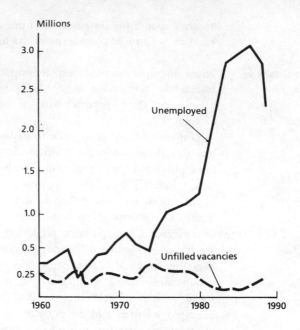

Fig.
9.7 Unemployment and job vacancies (number of registered unemployed and number of unfilled vacancies 1960–88) Sources: *Annual Abstract of Statistics* and *Monthly Digest of Statistics*

The curve itself showed no more than a statistical association – that between percentage unemployment rates and the rate of change of money wages. It was interpreted, however, as revealing the effect of aggregate demand on inflation. This is legitimate on two assumptions. First, that changes in aggregate demand *cause* changes in the level of unemployment in the opposite direction. In other words, the higher the aggregate demand, the lower the unemployment (and vice versa), so that unemployment becomes a measure of aggregate demand. The second assumption is that wage costs are an important element of final prices, so that as wage costs go up (give or take quite a bit for other forces) so must prices. Thus the Phillips curve provided an explanation of the influence of aggregate demand on inflation, through its influence on wage costs.

Figure 9.8 shows this relationship. The original curve that Phillips fitted to the date for the period up to 1957 is drawn, together with a series of points for subsequent years. The latter are marked with their years, except for 1958–66, for which the closeness of the cluster of points makes their individual identification both difficult and unnecessary. It is clear, however, that the observations for the decade after Phillips wrote his article suggest a fairly constant relationship between unemployment and money wage increases.

This relationship was shattered at the end of the 1960s by the money wage explosion when, for no obvious reason, wages rose faster and faster. Clearly the stable Phillips curve relationship that had lasted for a century had broken down.

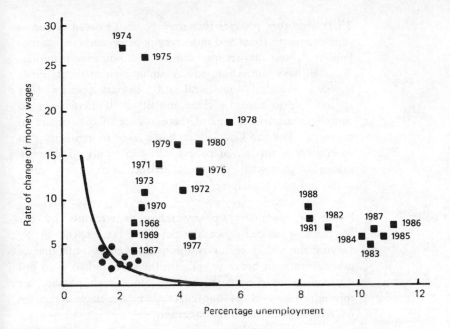

Fig. 9.8 The relationship between wage inflation and unemployment 1862–1983 (the curve is fitted to the period 1862–1957; the unlabelled dots cover the period 1958–66; the labelled squares cover the period 1967–1988) Sources: A W Phillips *Economica* 1958; *Annual Abstract of Statistics* and *Monthly Digest of Statistics*

By 1974, with unemployment not significantly different from the 1967 level, wage inflation had jumped from 4 per cent to nearly 30 per cent! The observations over that period are consistent with a major upward shift in the Phillips curve. Since that time the observations suggest that the pressure of aggregate demand, as measured by unemployment, still affects money wages but at a much higher level. The data for 1974 to 1988 trace out a fairly clear but different Phillips curve, showing that the rate of increase of money wages is less the higher is the rate of unemployment, but at a much higher average level of wage increases than existed in the earlier period.

The tools of macroeconomic policy

The effectiveness of government policy directed at the goals of growth, price stability and full employment depends upon a number of factors:

- The *ranking* of the goals, especially in so far as there are **trade-offs** between them.
- An understanding of the causes of unsatisfactory behaviour in the economy.
- The availability of up-to-date information upon which policy can be based.
- The tools (or **instruments**) used in pursuit of the goals.

Two main sets of tools can be distinguished:

- **fiscal policy**
- **monetary policy**

There are other policies that may be used instead of, or as supplements to fiscal and monetary policies, such as incomes policies, labour market intervention and indicative planning. We shall have something to say about each of them. First, however, we deal with fiscal and monetary policies. Our approach is to consider them initially as if there were no complications arising out of the existence of the balance of payments. For the UK, which has a large foreign sector in its economy, this is, of course, allowable only to simplify matters to start with. We discuss balance of payments policy at the end of this chapter.

Fiscal policy[1]

Fiscal (or budgetary) policy refers to attempts by the government to influence the level of total spending by varying the public sector component inversely with that of other sectors, in order to stabilise the total and so even out fluctuations in economic activity. Since such policies act through the level of aggregate demand, they are often referred to as **demand management**.

Fiscal policy can be used in a variety of ways. In the first place, taxes and subsidies can be varied to discourage spending on consumption and/or investment in times of excessive boom and, conversely, to encourage such spending when the level of economic activity is low. The government can make changes in the budget and, for speed and flexibility, it also has the power to vary tax rates on customs and excise duties by up to 10 per cent in either direction without the prior approval of Parliament. This provision is known as the **regulator**. It has not been used for many years, but can be invoked when required.

The second means of influencing total spending relates not to the private sector but to the government itself. There is no very good reason why the state has to balance its own budget, i.e. raising in taxation exactly the same amount as it spends. In times of boom it can run a budget surplus, while in periods of recession or depression it can run a budget deficit. Deficits tend to stimulate the economy because the government is putting more into it by way of spending than it is taking out in taxes. Surpluses tend to depress the economy (which might be a good thing if there is an overly strong boom) because they do the reverse. The extent to which the government and the nationalised industries borrow to finance an excess of expenditure over receipts is known as the public sector borrowing requirement (**PSBR**, or **PSDR** when negative – *see* page 146).

There is a third method by which the state can affect total

1 Fiscal policy is discussed in Lipsey and Harbury, *First Principles*, Chapters 31 and 42.

spending. It is particularly relevant in periods when the government is trying to reduce total demand. At times it is easier for the central government to issue instructions for the reduction of public spending than actually to reduce it, simply because programmes for spending are in many cases long-term and difficult to cut. **Cash limits** for particular categories of expenditure by government departments and local authorities were introduced in 1976. EFLs (external financing limits – see page 47) have the same function for the nationalised industries as cash limits. Both put limits on the amount that can be spent in a year. This method relates to the PSBR.

The overall impact of the government's fiscal policy is sometimes referred to as its 'fiscal stance'. In Britain this has often been assumed to be adequately measured by changes in the PSBR. This is not so, however, because changes in the PSBR are partly the result of alterations in the level of activity in the economy itself, as well as of changes in the government's fiscal stance. Fiscal policy is affected by the relationship between government expenditure and tax rates Changes in either alter the PSBR, but so does a change in the level of economic activity. A slump tends to lower tax revenues, because incomes fall, and to raise expenditure, especially on welfare payments. The combination of the two can raise the PSBR with no change in the government's fiscal stance. (To get round this problem economists often calculate a 'high employment budget balance', which is an estimate of what the PSBR would be on the assumption of current tax and expenditure policies and a high level of employment.)

Cyclical indicators It is vital for successful economic forecasting that *advance* signs of changes in any of the major components of economic activity should be available. This is because it is much more difficult to identify cyclical *turning points* than to project steady trends, whether upwards or downwards.

A great deal of research has been carried out to establish reliable **leading indicators** of cyclical activity for this purpose, i.e. statistical series which lead rather than lag behind movements in the general level of economic activity. Some of them, e.g. the rate of interest on three-month bills of exchange and the number of dwellings started, have an average lead of a year or more, while others, such as hire purchase credit extended and new car registrations, have a lead of only a few months. None is entirely reliable and the government uses composite index numbers of 'shorter' and 'longer' leading indicators, whose behaviour during the period 1968–88 is charted in Fig. 9.9.

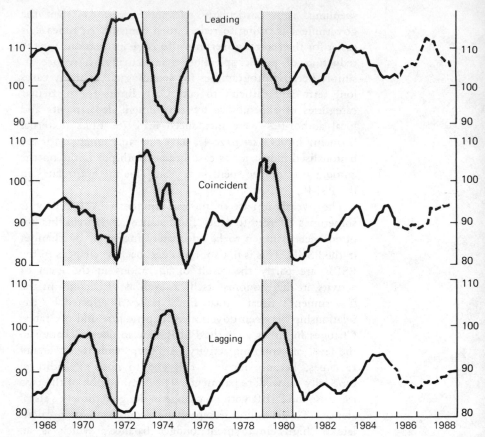

Fig. 9.9 Cyclical
indicators for the UK
economy 1968–1988
Source: *Economic Trends*

Monetary policy[1] The second set of instruments available to a government for
controlling the level of economic activity are grouped under
the general heading of monetary policy. This is operated by
the Bank of England (*see* pages 221–3). It seeks to influence
the amount of lending undertaken by the clearing banks and
other financial institutions, which itself depends both on the
willingness of the banks, etc., to lend and their customers to
borrow. These supply and demand aspects roughly correspond to the two main techniques available to the Bank. The
first involves what are called **open market operations** which
bring about changes in the liquidity of the banks. The
second, acting through **interest rates**, is directed more to the
amount of borrowing.

The technicalities of monetary policy are complex and
have changed substantially over the years. No attempt can

1 The theory and practice of monetary policy are discussed in Lipsey and
Harbury, *First Principles*, Chapter 37.

be made here to offer a comprehensive description of all of them. There have, however, been two landmarks in recent years which are notable for signifying changes in the emphasis of different facets of monetary control techniques. They occurred in 1971 and 1981 when the Bank of England published two important papers, entitled *Competition and Credit Control* and *Monetary Control – Provisions*, respectively.

Bank liquidity

Competition and Credit Control concentrated on the liquidity of the banks in a wide sense. A new concept was introduced – that of so-called 'eligible reserve assets'. Certain of the banks' assets were declared to be reserve assets and the banks were required to hold a minimum of 12½ per cent of their total sterling liabilities in one or other of them. The assets included were credit balances at the Bank of England (other than special deposits – *see* page 222), market loans, Treasury bills, a proportion of commercial bills of exchange and British government securities with less than 12 months to run to maturity.

The reserve asset system weakened the control of the Bank of England over credit creation by the commercial banks. This was because many of the reserve assets were also held by the non-banking private sector; thus the commercial banks could always replenish their reserves by buying some of the required assets from other private-sector sources. Indeed, the introduction of the system was accompanied by an unparalleled increase in the UK money supply.

The reserve asset system operated for nearly ten years until 1981, when *Monetary Control – Provisions* shifted the emphasis of the techniques of monetary policy towards the control of the growth of money and credit created by the banking system. There was some move towards a cash base system, in that banks and discount houses were required to hold a small percentage of their 'eligible liabilities' in a non-operational account at the Bank of England. The 1981 provisions were not limited to the clearing banks, but applied to a wider range of institutions, including also other banks and 'licensed deposit takers'.

Operation of monetary policy by the government has usually been related to specific monetary targets, i.e. to one or more of the measures of the money supply described in Chapter 8 (*see* pages 209–10). A favourite early target, M1, gave way to M3 (known prior to 1987 as sterling M3) as interest-bearing sight deposits became popular. However, as the Bank of England switched targets among the various monetary aggregates available, substitution took place, giving rise to what is called 'Goodhart's Law' (after Professor Charles Goodhart). The 'Law' says that, if the government aims to restrict growth of any particular monetary asset, then other monetary assets will take the strain and grow instead.

The validity of Goodhart's Law may be judged by the fact that in 1987 the government dropped the idea of specific targets for any broad monetary aggregates. Only the narrow money M0 (largely notes and coin) introduced in 1983 was specifically targetted.

The government's monetary policy objectives are set out each Budget Day by the Chancellor of the Exchequer in what has been referred to since 1980 as the **Medium Term Financial Strategy (MTFS)**. (*See* page 247.) The MTFS announced in April 1988, for example, set a target only for M0, though it was indicated that it would also be 'sensible to concentrate on measures of broad money, such as M4'.

Interest rate policy

The arrangements summarised in the previous section relate to the way in which the Bank exercises control over the money supply. Control over lending through interest rates was demoted by the 1981 paper. Traditionally the Bank had the power to change interest rates directly and thereby influence the demand for borrowing. This power arose from the Bank's function as 'lender of last resort'. In times of cash shortage, for example, the Bank could charge a rate of interest above the market rate, and this higher interest rate would then filter through to the rest of the financial system. Indeed, for over 200 years the weekly announcement of **bank rate**, the rate of interest at which the Bank of England was prepared to rediscount eligible bills of exchange (such as Treasury bills), was watched closely by financial institutions all over the world. After 1972 bank rate became known as **minimum lending rate (MLR)**, but any changes announced by the Bank were still regarded as evidence of whether the government wanted to see interest rates rise or fall generally. In 1981, however, this use of MLR was abandoned, though it can be restored in special circumstances, and was, in early 1985, to help support the £–$ exchange rate (*see* pages 254–5). This emphasised the relative importance newly attached to control of the supply of money rather than demand for it. The Bank continues to provide funds to the discount houses when they are in need, but does not formally publicise the rate at which it is prepared to do so, though this may often be inferred from its activities. Despite this, interest rate changes appeared to be the favourite tool of monetary policy in 1988.

Other techniques of monetary policy

A variety of controls and incentives for bank lending and other forms of credit have been employed from time to time, though they are currently in disuse. They include hire purchase credit controls (minimum allowable deposits and maximum allowable time for repayment); **special deposits** (frozen deposits the banks could be required to hold at the Bank of England) and **supplementary deposits** – also known as 'the Corset' – (whereby the banks were set target rates of growth for their deposits, and penalised if they overshot them).

Debates over macroeconomic policy

From time to time economists have debated many issues concerning macroeconomic policy. In this section we briefly discuss two:

- Is either fiscal or monetary policy to be preferred?
- To what extent should policy makers use discretion about how to respond to changes in the economy, rather than rely on automatic stabilisers?

Fiscal *versus* monetary policy

Fiscal policy developed out of ideas in the writings of John Maynard Keynes in the 1930s, while monetary policy came back into prominence later with the support, in particular, of Milton Friedman of the University of Chicago.

The view of many early Keynesian economists was that monetary policy was powerless to influence the economy, while fiscal policy was highly effective. Early monetarist economists held that fiscal policy was powerless to influence the economy, while monetary policy could exert a powerful influence – if it were directed to manipulating 'the' money supply.

Each of these views was based on a number of assumptions, including ones about the responsiveness of investment expenditure, and of the demand for money, to changes in the rate of interest. As a result of experience over more than four decades, most economists now agree that fiscal and monetary policies have important parts to play in whatever short- or long-term policies governments wish to pursue.

Discretionary *versus* automatic stabilisers

The original Keynesian view of macroeconomic policy saw the government constantly altering its policies in the face of constantly changing situations. Since Keynesians thought mainly of fiscal policy, this view was called **fiscal fine tuning**, but similar considerations apply to the use of monetary policy for the same purpose.

Fiscal policy attempts to influence the economy through controlling the level of total demand for all goods and services. The ideal objective is to stabilise aggregate demand at a level just sufficient to produce full employment, without causing excess demand to build up inflationary pressures from the demand side. Since private sector expenditure is constantly changing, this type of stabilising fiscal policy requires that the government's fiscal stance be continually adjusted in an offsetting manner. Such fine tuning was tried by many governments in the 1950s and 1960s. Experience over these decades suggests that fiscal fine tuning often worked to destabilise rather than to stabilise aggregate demand. Why was this so?

One reason why fiscal policy is difficult in practice is that the available data on which it must be based may be unreliable and out of date. We saw something of the reliability of some national income data in Chapter 7 (pages 187–90). If the government alters its fiscal stance, this will affect the economy's behaviour over the coming months. To adjust its stance in a stabilising way the government must know what private expenditure will be over the forthcoming months, not what it was over past months. Thus what the government really needs is information on *ex ante* or *planned* expenditures, whereas, apart from surveys by the Confederation of British Industry on investment intentions, almost all such information is of the *ex post*, *realised* kind.

Fortunately, much of the job of stabilising the economy against short-term fluctuations can be done without having to rely on policy makers' discretion, by using **automatic stabilisers**. These automatically raise government receipts or lower government expenditure during the upswing of a trade cycle, and have the opposite effects in the downswing. For example, unemployment benefits rise when people become unemployed, and fall when they are re-employed. Similarly, progressive taxes tend to take smaller bites during periods of recession and low incomes than during booms and periods of high incomes. Hence these help automatically to stabilise incomes and expenditures.

In the longer term, the economy sometimes settles in to prolonged periods of recession and persistent high unemployment. When this happens, careful diagnosis of causes and consideration of possible cures can be made. The use of fiscal and monetary policy is not then subject to the critique that applies when policies are used to offset short-term fluctuations. Discretionary policies may, nevertheless, be opposed by monetarist economists who feel the risk of relapsing into fine tuning is too great to justify using fiscal or monetary policy for stabilisation purposes. Instead they prefer to use such policies, within a broad package, to set the longer-term economic climate. This is where the Medium Term Financial Strategy (MTFS) fits in.

Medium Term Financial Strategy

From its inception by the Thatcher Government in 1980, the MTFS directed macroeconomic policy away from short-term goals of stabilisation towards longer-term goals of economic growth. Fiscal policy was to be part of a so-called **supply side** set of policies. The term 'supply side policy' is little more than a new name for *microeconomic* policies directed at improving efficiency (e.g. by deregulation and promoting competition) and strengthening incentives, which is where fiscal policy plays a role. Monetary policy was to be held on a steady long-term course designed to encourage growth without serious inflation. This new/old view of the government's main task is heavily market-orientated. It is to provide a stable economic 'environment' of law and order, a stable price level, and a tax system that does not seriously diminish or distort private sector economic incentives. The private sector is then intended to provide for average levels of employment and growth that are higher than could be achieved by active government intervention.

Fiscal policy in practice

The fiscal policy part of the MTFS was successful in meeting its own objectives:

- Government expenditures were cut.
- Nationalised industries were sold to private owners, (though they were also encouraged to meet their investment expenditures out of current revenues rather than borrowing, until they were privatised).
- The improved fiscal position was used partly to finance tax cuts to improve economic incentives, and partly to reduce the public sector borrowing requirement to reduce inflationary pressures.

In 1987 and 1988 income tax rates were substantially cut (*see* page 155) and the PSBR became negative — i.e. the government had a surplus and began to pay off the national debt (*see* page 146). Similar fiscal policies were followed in the 1980s by many EC countries, with a view to controlling budget deficits and encouraging long-term growth. By the end of the decade supporters of these policies could point to some fall in the level of unemployment, some increase in the rate of economic growth, and a fall in the size of the national debt. Over the decade, however, the abandonment of stabilisation policies had the short-term effects predicted by Keynesian economists. The EC countries were very slow to recover from the worldwide recession of the early 1980s. By contrast, the USA adopted a traditional Keynesian policy of raising expenditure and cutting taxes, and experienced rising deficits, and a rapid recovery from the recession.

Economists will long debate the long-term benefits of the

European policies and whether or not they were worth the short-term costs. Similarly, economists will debate the short-term benefits of the American policies, and whether or not they were worth the longer-term costs, whatever these turn out to be.

Monetary policy in practice

As far as the role of monetary policy within the MTFS is concerned, as already stated, this was to control the rate of growth of the money supply so as to allow for the needs of a growing economy, while avoiding the rapid growths that accompanied the inflations of the 1970s.

A central belief behind this thinking puts excessive monetary expansion as the primary cause of inflation. That a clear correlation exists between the rate of inflation and the money supply is not in dispute, as Fig. 9.10 shows by plotting the retail price index alongside M0, the currently targetted measure of the money supply in the MTFS. What is less clear is whether the statistical association is *causal*. Indeed economists of widely differing persuasions accept the correlation between monetary aggregates and inflation, but interpret the causal forces that give rise to it very differently. We should point out also that the statistics used in the construction of Fig. 9.10 are in crude, or nominal, form, whereas adjustments may sometimes be called for to assist in analysis, e.g. to allow for inflation (by expressing them in *real* terms). The evidence certainly lends itself to more than one interpretation.

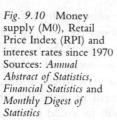

Fig. 9.10 Money supply (M0), Retail Price Index (RPI) and interest rates since 1970
Sources: *Annual Abstract of Statistics, Financial Statistics* and *Monthly Digest of Statistics*

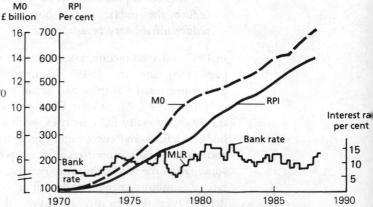

Whilst economists at the highest levels still disagree over the explanations of the data, there is no disputing that inflation and monetary magnitudes are closely related. There is also considerable agreement that an inflation cannot be sustained indefinitely without a corresponding increase in the money supply.

Among the problems experienced by those involved in trying to implement monetary policy within the MTFS, one turned out to be of prime significance. Which is 'the' monetary aggregate that the authorities should try to control?

The leading exponent of the new monetary policy, Professor Friedman, advocated controlling M1 as 'the' money supply. However, the experience of several countries in the 1970s showed that when M1 was in short supply people learned to use other monetary assets instead. These were assets included in M3 and other definitions of the money supply, but not in M1. So, central banks turned to controlling broader concepts of money, and soon a bewildering array of monetary magnitudes was defined and monitored. (*See* Chapter 8, pages 209–10.) 'The' money supply that was to be controlled moved from one magnitude to another, as Goodhart's Law (*see* pages 243–4) was confirmed. Towards the end of the 1980s, M0 (often called the 'monetary base') became the main target for UK monetary policy, while central banks in many other countries were looking at a wider array of assets, and concentrating on some very broad definitions of money.

Gradually it came to be accepted that there is a whole spectrum of closely substitutable monetary assets and no unique 'money supply'. To make matters even more difficult, the structure of the financial system was in the throes of profound structural changes, not only in the UK but worldwide (*see* Chapter 8, pages 220–1).

Among the relevant innovations were the gradual disappearance of the distinction between banks and building societies and between sight and time deposits. Furthermore, a whole new set of highly liquid credit instruments was being developed, such as certificates of deposit. Possibly most important of all, the revolution in communications, brought about by satellites and computers, led to the globalisation of the financial system. Funds moved effortlessly around the world in response to small changes in the conditions of credit. Would-be borrowers who failed to raise funds at home could easily turn to foreign money markets. Simple rules for controlling the money supply broke down, as the whole concept of the relevance of national credit conditions came under question.

As a result of all these changes, the naive monetarist position is no longer held by important central banks throughout the world. Today, central banks realise that to prevent the outbreak of inflationary pressures they must watch an array of supplies of monetary assets and of real interest rates. If these, collectively, indicate that monetary conditions are too slack, the central bank tightens its monetary policy. In the UK the Bank of England does this by raising the rate at which it is prepared to lend, and by purchases and sales of short-term securities in its open market operations.

Although naive monetarism has been rejected, so has naive Keynesianism – the view that money is unimportant to the macroeconomic behaviour of the economy. Central banks failed to locate a simple concept of the money supply which could be used as a lever for the control of the whole economy, but they did succeed, by tight monetary policies, in making the 1980s a decade of relatively low inflation throughout all developed countries.

The lessons of this decade appear to be two:

- Successful central banking cannot be reduced to blind rule-following. It remains an art, in which many economic indicators need to be studied and an array of policy instruments used.
- Given sufficient determination, a central bank can pursue a monetary policy that is sufficiently restrictive to hold inflation to low levels – although the short-term cost may be a recession with its accompanying high unemployment.

Other stabilisation
policies

Fiscal and monetary policies are not the only instruments that can be used in connection with the macroeconomic goals with which we are familiar. We shall look at three others. Prices/incomes policies, labour market intervention, and indicative planning.

Prices/incomes[1]
policies

The idea behind prices/incomes policies is that of setting targets limiting price and wage increases in an attempt to control inflation. Such policies were in favour when the Labour Party was in office, and a number of official bodies were established in the 1950s, 1960s and 1970s (all now defunct) to negotiate wage and price increases between employers' organisations and trade unions.

Part of the problem when discussing prices and incomes policies lies in the fact that the circumstances in which these policies have been used have varied greatly. We can distinguish three major uses for incomes policies. First, they may be employed to suppress demand inflation. However, if the excess demand is not removed the inflation is merely *suppressed* and will recur once the restrictions are removed.

The second major use of incomes policies is as an adjunct to restrictive fiscal and monetary policies to help break

1 See Lipsey and Harbury, *First Principles*, Chapter 42.

entrenched inflation. If inflation has been going on for some time and is *expected to continue*, it develops a momentum of its own. If everyone expects the general level of wages and prices to increase, they raise their own wage or price to keep in step, and this causes the very inflation they were expecting. Incomes policies may then try to interrupt the inflationary process by lowering people's expectations of the future course of prices and wages. If successful, the inflation can then be attacked with new fiscal and monetary policies much faster than by demand restraint alone.

The third and final use of incomes policies is as a *permanent* measure. If it is true, as some economists allege, that the market processes of wage and price determination themselves impart an inflationary bias into the proceedings, because of the predominance of large firms and trade unions, then some form of permament incomes policy may be needed to restrain inflation.

Incomes policies appear to have been most effective in the short-term and to have broken down when under pressure for too long. It also seems improbable that they could ever be completely effective in Britain's complex economy. The pay of some groups of workers is relatively easy to control, e.g. those in the public sector, while that of others may be virtually uncontrollable, e.g. the self-employed. Tight incomes policies are difficult to enforce and the same can be said of price controls. The black economy (*see* page 191) and black markets for goods tend to flourish when pressures are applied with great rigour. Finally, it may be said that trade union support is likely to be critical for the success of incomes policies, but the faith of that movement in free collective bargaining is traditionally strong and may be difficult to change.

Labour market intervention

Some economists have argued that a significant part of unemployment is due to the imperfect functioning of the labour market. Beyond reasonable doubt, the market for labour does not behave like the perfectly competitive markets for some industrial raw materials where prices fluctuate continuously to equate supply and demand. This is an institutional fact of labour markets the world over.

The argument goes on to attribute much of the high level of unemployment in countries such as Britain and France in the 1980s to the general level of wages being too high. On this view wages have absorbed so high a proportion of total revenue that less efficient firms have been forced to close down, causing the level of unemployment to rise. Some of these economists blame the increased power of trade unions for many of Britain's economic troubles. As we saw in

Chapter 4 (*see* pages 103–4), the incidence of strikes in support of wage claims from the beginning of the 1970s until the mid-1980s was well above that of the 1950s and 1960s (though it was still below that of the worst interwar years).

The settlement of wages in the UK has for long been based upon the principle of free collective bargaining. There has, however, always been a public interest in helping to achieve a fair balance between the parties and in avoiding disputes. An early measure was the establishment of joint industrial councils for industries which had not provided their own negotiating machinery. More recently, in 1974, an independent **Advisory Conciliation and Arbitration Service** (known as **ACAS**) was set up, together with a permanent Central Arbitration Committee, to which disputes may be referred by agreement. In the most serious cases the Secretary of State for Employment can appoint a special court of inquiry, or committee of investigation. Their recommendations are not legally binding, but often lead to settlements. (For disputes involving individual workers and dealing with cases of unfair dismissal, sex and racial discrimination, etc., there are industrial tribunals and an Employment Appeals Tribunal.)

Many and varied attempts have been made to influence the legal and institutional background within which collective bargaining takes place. Invariably they reflect the philosophy of the governments which made them.

Recent changes in the law – in a number of Employment and Trade Union Acts brought in by Conservative governments in the 1980s – have been directed at curtailing the powers of trade unions to call strikes or take other industrial action, and protecting the rights of individual workers who prefer not to belong to a trade union.

Since 1984, unions have been required to maintain a register of members' names and addresses and the idea of secret ballots, having already been encouraged, became required for some purposes. Most significantly, any union calling a strike loses indemnity from civil action – with the effect (as ACAS reported in 1988) that secret ballots in such cases are now firmly established. Issues on which secret ballots have to be held include elections to the main executive committee and the use of union political funds. Legal protection was also removed from unions operating closed shops (*see* page 101) which make union membership a requirement for employment.

Indicative planning A policy of expanding aggregate demand to foster economic growth and full employment can fail because of unforeseen supply-side bottlenecks. A centrally planned economy might, at least in theory, avoid such problems, but for a mixed economy like the UK, where major sectors are in private hands, this is certainly not the case. Moreover, because of the great complexity of the economic network and the high degree of interdependence among its constituent parts, British governments have tried to introduce some machinery which, by co-ordinating plans for several industries, might assist firms to formulate more realistic plans for themselves.

Indicative planning is the term used to describe such combinations of consultative machinery and sectoral projections, e.g. for labour supply, productivity and important requirements, which might lead to the setting of attainable targets for economic growth and other macroeconomic variables.

In some ways the National Economic Development Council (*see* page 171) might be said to do a little rudimentary planning; but a single, more ambitious attempt at planning in the UK was made in 1965. The Labour Government of the day set up a new Department of Economic Affairs (DEA) and published a detailed National Plan, with a 4 per cent growth rate for the economy for the remainder of the decade. The plan was abandoned a year later and the DEA abolished. Moreover, even countries such as France, which used indicative planning in earlier years, have not returned to it.

International economic policy[1]

Balance of payments problems arise whenever the government considers that they exist. There are no simple rules for making such a judgment. Sometimes a large deficit on the current account will be regarded as unsatisfactory. This may be so when it results from heavy foreign borrowing to finance current consumption, as was the case in the USA in the late 1980s. At other times, a large current account deficit will be regarded as satisfactory. This may be so when it is accompanied by an inflow of foreign capital attracted by a strong and growing domestic economy. Many observers felt that this was the case in the UK in the later 1980s, though some revised their view when the deficit grew rather large.

In making such judgments, it is important to remember that the balance on capital account must be matched by an equal and opposite balance on current account. Thus a large increase in net capital imports will be matched by a large reduction in the surplus (or increase in the deficit) of visible and invisible trade. (*See* pages 198–9).

We have seen that a deficit on the current account does not

1 See Lipsey and Harbury, *First Principles*, Chapter 43 on exchange rates and Chapter 44 on macroeconomic policy.

necessarily imply a balance of payments problem. A rapid deterioration in the current account, however, may give rise to problems if it causes a speculative outflow of short-term capital.

It must also be recalled that, when we were discussing the goals of macroeconomic policy at the beginning of this chapter (*see* page 231), we described the balance of payments as a secondary goal in contrast to the primary goals of growth, price stability and full employment. It is regarded as secondary because the balance of payments may act as a constraint on the achievement of the primary goals, rather than being in itself desirable.

Exchange rates

Of crucial importance to the whole question of the nature, and even the existence, of balance of payments problems is whether the exchange rate between domestic and foreign currencies is fixed or freely floating. When the exchange rate is floating, as sterling has been since 1972, its external value is determined by the forces of supply and demand, which may keep the balance of payments in equilibrium.

Unfortunately, market-determined exchange rates fluctuate quite considerably. The monetary authorities of many countries worry that the short-term fluctuations in import and export prices create uncertainty among traders, so exerting a depressing effect on the volume of world trade. As a result many governments (operating through their central banks) accept as a goal of policy sufficient intervention to reduce short-term fluctuations in the exchange rate, due mainly to movements of short-term capital, but do not try to resist long-term pressures due to such factors as differing rates of inflation and productivity growth among nations.

In the Bretton Woods system of fixed exchange rates that ruled from 1945 to the early 1970s, and which will be discussed shortly, an overriding object of policy had to be to maintain a 'satisfactory' balance of payments position for sterling, in the sense that there was no strong pressure forcing the exchange rate up or down. Under fixed rates the need to maintain a satisfactory balance of payments position can seriously interfere with the achievement of one or more primary policy goals. This has happened quite frequently in the past. Expansionary policies aimed at the promotion of economic growth led to pressures on the balance of payments as imports rose with rising incomes, exports declined in the face of rising prices and high domestic demand, and capital flowed out of the country because of adverse expectations among investors. The result was that the government of the day at times slammed their expansionary policies into reverse in what came to be called 'stop-go'.

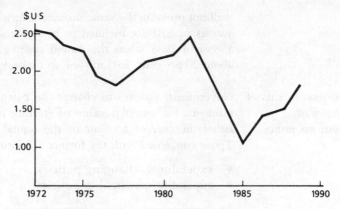

Fig. 9.11 Exchange rate between sterling and US dollars 1972–88 (number of dollars obtained for £1; annual averages) Sources: *Annual Abstract of Statistics* and *Financial Statistics*

In free market conditions the best single indicator of the strength of the forces of supply and demand on the balance of payments is the rate of exchange between currencies. Figure 9.11 shows the course of the US dollar–sterling rate since 1972. The diagram charts four phases of the recent history of sterling:

(a) its depreciation in the years up to 1977, when the current account of the balance of payments was in deficit;

(b) its strength up to 1981 due to a combination of internal and external influences – government policy, North Sea oil, weakness overseas and high domestic interest rates;

(c) its renewed depreciation from 1981–85, largely because of relatively high interest rates in the booming US economy; and

(d) the strength of sterling since 1985. In this most recent period, interest rates were relatively high in the UK, and capital flowed into the now more buoyant UK economy as anticipation of draconian measures to deal with the US deficits caused people to be unhappy about holding dollar assets.

The exchange rate between sterling and other currencies influences the level of imports and exports. A lower rate for sterling helps exports, because foreign importers have to pay less of their own currency for goods priced in sterling. It also helps keep imports down, because British consumers have to pay more pounds for goods priced in foreign currencies.

We have seen something of the recent history of the sterling – US dollar exchange rate. But of more relevance is the value of sterling as compared with the whole range of currencies of our major trading partners. One such measure, called the sterling Exchange Rate Index (ERI), measures overall changes in the sterling equivalent of a 'basket' of such currencies. ERI tends to mirror the sterling–dollar exchange rate but, because all other currencies in the basket may very well not move in the same direction, upward and downward swings in ERI are inclined to be moderate. Thus, between 1986 and 1988 when the pound rose against the dollar by about 20 per cent, ERI moved up by only about 10 per cent.

The instruments of balance of payments policy

Government policies to change the balance of payments or influence the external value of sterling may be directed at either the current account or the capital account, or both. Those concerned with the former fall into two categories:

- **expenditure–changing policies**
- **expenditure-switching policies**[1]

The mechanism of expenditure-changing is achieved by the use of the instruments of fiscal and monetary policies discussed earlier (*see* pages 240 ff). The tools for expenditure-switching are two-fold:

- **commercial policy**
- **altering the exchange rate**

Commercial policy

Under the general heading of commercial policy are all the means of reducing imports (or increasing exports) other than changing the exchange rate. The major tools here are tariffs and other import restrictions, both of which were dealt with in Chapter 5. It needs to be added that since the UK joined the EC these two tools cannot be used against member countries. Similarly Britain's membership of GATT (*see* page 128) inhibits the raising of trade restrictions against imports from other GATT participants, except for temporary alleviation of balance of payments problems.

Changing the exchange rate

The second technique for expenditure-switching involves changes in the exchange rate. Sterling is said to be *depreciated* (or *appreciated*) when its value falls (or rises) respectively on freely fluctuating exchange rate markets, but it is said to be *devalued*, or *revalued*, when its fixed rate is changed downwards (or upwards) respectively in a regime of fixed exchange rates. Depreciation of the currency lowers the price of sterling to foreigners. It means that importers in the rest of the world can buy more sterling with their own currencies. This helps to stimulate the UK's exports, while at the same time raising the domestic price of imports into the UK and inhibiting the quantity bought. Whether or not such devaluation raises the *value* of exports or lowers the *value* of imports depends, among other things, on how responsive demand and supply are to price changes.

Prior to 1972, the UK maintained a fixed rate of exchange for sterling, and devaluation was sometimes used to help the

1 See Lipsey and Harbury, *First Principles*, pp. 546–8.

balance of payments. The last occasion on which this happened was the 15 per cent devaluation of 1967. Since there are long lags in the adjustment of trading relations to price changes, this did not bring about an immediate improvement in the balance of payments. It was two years before any substantial benefit was felt. This was aided by the government's adoption of policies of fiscal and monetary restraint. Such supplementation is usual to prevent the erosion of any benefits following on from the devaluation, which is in itself expansionary because it increases the demand for domestic output.

When the UK abandoned a fixed exchange rate in 1972 the policy decision of whether or not to devalue was no longer needed, since the external value of sterling was free to be determined on the open market. Since then, however, the Bank of England has often intervened to try to iron out short-term fluctuations in the exchange rate. When the Bank intervenes in a free market to influence the value of sterling, but not to support a pre-announced pegged rate, it is referred to as a managed or a 'dirty' float.

Managing a floating exchange rate (or maintaining a pegged rate) requires reserves of foreign exchange. When the Bank of England is supporting sterling it buys that currency and sells foreign exchange, thereby reducing its reserves; when it is holding down the price of sterling it sells sterling and buys foreign exchange, thereby adding to its reserves. With a dirty float the Bank has to decide whether or not to resist pressures for a depreciation (or an appreciation) when they develop. The Bank will be more likely to resist if it thinks the pressures are short-term rather than long-term.

As regards the capital account, there are again two policy instruments:

- exchange control
- monetary policy

Exchange control Exchange control, a technique directed at the capital account, aims to restrict the purchase and sale of foreign exchange for *all* purposes, including both visible and invisible transactions and capital movements. The machinery for the operation of exchange control in the UK was run by the Bank of England, to whom applications for foreign currency used to be made.

Exchange controls may be general, applying to all foreign currencies, or discriminatory, affecting only currencies in particularly short supply ('hard' rather than 'soft' currencies, in the jargon). In the UK, exchange controls were imposed on the outbreak of war in 1939 to limit the use of currencies to essential purposes. They were progressively relaxed after the war, though more quickly for non-residents than for residents. Complete abolition of exchange controls came in 1980, since when it has no longer been necessary to obtain permission from the Bank of England to buy foreign exchange for any purpose.

Monetary policy

The second technique for influencing capital movements is monetary policy. Raising interest rates tends to encourage capital inflows and/or to discourage outflows; lowering interest rates tends to encourage outflows and/or to discourage inflows. It is important to notice in this context that it is not the absolute level of interest rates in the UK that matters, but UK rates *relative* to those ruling elsewhere. (Investors want to know if they can make more or less by lending their funds in the UK rather than in other countries.) Since there is a large volume of short-term capital in world markets seeking the highest return, interest rate manipulation can be an extremely effective device, though its implications for domestic policy must be taken into account. In 1988–89, for example, when the balance of payments was under pressure, the UK government's policy of high interest rates slowed down the economy. It also had marked redistributive effects, adversely affecting, in particular, borrowers locked into heavy mortgages taken out during the preceding house price boom.

Reserves

Reserves are required, as we have seen, to enable the Bank of England to intervene in the foreign exchange market. In 1988 the UK's official international reserves were at a relatively high point, standing at a figure of about £30 billion, representing approximately 30 per cent of the cost of a year's imports. Such a sum may appear small by that standard, although in comparison with potential *deficits* on current account it seems larger. Even so, in some years reserves have been less than current account deficits. Moreover, investors are liable to notice and respond to any substantial depletion of the reserves and their actions may aggravate the balance of payments position further.

International co-operation

During the 19th century exchange rates between the major currencies in the world were fixed through a system known as the **gold standard**. Each country's currency was freely convertible into a fixed amount of gold, which effectively fixed the exchange values of the currencies in question in relation to each other.

The gold standard broke down during the interwar years, and in the depression of the 1930s nations resorted to competitive devaluations and exchange controls to try to protect themselves from balance of payments deficits. As time went on such actions tended to cancel each other out, while world trade spiralled downward. Such 'beggar-my-neighbour' attitudes benefited no one and during the Second World War the representatives of the majority of countries on the 'allied' side met at an international conference at **Bretton Woods**, New Hampshire, out of which grew a system, akin in some ways to the gold standard, which operated during the following 20 years.

Bretton Woods

The Bretton Woods Agreement of 1944 set up two international institutions, the International Bank for Reconstruction and Development and the International Monetary Fund (IMF). The former was discussed in Chapter 5 (*see* page 130).

The prime objective of the charter establishing the IMF was to return to a system of fixed exchange rates, with the important proviso that they would be adjusted in the light of long-term changes in economic conditions. Such a system is of the **adjustable peg** type previously referred to. It aims to eliminate short-term instability and competitive devaluations, while incorporating arrangements to accommodate structural changes in the relative strengths of different currencies brought about by differential rates of inflation, economic growth or any other cause.

The Bretton Woods system had to cope with three main problems. First, reserves did not grow as fast as trade. By the late 1960s international reserves were distinctly inadequate. Second, very large speculative movements of capital occurred whenever people believed that a realignment of exchange rates was needed. Capital fled from currencies expected to be devalued into currencies expected to be revalued. Third, and largely to the surprise of the architects of the system, countries tended, mostly for domestic political considerations, to cling to their existing exchange rates. They accepted devaluations and revaluations only when literally forced into them by an irresistible flood of capital – away from currencies that were clearly overvalued and into currencies that were clearly undervalued.

During the first postwar decades the Bretton Woods system was aided by the very large gold reserves of the USA, but by the late 1960s the United States' balance of payments position had deteriorated to such an extent that it decided to suspend the convertibility of dollars into gold. Confidence in the dollar (and in sterling, the other major reserves currency of the time) lapsed. The dollar was eventually devalued (by 7.9 per cent) in 1971 and again in 1973. Dollar devaluations and the suspension of convertibility were the signal for the virtual collapse of the IMF rules as originally laid down. An agreement signed at the Smithsonian Institute in Washington in 1971 established new parities, but they were not long lived. Within a couple of years most countries had decided to allow their currencies to float (the UK in 1972, as we have seen), although trying to 'manage' them in the interests of short-term exchange stability.

The International Monetary Fund itself did not, however, collapse. It adapted its rules to the new situation, and in 1974 issued three new guiding principles for countries managing their exchange rates:

- Accepting the need for the avoidance of sudden large movements in the value of currencies
- Calling for the establishment of target exchange rates for the medium term.
- Recognising that exchange rate management involves joint responsibilities (to prevent countries adopting mutually inconsistent exchange rate policies such as occur, for example, when country A wants to lower the value of its currency relative to that of country B, while B is trying to do the same thing relative to A's currency).

Special drawing rights

One response by IMF members to the shortage of international reserves was to find ways of increasing them. A major step in this direction was the introduction of so-called **special drawing rights (SDRs)** in 1970.

SDRs are drawings rights, fixed initially in terms of gold. They were allocated by quota to member countries who could use them to support their existing exchange rates. In the years that followed, the SDR system was extended in several ways, including valuing SDRs in terms of a 'basket' of currencies, reducing the restrictions on the purposes for which SDRs could be used, and raising the rate of interest payable on SDRs to levels comparable to those in world markets. The quotas available to member countries were also increased, to aid countries affected by the oil price rises in 1974 and 1981. The result of these measures was to ease world liquidity problems, though one should not exaggerate their quantitative importance. SDRs currently account for only a small portion of total world reserves of gold and other currencies.

European monetary co-operation

On several occasions in the post-war world the monetary authorities of major trading nations have met and agreed to help each other with loans to tide over temporary balance of payments difficulties that threatened their exchange rates. One arrangement of particular importance is the **European**

Monetary System (EMS), launched in 1979 (as a development from a rather unsuccessful European Monetary Union).

EMS

The EMS seeks to provide a degree of exchange rate stability for the currencies of participating member states in the EC. Three components are involved:

(a) Denomination of a European Currency Unit (ECU) (already referred to, *see* page 206) consisting of a basket of currencies of participating members
(b) An agreed Exchange Rate Mechanism (ERM), whereby exchange rates between currencies are kept within fairly narrow limits of agreed parities
(c) A European Monetary Co-operation Fund (EMCF) which receives 20 per cent of the foreign exchange reserves of participating nations (in exchange for ECUs) and which can be used to support individual currencies.

Under the EMS, exchange rates for currencies are not allowed to deviate from the agreed parities by more than 2¼ per cent either way. If these limits are reached, then central banks are obliged to intervene to prevent the rate for a currency outstepping the limits. Thus if one currency, say the Italian lira, falls to its limit against, say, the D Mark, the German central bank enters the foreign exchange market to buy lire, and the Italian central bank sells D Marks (using borrowed funds if necessary).

The EMS is, thus, intended to prevent excessive fluctuations in exchange rates. However, adjustments are bound to be necessary if economic conditions, especially rates of inflation, diverge substantially among participating nations. Hence a mechanism is built into the system to try to avoid this happening. It operates through what are called Divergence Indicators.

When the value of a currency diverges from parity to reach a threshold of 75 per cent of its maximum permitted spread in relation to the ECU, there is a presumption that the governments concerned will take appropriate remedial action: for example, to contain inflationary pressure, if that has caused its exchange rate to fall; or to accelerate economic growth, if slow expansion has caused its exchange rate to rise.

Given that it has been operating in a world of relatively low inflation rates, experience with the EMS has been of modest success. However, realignment of currencies to new parities (which have to be agreed among all participants) has occurred on rather a large number of occasions. (For example, the D Mark has been revalued upwards seven times, and the Italian lira devalued five times between 1979 and 1987.) This suggests perhaps that the requisite adjustments in domestic policies called for by the Divergence Indicators have not been too effective.

The UK, while participating in the ECU and EMCF, held out against joining in the ERM, principally because of the implications membership would have for autonomy over its domestic economic policies. It would appear to be only a matter of time before the UK becomes a full member of the EMS. The Single European Market of 1992 (*see* page 125) hardly makes sense unless this happens.

<table>
<tr><td>

The world debt problem

</td><td>

The foregoing discussion of international agencies which deal with the balance of payments problems of individual countries must be seen in the context of a major problem of international indebtedness, which reached a quite massive scale by the early 1980s.

The origins of the problem are usually traced to the 'oil price shock' of 1973–74, when the OPEC countries quadrupled the price of oil (*see* page 195) which severely hit non-oil producing developing countries, raising their import prices and reducing their export markets. Anxious to maintain their growth rates, these developing countries needed to borrow to finance the deficits in the current accounts of their balances of payments. Private commercial banks were glad to oblige, partly by recycling the large credit balances of the oil exporters, because investment prospects in the industrialised countries had, at the same time, taken a turn for the worse.

The situation was already dangerous. It became disastrous after 1980. There were two main reasons for this. The first was that there was a second oil price shock. The price of oil more than doubled between 1979 and 1980. In the second place, the slowdown of growth rates in most industrialised countries in the 1980s severaly curtailed the debtor countries' ability, through export earnings, to repay their debts. The burden of debt was not at all helped by the rise in real interest rates which was taking place. It has also to be appreciated that every time a debtor was unable to meet even the service interest charges on the debt, these charges were added to the outstanding principal sum.

The scale of the problem continued to escalate to horrendous proportions. The total of developing countries' external debt is estimated to have risen from $200 billion in 1973, before the first oil price shock, to $1200 billion in 1988. Looking at the size of the total debt burden, however, hides an important consideration. The debtors fall naturally into two groups. One group, the so-called middle-income

</td></tr>
</table>

debtors, includes Argentina, Brazil and several other South American countries, as well as Mexico, Morocco, the Phillipines and Yugoslavia. Their debt is largely owed to private banks in developed countries. The second group consists of a very much poorer set of countries, known as sub-Saharan Africa, comprising all African states south of the Sahara, with the exception of Nigeria and South Africa itself. Their debt is largely owed to governments and international organisations. Although the per capita debt of the former group is nearly four times that of the sub-Saharan countries, their per capita income is, on average, over five times greater, making the repayment problems of the poorest group extremely crippling.

Neither creditors nor debtors tend to benefit from the latters' bankruptcy. Hence both sides have sought long and hard for ways of alleviating the situation. Negotiations have involved the International Monetary Fund, the World Bank, commercial banks and governments in the creditor and debtor nations. The so-called Paris Club (which first met as long ago as 1956) has been involved in trying to co-ordinate action. In 1988 its members reached a new agreement for the poorest sub-Saharan group of countries – allowing much longer (up to 25 years) for repayment of debt (so-called 'rescheduling'), reducing interest charges by up to 3½ percentage points, or even writing-off a third of the total debt volume. However, until debtors can generate sufficient income, the problem will not go away. Hence the importance attached to attempts to channel effort in directions that will yield good returns.

| Concluding remarks: macroeconomic policy – a perspective | This has been a long chapter. It has touched upon some of the most interesting, complex and controversial issues in modern economics. We cannot, therefore, provide the reader with a neat summary of the chapter's contents. We expect you found it difficult. It is. The best brains in the world have not been able to solve all the problems we have considered and to come up with policy combinations for the simultaneous achievement of the multiple aims of full employment, price stability and satisfactory economic growth – especially for a country with a large overseas sector. |

It must, moreover, be understood that the division of economic policy into separate micro- and macroeconomic compartments (corresponding to Chapters 6 and 9 in this book) is artificial. We earlier described the goals of micro-policy as efficiency and equity. Yet it takes no great intellectual effort to realise that growth and efficiency are inextricably entwined and that all macro-policies have distributive implications, and therefore involve considerations of equity.

Economic policy formation in the real world must, to an extent, be based on normative judgments. The Keynesian-Monetarist controversy of recent years, for example, was perhaps as much ideological as 'scientific' in base. If we understood better how the economy worked, all of the issues could be quickly settled by recourse to the facts, in the way that some of the issues have been. However, we are still learning (as we always shall be). That may not be very comforting for those who hope for final solutions to all the economy's problems, but at least it makes economics a fascinating subject, for us anyway and, we hope, for you too.

Questions and exercises

For key to symbols indicating suggested sources *see* pages xi–xii.

1 Calculate the year-to-year changes in national product in real terms for each of the years since 1980 for the following countries: UK, USA, Japan, France, West Germany. Which countries can be identified as having:

(a) the highest growth rate in any one year;
(b) the highest growth rate over all years, on average;
(c) the most variability in growth rates;
(d) the lowest rate of growth over the whole period, on average?

Compare your results with Fig. 9.3 on page 232. (*NIER, IFS*)

2 Prepare a graph, on the lines of Fig. 9.5, to show the changes in consumer prices between 1985 and the most recent year for which statistics are available for the same countries. Comment on any changes which you find in the rank order of countries. (*NIER, IFS*)

3 (a) Estimate how your family expenditure is allocated among the major categories of goods and services which are used for the collection of data for the Retail Price Index. Compare your family's allocation with that for the whole country, which is given as the 'weights' in the appropriate table in *AS* (to convert the weights to percentages, simply divide by 10).

(b) Try to estimate whether the cost of living changed more unfavourably for your family than for the average family. Do this by looking, one by one, at each commodity group – noting whether its price change was above, or below, the change in the RPI and whether the item was a more important, or a less important, component of your expenditure than it was for the average family. (*AS*)

4 Prepare a table to show the trends in the percentage

unemployment rates in France, West Germany, Italy, Japan, USA and UK over the past five years.

(a) Which country has reduced its unemployment rate most (or increased the rate least) over the period?
(b) Which country has reduced its rate least (or increased its rate most) over the period?
(c) Which country has the highest rate, on average, over the period?
(d) Which country has the lowest rate, on average, over the period?

Are there any lessons for economic policy to be drawn from your results? (*NIER*)

5   Construct a graph, on the lines of Fig. 9.8, to show percentage changes in the index of consumer prices associated with unemployment rates for each year in the 1980s. In what important respect should your 'Phillips curve' require different interpretation from the relationships shown in Fig. 9.8?

6   Obtain current data for each of the standard regions of the UK to show:

(a) the ratio of numbers unemployed to unfilled vacancies, and
(b) the percentage rate of unemployment.

Rank the regions according to the two criteria and comment on your results. (*RT, MDS*)

7   Draw a graph for the past ten years showing the course of M0, M3, M4, M5 and the retail price index. Which of the measures of the money supply seem to be most closely correlated with the RPI? Refer to the coverage of the last budget of the Government in the national press to find out which, if any, money supply aggregates is to be targetted for the current year. Does your graph suggest that the Chancellor of the Exchequer has made a reasonable choice? (*AS, EPR, T, FT*)

8   Obtain figures for the past five years of the following:
(a) the surplus or deficit on the current account balance of payments;
(b) ERI (sterling exchange rate index);
(c) sterling-US dollar exchange rate.
Which series, *(b)* or *(c)*, is better correlated with *(a)*. Why? If neither is correlated with *(a)*, what could be a possible explanation? (*AS, FS, ET, NIER*)

9   Prepare a graph showing movements in the following over the past ten years:
(a) M3;
(b) the banks' base rate/bank rate series;
(c) the current account balance.
Plot on a graph and observe any statistical associations. Do they suggest that UK macroeconomic policy was affected by the balance of payments situation over the period? (*NIER*)

Appendix

Table A9.1 Growth rates of GDP*, selected industrial countries, 1964–87. Average annual rates per period.
Source: *International Financial Statistics*

	1964–68	1969–73	1974–78	1979–87
United States	4.92	3.48	2.80	2.40
Canada[1]	5.88	5.68	3.24	2.74
Australia	5.70	5.50	2.24	3.41
Japan	11.70	8.94	3.38	4.03
New Zealand[2]	3.46	4.56	0.74	2.30
Austria	4.36	5.68	2.60	2.01
Belgium	4.34	5.94	2.46	1.57
France	5.20	5.88	3.08	1.83
West Germany	4.14	4.88	2.10	3.17
Ireland[1]	4.10	4.84	4.20	1.91
Italy	5.12	4.64	2.20	2.57
Netherlands	5.56	5.16	3.58	1.40
Norway	4.52	4.10	4.86	3.51
Spain[1]	6.60	6.80	2.98	1.51
Sweden	3.94	3.92	1.42	2.04
Switzerland[1]	3.54	4.46	− 4.40	2.10
United Kingdom	3.30	3.18	1.34	1.80
Industrial countries (average)	5.18	4.58	2.62	2.60

* See page 187 for definition of GDP.
[1] Average 1979–86
[2] Average 1979–85

Table A9.2 Index numbers of consumer prices for selected countries, 1978–88 (1980 = 100)
Source: *National Institute Economic Review* (November 1988)

Year	US	Canada	Japan	France	West Germany	Italy	UK
1978	79.2	83.1	89.4	79.4	91.2	71.9	74.7
1979	88.1	90.8	92.5	87.9	94.9	82.5	84.8
1980	100.0	100.0	100.0	100.0	100.0	100.0	100.0
1981	110.3	112.5	104.9	113.1	106.3	117.8	111.9
1982	117.1	124.6	107.7	126.6	112.0	137.2	121.5
1983	120.8	131.8	109.7	138.6	115.7	157.3	127.1
1984	126.0	137.6	112.2	149.2	118.4	174.3	133.5
1985	130.5	143.0	114.4	157.9	121.0	190.4	141.6
1986	133.0	149.0	114.9	161.9	120.8	201.4	146.4
1987	137.9	155.0	114.7	167.2	121.1	211.0	152.5
1988*	142.7	161.0	114.7	171.1	122.3	220.2	159.0

* First half of year

Table A9.3 Unemployment rates (per cent), selected countries, 1978–88.
Source: *National Institute Economic Review* (November 1988)

Year	US	Canada	Japan	France	West Germany	Italy	UK
1978	6.0	8.3	2.2	5.2	3.5	7.1	5.9
1979	5.8	7.4	2.1	5.9	3.2	7.6	5.0
1980	7.0	7.4	2.0	6.3	3.0	7.5	6.4
1981	7.5	7.5	2.2	7.4	4.4	8.3	9.8
1982	9.5	10.9	2.4	8.1	6.1	9.0	11.3
1983	9.5	11.8	2.6	8.3	8.0	9.8	12.5
1984	7.4	11.2	2.7	9.7	7.0	10.2	11.7
1985	7.1	10.4	2.6	10.2	7.2	10.1	11.2
1986	6.9	9.5	2.8	10.4	6.5	11.0	11.2
1987	6.1	8.8	2.8	10.6	6.5	NA	10.3
1988★	5.4	7.8	2.5	10.5	6.6	NA	8.2

★ First half of year

Table A9.4 Growth rates, unemployment, inflation, money stock and interest rates, UK 1978 88
Sources: *Annual Abstract of Statistics, Financial Statistics, National Institute Economic Review, UK National Accounts*

Year	Growth rate (% change in GDP) Real	Unemployment (%)	Retail Price Index (% change on previous year)	Money stock M0 £ bn	Interest Rates † (%)
1978	+ 3.0	4.4	7.4	9.8	12.5
1979	+ 2.7	4.0	11.4	11.0	17.0
1980	− 2.2	5.0	21.0	11.6	14.0
1981	− 1.1	8.3	11.3	11.8	14.5
1982	+ 1.8	9.6	9.2	12.3	10.25
1983	+ 3.7	10.6	3.7	13.1	9.0
1984	+ 1.7	10.7	5.0	13.5	9.62
1985	+ 3.8	10.9	6.1	14.1	11.5
1986	+ 3.0	11.2	3.4	14.7	11.0
1987	+ 4.2	10.0	4.2	15.4	8.5
1988★	NA	8.0	6.8	16.6	12.0

Notes:
† Minimum Lending Rate to 1981, then London Clearing Banks' Base Rates
★ Provisional

Index

References in bold type indicate main sources.
References in italics are to statistical tables in Appendices.

An Introduction
to the
UK Economy

Third edition